F
RA
967
B87
1992

Hospitable Design for Healthcare and Senior Communities

Hospitable Design for Healthcare and Senior Communities

Albert Bush-Brown
Dianne Davis

VNR VAN NOSTRAND REINHOLD
_____ New York

Copyright © 1992 by Van Nostrand Reinhold

Library of Congress Catalog Card Number 91-8445
ISBN 0-442-23959-9

Printed in the United States of America

Van Nostrand Reinhold
115 Fifth Avenue
New York, New York 10003

Chapman and Hall
2-6 Boundary Row
London SE1 8HN, England

Thomas Nelson Australia
102 Dodds Street
South Melbourne 3205
Victoria, Australia

Nelson Canada
1120 Birchmount Road
Scarborough, Ontario M1K 5G4, Canada

16 15 14 13 12 11 10 9 8 7 6 5 4 3 2

Library of Congress Cataloging-in-Publication Data
Bush-Brown, Albert.
   Hospitable design for healthcare and senior communities/Albert Bush-Brown, Dianne
Davis.
      p.   cm.
   Includes bibliographical references and index.
   ISBN 0-442-23959-9
   1. Health facilities—Design and construction. 2. Interior decoration. I. Davis,
Dianne. II. Title.
RA967.B87   1992
747'.855—dc20   91-8445
                                                                         CIP

Contributors

George Baker III, Ph.D., President, Nathan W. and Margret T. Shock Aging Research Foundation and Baker & Associates, Silver Spring, Maryland

Wilt Berger, President, Edwin Bell AIA, Miller, Hanson, Westerveck, Bell Architects, Minneapolis, Minnesota

Herbert Bienstock, AIA, Senior Partner, NNBJ/Rosenfield, New York, New York

Noel J. Brady, M.S. Arch., St. Joseph's, Drumalee, Cavan, Republic of Ireland

Jerry Breakstone, Affiliate Associate Professor, School of Architecture, Washington University, St. Louis, Missouri

Joseph B. Breed IV, Assistant Administrator, The Hebrew Home for the Aged at Riverdale, Riverdale, New York

Miner L. Brown, CFACHEA, Administrator, Meridian Healthcare Center at Brightwood, Brooklandville, Maryland

Albert Bush-Brown, M.F.A., Ph.D., Hon. AIA Chairman, Albert Bush-Brown Associates, Barnstable, Massachusetts

Margaret P. Calkins, M. Arch., Heather Hill, Inc., Chardon, Ohio

Janet R. Carpman, Ph.D., Partner/Principal, Carpman Grant Associates, Environmental Design Consultants, Ann Arbor, Michigan

Edith S. Claman, ASID, President, Primarily Seating, Inc., New York, New York

Martin H. Cohen, FAIA, Principal, Martin H. Cohen, FAIA, Armonk, New York

Richard T. Conard, M.D., National Foundation on Gerontology, Bradenton, Florida

Spero Daltas, FAAR, Spero Daltas and Associates, Inc., Rome, Italy

Dianne Davis, M.A., P.D., Senior Principal, Hospitality Healthcare Designs, New York, New York

Horace D'Angelo, Jr., President, Caretel Corporation, Romeo, Michigan

David Demko, Ph.D., Gerontologist, Boca Raton, Florida

James R. DeStefano, FAIA, RIBA, DeStefano/Goettsch, Chicago, Illinois

Susan C. Drew, AIA, Associate Partner, Gruzen, Samton, Steinglass, New York, New York

David M. Dunkelman, Executive Director, Rosa Coplon Jewish Home and Infirmary, Buffalo, New York

Rose Duran-Harvey, Manager, Employee Development, Department of Human Resources, Mount Sinai Medical Center, Miami Beach, Florida

James E. Eden, Ed.D., General Manager and Vice President, Senior Living Services Division, Marriott Corporation, Washington, D.C

Arvid Elness, AIA President/CEO, Arvid Elness Architects, Inc., Minneapolis, Minnesota

Mark Engelbrecht, AIA, Principal, Engelbrecht & Griffin, Des Moines, Iowa

Bruce I. Fisher, Chief Financial Officer, New Haven Medical Hotel, New Haven, Connecticut

David A. Frank, AIA, Partner, Korsumsky Krank Erickson Arch., Inc., Minneapolis, Minnesota

Joseph Franko, Director of Marketing, The Clinic Center Hotel (Cleveland Clinic), Cleveland, Ohio

Jean Marc Gauthier, AIA, Architecte D.P.L.G., Paris, France

David Ginsberg, FAIA, Executive Vice President / Chief Planning Officer, The Presbyterian Hospital in the city of New York, Columbia-Presbyterian Medical Center, New York, New York

William Glass, AIA Project Manager, Senior Living Services Division, Marriott Corporation, Washington, D.C.

Lewis S. Goodfriend, P. E., Principal, Lewis S. Goodfriend & Associates, Morristown, New Jersey

Malcolm Grear, Helen M. Danforth Distinguished Professor, R.I.S.D.; CEO, Malcolm Grear Designers, Inc., Providence, Rhode Island

Shaun T. Griffin, Poet and Disability Advocate, Turning Point, Inc., Reno, Nevada

David A. Guynes, President, Guynes Design Inc., Phoenix, Arizona

Imre Halasz, Professor, Architecture, MIT, Cambridge, Massachusetts

Mary Harrison, Regional Administrator, Life Care Services, Abby Delray South, Delray Beach, Florida

Precia Harthcock, President, PRH Interior Design, Benica, California

Thomas R. Hauck, AIA, The Eggers Group P.C., New York, New York

Janet Hays, Marketing Associate, NBBJ/Rosenfield, New York, New York

Carolyn Kizer, Pulitzer Prize winner for Poetry, Sonoma, California

Ronald Kollar, Assistant Vice President, Planning and Design, Classic Residence by Hyatt, Chicago, Illinois

Albert Richard Lamb, Partner, Rick Lamb Associates, Cambridge, Massachusetts

Jeffrey H. Los, AIA, Vice President, Cannon, St. Louis, Missouri

Christian A. Mason, MBA, Vice President, Operations, Sun Retirement Corporation, Salem, Oregon

Joseph A. McDonnell, Sculptor, Cold Spring, New York

Philip A. Monteleoni, Associate Partner, Skidmore, Owenes & Merrill, New York, New York

Donald L. Moon, President, Friends Retirement Concepts, Inc., Lower Gwynedd, Pennsylvania

Bradford Perkins, AIA, Partner, Perkins, Geddis, Eastman Architects, New York, New York

Stevan D. Porter, MBA, District Director—Sales and Marketing, Embassy Suites Hotels—Southern California, Irvine, California

Barbara Proven, Activities Director, Life Care Services, Abby Delray South, Delray Beach, Florida

Robert B. Rees, Vice President, Baptist Hospital of Miami, Miami, Florida

David Rockwell, AIA, Principal, Haverson-Rockwell Architects, P.C., New York, New York

Stephen R. Roizen, Administrator, The Willows at Westborough, Westborough, Massachusetts

Zachary Rosenfield, Partner, NNBJ/Rosenfield New York, New York

Wayne Ruga, AIA, ASID, President, Wayne Ruga Architect, Inc., Martinez, California

Robert J. Shakno, President and CEO, The Mt. Sinai Medical Center, Cleveland, Ohio

Richard Somerset-Ward, President, RSW Enterprises, New York, New York

Ronald P. Steger, General Manager, New Haven Medical Hotel, New Haven, Connecticut

Earl S. Swensson, FAIA, Chairman of the Board, Earl Swensson Associates, Nashville, Tennessee

Lynn Tamarkin Syms, President, Tamarkin Design Associates, Inc., New York, New York

Glen Tipton, AIA, Senior Vice President, Cochran, Stephenson & Donkervoet, Inc., Baltimore, Maryland

Martin Trueblood, Vice President, Development Consulting, American Retirement Corporation, Williamsburg, Virginia

Martin S. Valins, Dipl. Arch. RIBA, Martin Valins & Associates, London, England

Barbara J. Watt, R.N., ASID, Senior Interior Designer, Marriott Corporation, Washington, D.C.

Karen Myers Ziccardi, ASID, President, Interior Design Development, Inc., Costa Mesa, California

CONTRIBUTORS OF PHOTOGRAPHS AND ILLUSTRATIONS

Adjustable Fixture Co., Milwaukee, Wisconsin

Backen Arrigoni & Ross, Inc., San Francisco, California

Byron Bell, AIA, Partner, Farrell, Bell & Lennard, New York, New York

Bohm-NBBJ, Columbus, Ohio

Buttrick White & Burtis, New York, New York

Casa del Mar, Boca Raton, Florida

Cedars Medical Center, Miami, Florida

Cini-Little International, Inc., Cleveland, Ohio

Cookle Douglas Farr, Jackson, Mississippi

CTB/Childs Bertman Tseckares & Casendino, Inc., Boston, Massachusetts

Culpepper McAuliffe & Meaders, Atlanta, Georgia

Paul Darrall, Santa Monica, California

Design I Interiors, Los Angeles, California

DiLeonardo International, Inc., Warwick, Rhode Island

Ewing Cole Cherry Parsky, Philadelphia, Pennsylvania

Fusch-Serold & Partners, Inc., Dallas, Texas

Hansen Lind Meyer, Inc., Iowa City, Iowa

Healthcare Medical Center of Tustin, Tustin, California

Honeywell, Inc., Golden Valley, California

Hoskins, Scott, Taylor & Partners, Inc., Boston, Massachusetts

Huyens Di Mella Shaffer, Boston, Massachusetts

Khuly Alvarez Associates, Inc., Miami, Florida

Klick Inter Arch Designs, Minneapolis, Minnesota

Life Designs, Salt Lake City, Utah

Jain Malkin, Inc., La Jolla, California.

Martin Organization, Philadelphia, Pennsylvania

Miami Heart Institute, Miami, Florida

Richard McDermott Miller, New York University Medical Center, New York, New York

Palmcrest House—Senior Eye Gallery, Long Beach, California

Tim Prentice, Sculptor, West Cornwall, New York

Arthur Schuster, Inc., St. Paul, Minnesota

Shepard Legan Aldrian, Minneapolis, Minnesota

Sherertz, Frankin, Crawford & Staffner, Roanoke, Virginia

Soderstrom Architects, Inc., Portland, Oregon

Sullivan Associates, Inc., Philadelphia, Pennsylvania

SwimEx Systems, Inc., Warren, Rhode Island

Tadder Associates, Inc., Baltimore, Maryland

The Christian Partnership, Inc., St. Louis, Missouri

Treffinger, Walz & McLeod, San Rafael,
California

TRO/The Ritchie Organization, Newton,
Massachusetts

Wallace, Roberts & Todd, Philadelphia,
Pennsylvania

Rober Wendler & Paul Pizzo Architects, New
Haven, Connecticut

Contents

Foreword

The most intensive debate over our nation's healthcare system since the enactment of Medicare and Medicaid in 1965 may reach its climax before long. Legislation is pending in the United States Congress that would guarantee every American access to affordable, quality healthcare services. This is not the first time such legislation has been introduced; indeed, various proposals have been introduced and considered for many years.

This may well be the first time, however, that a majority of the people of this nation—including consumers, businesspeople, healthcare providers and elected officials—have agreed that our healthcare system has broken down and must be fixed. While there is considerable disagreement over the kind of reform needed, there is a strong consensus that the time for reform is now.

Much of the changed mood can be attributed to rapidly escalating costs and inadequate access to healthcare services; indeed, the legislative debate has centered around ensuring access to health insurance and instituting cost containment measures. The current drive for reform is motivated by two major factors: deep concern over the potentially imminent collapse of our healthcare system, and a desire to address the very real, painful and growing human consequences of a failing system: 34 million Americans have no health insurance at all; millions of other Americans are underinsured; and countless others who do have adequate insurance coverage worry that the premium cost may soon be beyond reach.

Another serious problem, which is also the focus of much concern, is our growing aging population. Whether healthy or ill, older people have physical and emotional needs that have not been adequately addressed by a society that is increasingly fragmented and isolated. The days of the elderly grandparent living with her child and grandchildren are largely gone: the true portrait of America today is an elderly widow or widower living alone at home or in a nursing home. Mobility, distance, divorce, estrangement—even personal choice—may contribute to this situation.

Whether we wish to alter this course or not, we must recognize the nature of society today. Our institutions should enhance the quality of life of the people they serve, and this is no less true in the health or long-term care setting.

Dianne Davis and Albert Bush-Brown have added a new and significant dimension to the current healthcare debate. Their central premise—that healthcare institutions must recognize "two great human needs, our need for privacy and our need for membership" through "hospitable . . . design and services" —is a reminder that the healthcare system we are working to fix involves not only the physical but also the emotional, spiritual, and psychological well-being of the individual. We must remember that while universal access to the healthcare system is necessary, the success of any system will depend on whether we can truly respond to both the physical and mental health needs of the ill and aging individual.

In 1923, Albert Schweitzer wrote that "the tragedy of man is what dies inside himself while he still lives." Dianne Davis and Albert Bush-Brown show us one way that our healthcare system can help foster in the individual the spirit, will, energy, and desire to live healthy and well.

Claiborne Pell
U.S. Senator

This book discusses the design of hospitals, ambulatory care centers, special treatment centers, nursing homes, senior living communities (SLC), continuing care retirement communities (CCRC), and medhotels.

Organized in nine parts, more than ninety essays and 218 illustrations champion a single theme: our plea for healthcare institutions that are hospitable in their design and services. We advocate the design of a caring, intimate, and enriching experience.

Where heretofore the imagery has been that of the medical technician (clinical, aseptic, efficient) and the bedridden patient (confinement, isolation, immobility), we urge designers, developers, administrators, and public officials to build healthcare facilities that are spatially generous and congenial, and to offer hospitable services that motivate activity, companionship, membership, and a will to enjoy a future.

Intended to challenge traditional forms and inspire new models, the text is organized by topics rather than by building types. Where a conventional outline might open with hospitals and intensive care units, then introduce clinics, nursing homes and ambulatory care centers, and end with CCRCs, this outline offers a series of topics, such as circulation, spatial design, color, and lighting, which occur in all healthcare building types. Admittedly, some topics are more transferable than others; for example, while foodservice is a universal topic, our particular advice—that dining be a social and cultural experience—is not as valuable for an Alzheimer unit as it is for an SLC, CCRC, or birthing wing of a hospital.

Overall, we ask how to satisfy two great human needs, our need for privacy and our need for membership. Several essays inquire into how to design healthcare communities that foster those two essential conditions for hospitality.

Our intent is to focus on hospitable design, no matter its origin or application. If hotels offer services hospitals can adopt, if an airport concourse suggests an alternative to nursing home corridors, if lighting is best in select restaurants, if an artist's studio suggests how a CCRC might shape space for creative work, then those nonmedical models are introduced with the intent that they be adapted to various healthcare settings.

Hospitable design starts with a holistic concern for patients. None of us is merely a lymph, circulatory, skeletal, or nervous system. Our sentient, intelligent, and spiritual functions defy such specialists' physiological analyses. We are also contextual and social. While we relish privacies, we thrive on relationships with family and friends. And we are also creative. Therefore, we do not restore or sustain our health by medicine alone. The clinical imagery does not account for the feistiness of the 87-year-old Max Lerner, whose "continuing high spirits," after cancerous lymphoma, chemotherapy, prostate cancer, pulmonary cancer, and a heart attack, his daughter attributes to his fantasy: "My father can't imagine a world without him." Beyond surgery and medicines, there are cultural, social, intellectual, spiritual, and creative agents.

How to integrate those agents into the clinical model is the theme of this book. It is informed by current trends: colossal urban and regional hospitals that are becoming larger, more impersonal, more expensive, and more remote; a growing need for short-term stays at such technically sophisticated hospitals for intensive care and diagnostic, remedial care; a greater need for alternate models for short-term and repeated treatment; a growing need for special institutions that will cope with the rising incidence of depression, alcoholism, AIDS, or Alzheimer's disease; and the rapid growth of the aged population, which needs better healthcare delivery and community planning.

By "community planning," we intend to convey the need to build villages and neighborhoods where residences attract and satisfy both younger families and older people, with different common facilities provided for the different generations. We oppose segregation of elderly people and advocate mixed-use, multigenerational community planning.

We are deeply concerned for the ill and aged; our compassion is especially moved by those millions of Americans who are also impoverished. At best, their fate may be a crowded nursing home where a morbid cloud hangs over everyone. Yet, this book is avowedly directed at providing hospitable healthcare for those families about and above the middle income level simply because models exist. These models will work at all income levels, but their adaptation requires a national resolution of the debates over Social Security, health insurance, Medicaid, Medicare, and community planning. Toward that goal, essays are directed at chief obstacles preventing the development of a national program: zoning, codes, and finances. Until those barriers are eased, the American provision for care of the ill and elderly will not work well for families at any economic level, whether afflicted by accident, congenital deformity, cancer, heart disease, AIDS, alcoholism, or age. There is good reason to be hopeful. Examples of hospitable design for healthcare and senior communities abound amid a rising demand for more.

The chief obstacle to developing a national healthcare program is the ideological commitment of our market-driven society against any initiative grounded in solely social value. Nowhere in America will our marketing of the "Good Life"—advertised as endless youth, buoyant health, lucrative work, abundant leisure, "fast foods," aggressive sports, transient sex, and on-the-road mobility—miss reality's mark so widely as for the generation who will dominate the 21st century: elderly people. Unemployed, unengaged, lonely, often infirm and seldom without financial worries, the elderly live in an unsympathetic, unresponsive social setting, and that alienation is broadcast by "Good Life" TV and radio commercials every few minutes.

Social alienation is made worse by the physical conditions the elderly encounter. From transit obstacles they cannot negotiate on their way to distant markets and hospitals, to food and drug labels they cannot read, the aged will suffer badly from our cities' physical obsolescence, colossal scale, and lack of communities and neighborhoods where local organizations and institutions provide services and help. Our suburbs are not more fortunate. The freestanding house, automobile, and "commercial strip" reflect our preoccupation with the "Good Life" for perpetual youth.

The elderly and infirm in America are deeply hurt by the "Good Life's" social atomism. We have nearly lost our will to build neighborhood institutions and communities. When the historian James Truslow Adams described the "American Dream," in 1927, he described it as an individual's ability to realize self-fulfillment (life, liberty, happiness) because of the special American social condition—our governmental, economic, religious, and legal foundations for making communities. Since individual success rests on communal strengths, as Adams recognized, care is needed for the institutions and communities that nurture individual self-fulfillment. Hence, philanthropy and social invention have been peculiarly American social obligations, exemplified by the benefactor, Andrew Carnegie, who acted on the belief that private wealth should be invested in commonwealth.

To that belief we owe numerous hospitals, schools, colleges, universities, parks, churches, orchestras, museums, libraries, zoos, and gardens. Philanthropy has been inventive and responsive: settlement houses for immigrants, colleges for women, scientific and technical institutes, and asylums for invalids with chronic debilities. The YMCA and YWCA are emblems of American enterprise: private institutions and communities that offer public services and membership.

Unless we show comparable social, financial, and architectural invention today, after decades of little invention and much strain on the institutions we inherited, life for all ages— the elderly, the ill, the young, and all the middle-aged workers who support the others—will become intolerable. Leadership (and here we must fault successions of presidents, governors, mayors, and Secretaries of the Federal

Department of Housing and Urban Development) must somehow change the popular idea of the "Good Life" (and its consequent imagery for cities and healthcare institutions), so that the "American Dream" countenances our aging, often infirm and poor populations.

Central in the imagery that needs moderation is the colossal research hospital with sophisticated technicians, state-of-the-art equipment, and clinically minded specialists. Necessary and desirable as they certainly are, such medical centers dominate urban planners' thinking, to the exclusion of other vehicles for healthcare. Capital costs for buildings and a CAT-scanner or MRI, combined with rising costs for operations (insurance, research, teaching, unionized personnel, and healthcare specialists) urge planners to think of aggregation and centralization in comprehensive ʹmedical centers. These are not planned for lifecare, and their model will not meet the needs of aging Americans.

Supplements and alternatives to the comprehensive medical center should enter our healthcare imagery. One is the recovery hotel, where postoperative patients recuperate in more congenial, less costly facilities. Another is the inn, hotel, or suite that enables cooperative care of patients by a family member or friend. A third is a new version of home care, such as "district nurses" formerly conducted. A fourth is the ambulatory medical and surgical clinic. A fifth is the day-care center for those adults living with relatives who work during the daytime. A sixth is the hospice for terminal care. A seventh is any of several versions of the lifecare community, notably the continuing care retirement community (CCRC). Small, local, responsive and accessible, those supplements to the comprehensive medical center should be integrated vertically into a system of urban and regional healthcare delivery.

Such integration of a variety of healthcare institutions will require a second change in the imagery underlying planning, namely zoning. Today, most zoning legislation attempts to protect property values and public welfare by prescribing which uses may occur on various land areas. Reasons of density, pollution, sunlight, air, noise, and natural (including scenic) value support zoning laws that separate uses. Mixing uses makes social, cultural, and economic sense: CCRCs on university campuses; ambulatory clinics in office buildings; adult day care centers in commercial areas; shopping malls with apartments for the elderly; apartments, YMCAs, and nursing centers above parking garages.

Given zoning opportunities to build mixed-use developments, American enterprise will quickly invest in lifecare institutions, of which the most promising, the CCRC, offers private residence, membership in a community, medical care, and a contract providing lifetime healthcare.

The principal and generative insight needed by national and local leaders is that successful lifecare requires social and architectural nurture of privacy and membership within stimulating communities that are integrated into both their local urban contexts and their regional medical systems. Unlikely as it may seem, we found hospitable design and care in a private institution dedicated to poor elderly men and women who are blind and have Alzheimer's disease. If it is possible in that tragic circumstance, hospitable healthcare is possible everywhere. ∎

Acknowledgments

Like other books that advocate expanded goals for evolving professions, *Hospitable Design for Healthcare and Senior Communities* started from a simple, neglected premise: that medical settings should be hospitable. That idea inspired Professor Davis, whose insight into possibilities for more congenial hospitals was informed by her knowledge of fine hotel and restaurant services. From that beginning, the theme developed rapidly: first, with the enlistment of Albert Bush-Brown, Hon. AIA, as co-author, to introduce architectural design and social planning, and, thereafter, with invitations to nearly a hundred experts to contribute essays and illustrations. Throughout two years' travel and study, the authors were generously helped by these contributors and also by many designers and managers of healthcare facilities who are credited in the text and captions.

Editors of journals were especially helpful: M. J. Madigan of *Restaurant Hotel Design International*, Donna Boss of *Food Management*, James Bowe of *Contemporary Long-Term Care*, Mary Chamberlain of *Modern Healthcare*, Charles Bernstein of *Nation's Restaurant News*, Sara O. Maraberry of *Contract*, and Edith Tucker of *United Retirement Bulletin*.

Professional associations and organizers of conferences and exhibitions responded readily to requests for information: The American Association of Retired Persons, American Association of Homes for the Aging, National Association of Senior Living Industries, and American College of Hospital Administrators. An organizer of seminars on healthcare design, Wayne Ruga, AIA, ISID, was an early ally, as was James Marquart, President of the New York State Hospitality and Tourism Association. The Educational Institute of the American Hotel and Motel Association provided opportunities to organize seminars during the annual International Hotel/Motel and Restaurant Show.

Many architectural and interior design firms were extraordinarily informative and helpful; we thank Charles Griffin, AIA, and Mark Engelbrecht, AIA, of Engelbrecht & Griffin; Dennis Cagan of Design One Interiors; Thomas Hauck, AIA, of The Eggers Group; John Klick, AIA, and Colleen Schmaltz, ASID, of Klick Inter Arch Design; Jain Malkin, of Jain Malkin, Inc.; Donald Dissinger, AIA, of Ewing Cole Cherry Parsky; Richard Donkervoet, AIA, and Glen Tipton, AIA, of Cochran, Stephenson & Donkervoet and their British affiliate, Martin Valins, RIBA, of Martin Valins + Associates. William Glass, AIA, then head of Design, Senior Living Division, Marriott Corporation, now consultant to CS&D, was especially charitable in suggesting new models. Martin Cohen, FAIA, kept us informed about the AIA's Task Force: "Facilities for Aging: Agenda for Action in the 1990's."

Organizers and managers of healthcare facilities welcomed our study. Especially informative were Jessie Lee, of Life Care Services, who manages the North Hill Continuing Care Retirement Community in Needham, Massachusetts; Stephen Roizen, Administrator of The Willows at Westborough, Massachusetts; Mary Harrison, Florida Regional Director for Life Care Services; Aaron Fodiman, President of the Kapok Corporation in Clearwater, Florida, who developed the concept of joint venture between a restaurant and senior living community; and James Eden, Vice President for Senior Living Division, Marriott Corporation.

As our essays developed, we sought advice from Marion DeJur (Professor Davis' mother and widow of a physician); Judith Harris, consultant in medical communications; Carolyn Doppelt Gray (then a Deputy Assistant Secretary [acting] for the United States Department of Health and Human Services [Office of Human Development Services]), now attorney with Saul, Ewing Remick & Saul; Paula Terry of the National Council on the Arts; Miner

Brown of Meridian Healthcare; Dr. Jules Feingold, founder of Palmcrest Home and Senior Eye Gallery (the first professional gallery within a retirement center and convalescent hospital) in Long Beach, California; and Richard Westin of Western Financial Group, which specializes in hotel conversions.

Periodically, we reviewed the book's scope and outline with four wise counselors, Marvin Spira, Leonard Rubin, Harriet Morgan and Martin Hassner. As always, special friends Thomas R. Hauck, AIA; Walter A. Netsch, FAIA; G. E. Kidder Smith, FAIA; Benjamin A. Thompson, FAIA; and John Spencer, former President, Barclays Bank of New York, gave luster and sparkle to our ideas. We thank Helene Santos for her diligence with illustrations and her assistance in typing much of the text.

Inevitably, we received more ideas and documents than we could use. Of more than 900 photographs, the book displays less than a third. To more than a dozen design firms, unmentioned in the text, we give thanks for their prompt and constructive response.

Since we make an urgent plea for reform of the national healthcare system, we welcome the Foreword written by U.S. Senator Claiborne Pell. Chairman of the Committee on Foreign Relations, Senator Pell also chairs the Subcommittee on Education, Arts and Humanities and is a member of the Committee on Labor and Human Resources, the Subcommittee on Aging, and the Subcommittee on Children, Families, Drugs and Alcoholism. His endorsement of our thesis—*that healthcare institutions must recognize our need for privacy and our need for membership through hospitable design and services*—is greatly appreciated, for we hope to see that premise recognized in the current Congressional healthcare debate.

Lilly Kaufman, Executive Editor for Architecture, Design, and Hospitality within Van Nostrand Reinhold, was our earliest, steadfast champion, and her colleagues, Amanda Miller, Liz Geller, Kenneth Allen, and Louis Vasquez, have guided the book's production with skill, humor and alacrity, even when the manuscript arrived five months early.

One group of supporters needs special thanks, namely, those who gave us the time and services needed for writing and editing. For Professor Davis, Senior Principal of Hospitality Healthcare Designs, thanks go to the New School for Social Research (which sponsored the first seminar, "Hospitality and Beyond," that addressed combined healthcare and hospitality design and services). New York University (for the opportunity to create the Center for the Study of Foodservice Management), and International TEAM Associates. Dr. Bush-Brown is grateful to Barclays Bank of New York (where he chairs the Regional Advisory Boards and was non-executive Chairman of the Board), Skidmore, Owings & Merrill (for whom he wrote *SOM 1973–1983*); Andry Montgomery, Inc. (where he was Chairman); and Hill & Knowlton (Senior Counselor)—who in multiple, generous ways, provided colleagues, ideas, space and time to work upon this book.

With gratitude to all.

Albert Bush-Brown
Dianne Davis

Introduction

Although Americans must make hard choices about future healthcare delivery, we have many excellent models and a rising will and ability to create more. To dwell on the lapses, whether forlorn nursing homes or sordid clinics, is unjustified. Expanding hospitals in Atlanta, New Orleans, and San Francisco give heartening reassurance that effort, ideas, and money are being directed at perfecting healthcare. Houston, Boston, New York, Cleveland, and Miami are internationally renowned centers of advanced medical care.

Less recognized are the smaller but admirable models for intermittent and long-term care at the community level. Yet at Fountain House in Manhattan, the architecture and program demonstrate how severely depressed adults may be helped to functional independence. At Massachusetts General Hospital in Boston, one of the many burn centers established by the Shriners is a model of medical and hospitable care. The cooperative care program within New York University's hospital in New York City suggests how a patient needing acute care may be assisted by family members and friends. Were they better known, the Hospice in Boca Raton, Florida, two continuing care retirement communities (CCRCs) at Kennett Square, Pennsylvania, the Alzheimer Center in the Riverdale, New York, Hebrew Home for the Aged, the clinic of the Menninger Foundation in Topeka, Kansas, and the maternity wing of Miami Baptist Hospital would all suggest exemplary directions for a national healthcare system.

Our study of those encouraging models suggests two observations, which explain the emphasis and organization within this book. First, to restate the Preface: The chief and seminal insight needed by national and local planners is that successful healthcare and lifecare requires social and architectural nurture of privacy and membership within stimulating communities that are integrated into both their local contexts and their regional medical systems.

Second: Design for healthcare and senior communities must start fundamentally with a full program of spatial needs, followed by site planning, and completed by shaping and connecting the needed spaces, always with sensitivity to proportion, scale, light, acoustics, color, and furnishings. While some essays—for example, those about circulation, color, chairs, and light—speak of interior design, scant attention is directed to interior "decoration" or "furnishing," which, we believe, can succeed only when the decorator's and furnisher's useful roles are performed within the fundamental architectural service—providing fine spaces and sequences of space. In one sense, no essay addresses interior design; in a more profound sense, this book discusses nothing else: the architectural conditions for achieving useful, fine interior spaces.

Those two observations about a national healthcare goal and architectural design lead us to state twenty-seven provocative propositions that appear and reappear as premises in the essays:

1. The successful healthcare institution today must be designed to offer hospitable space and be organized to provide congenial, amenable services. (See especially Parts I, II, III, VIII).
2. While it will continue to be a model for research, education, diagnosis, and remedial intervention, the colossal, comprehensive regional or urban medical center will specialize in emergency, intensive, and critical care for patients whose hospitalization is brief (Parts IV, V, VI).
3. A close definition of markets suggests that such comprehensive hospitals will be augmented by various community-scaled in-

stitutions offering postoperative care, routine diagnostic and surgical procedures, ambulatory care, adult care, and long-term care (Parts VI, IX).

4. The clinical or laboratory model does not satisfy long-term patients' needs nor anticipate the requirements of the elderly, who are the largest group of healthcare consumers (Parts I, II, III, IV, VIII).

5. The imagery of the immobilized, confined, and isolated patient must be replaced by one that nurtures physical, social, and intellectual activity (Parts II, III).

6. The arts of music, dance, painting, and sculpture are beneficial agents for restoring and sustaining health, and creative, not merely passive, aesthetic experience should be encouraged (Part III).

7. Architectural sterility, even senility, promotes places where nothing moves, nothing is present, and therefore nothing occurs (Parts I, II, III, IV).

8. Spatial planning must reflect patients' need for both privacy and community (Parts II, IV).

9. A sense of membership must be nurtured by sequences of common or public spaces related to concourses (Parts II, III, IV).

10. Circulation patterns should reduce conventional arrangements of corridors, elevators, and stairs, and introduce dedicated paths, concourses, atriums, and agoras (Part IV).

11. Moving patients to central services is often not so beneficial as arrangements that deliver decentralized services to groups of patients residing in clustered spaces (Part IV).

12. Generous spatial design, augmented by natural light, is a fundamental origin of hospitable environment (Parts IV, V).

13. Designers must rid themselves of spatial enumeration and diagrams that are collections of boxes (Parts III, IV, V).

14. Detailed planning and furnishing of patients' rooms should reflect practical conditions, such as acoustics and lighting, and newly wanted services, such as facsimile and other machines that enable patients to conduct their affairs (Parts V, VI).

15. Hospitable design requires imaginative attention to landscape, lighting, color, graphics, furniture, and hardware (Parts III, IV, V, VI, VII).

16. Specialized healthcare requires explicit models for the hospice, medhotel, adult day-care center, and ambulatory care center (Part VI).

17. Old hotels and mansions offer useful, attractive spaces for senior communities (Part III).

18. A rising incidence of AIDS, depression, alcoholism and drug addiction requires special agencies and, often, spaces devoted to cooperative care involving family members and friends (Parts II, III, IV, V, VI).

19. The CCRC is a developing but intricate building type that holds great promise for long-term care of the elderly (Parts II, III, IV, VIII, IX).

20. The design of communal spaces requires hierarchies of meeting places and visual reciprocities (Part III).

21. Patients and residents should be encouraged to participate in planning institutional policies (Part VIII).

22. Hospitable design aids in the satisfaction and retention of staff (Parts VIII, IX).

23. The goal of hospitable healthcare will be advanced by educating administrators, trustees, and public officials (Part VIII).

24. Hospitable healthcare requires changes in building codes, regulations, zoning, and financing (Part IX).

25. Beneficial directions for urban development and community planning are suggested by both the campus-style and high-rise healthcare communities, especially the senior living communities (SLC) and the CCRC (Parts II, III, IV, IX).

26. The college or university campus offers potential sites and services for CCRCs (Part IX).

27. Imaginative designers are proposing models where healthcare is integrated within urban communities that provide multigenerational housing and medical care in the context of commercial, social, and cultural institutions (Parts III, IV, V, IX).

These twenty-seven propositions suggest the chief themes, but the essays can also be read to derive other topics: regional style as an aid in marketing; adoption of the concierge and other ideas from successful hotels; the advantages of modularized design; the need for training and motivating personnel; and the brutal insensitivity of hardware and equipment manufactured without regard for the aged or disabled. Indeed, the essays range across nearly all the features that will encourage hospitable design for healthcare and senior living communities. ■

Part I

Advocacy for Hospitable Design

Following up on the large themes stated in the Preface and Introduction, Part I discusses two questions: What is hospitable design? What are its economic and therapeutic advantages?

1/Strategies for Hospitable Design

Albert Bush-Brown

As an advocate of hospitable design, I would love to claim, as all architects, interior designers, and graphic artists would, that good ordering of environment promotes health, and bad design deters health. We want to say that right design is curative, restorative, and beneficial. Unfortunately, such bountiful results from a spatial composition, color scheme, symphony of sound, or pattern of lights are not demonstrable.

Let us be modest: Good design is an ally in healthcare; it can be a *fundamental* ally; it can support personal, social, and technical services. But good design is not the only generator of health. Surgery, radiology, and chemistry are powerful agents. Laughter and faith also help. Even in a dark and shapeless room, the hand that touches and holds has a magic to heal no architect can match.

Recall the Hawthorne experiment. This experiment took place after Western Electric officials, who had been worried about low productivity, defective products, absenteeism, and turnover, learned that assemblers of telephones were complaining about insufficient light. When footcandles in one laboratory were raised, output rose, incidence of defective equipment dropped, and absenteeism declined. Later, when footcandles were lowered, production still rose, and absenteeism and turnover continued to decline. Footcandles no longer mattered. Treated special, that laboratory's workers had become a team, proud of the quality and quantity of their production, unwilling to let the team down. Lighting was a catalyst; management's care and concern for environment fostered morale and changed social behavior.

Believing that design, as a catalyst, influences social conduct, we may still claim too much for its healing, therapeutic value. That is especially likely if we think of design as decoration. What colors for walls; which patterns

Baptist Hospital of Miami, Miami, Florida. (Photo: Medical Services, courtesy of Robert Rees)

for floors, where should paintings be hung, should there be a chandelier? That is all superficial. True, the sunny palette and generous room please us, and we are offended by the crude, noxious, putrid, and bilious. But good design does not start simply from rejecting such blatant offenses, nor, indeed, from selecting pretty patterns.

Rather, hospitable design starts from *basic decisions about how to organize people, give them appropriate spaces, situate caring services, and enable people to work effectively with each other.* That is not superficial. It insists upon profound origins for design.

3

Considering design in that way—as an organization of basic decisions about people—I would ask first about your healthcare facility, "Whose welfare dominates? Who, really, is served? Who is the client?" If, as a patient or guest, I drive up to your hospital and find that the only open, accessible parking spaces are reserved for the Director, Assistant Directors, and sundry physicians who arrive once a day, I know that the patient or visitor is less important. If I encounter elevators jammed by technicians, telephones tied up by custodians, distracted receptionists, baffling corridors, and visitors pleading with paper-burdened nurses to bring a medication or order a clean sheet, then I ask, "Whose welfare dominates, mine as patient, or the accountant's, the technician's, the physician's, the custodian's—or perhaps no one's?" Are we all meant to compete? Good design should champion the patient first, the patient's wardens and servants second. What technical or entrepreneurial arrogance suggests that the patient should be second-class? Do you serve patients or medicine or profit?

Considering design profoundly prompts two more questions: What is the *program?* and

What spaces are wanted? The basic needs are obvious: so many patients' rooms, so many offices and examining rooms, a laundry, kitchens, nurses' areas and laboratories. While the shape and location of patients' rooms and the laboratories will attract much attention, those conventional spaces will not suffice. The hospitable program for any marketable long-term healthcare community today includes amenities: a library, dining rooms, gift shops, studios and workshops, places for music, lectures, and film, and places for exercise and games. Mere cells for patients and laboratories for technicians will provide neither the services nor the morale essential to healthcare. The clinical program alone does not include hospitality and all its supporting services. It does not countenance that the patient or resident is a whole person with diverse talents and debilities, with unique hopes and fears, and with need for associations and privacies.

Therefore, my next questions ask about the shape and quality of *communal* spaces. Are they mean afterthoughts, some leftover lobby where a windowless meeting room is tucked in, some cramped room where wheelchaired pa-

Baptist Hospital of Miami, Miami, Florida. (Photo: Medical Services, courtesy of Robert Rees)

tients are forced to watch television, some low-ceilinged corridor where residents or staff line up to enter a cafeteria? Or are they instead ample and cheerful, a convivial lounge, a terrace with a view, a quiet library, an interesting exhibit, or a creative studio? To refer again to the Hawthorne experiment: If the curative function is to lift morale and a will to be vital, then healthcare spaces must inspire pride in belonging to a successful community.

The most critical point in that endeavor is circulation. How (my next question) shall circulation resolve conflicting demands? The need for privacy competes with the need for access. Providing two separated ways, one for staff, another for patients, competes with the need for economy. Traditionally, private spaces are organized in healthcare facilities along central public corridors. Passageways are then encumbered by patients, guests, nurses, physicians, custodians, technicians, food, laundry, and equipment—all competing. Successful alternatives to the double-loaded corridor exist in the cluster, atriums, agoras, and concourses. The tall, wide, airy space lessens confinement and eases flow. It is a natural lo-cation for lobbies, staircases, reception areas, and major intersections, which then become gathering and interchange points that encourage exchange and foster membership.

Such tall nodal spaces, a further point, offer more than directional and social value. They readily accommodate services and concessions such as cafes, restaurants, gift shops, libraries, and studios. When a hospital sets itself the objective of serving the patient and family, the restaurant, health spa, and conference rooms will have a wholly fresh imagery. When they are well-located and well-designed, the fine restaurant, auditorium, or spa inside a hospital becomes a source of revenue and membership.

Natural light is the tall space's ally. Seek natural light. Break the confinement and monotony of ordinary halls and rooms. Puncture walls and roofs; draw light along floors and stairs, at rooflines, in ridges, at corners, even at peaks. Catch the dawn and sunset. Then spaces will be vibrant.

Another point is a caution: Curb the tendency to demand flexibility. You will hear designers advocate "universal space" with flat

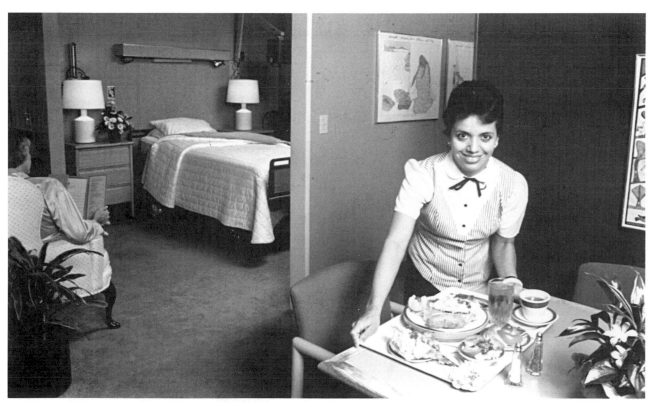

Baptist Hospital of Miami, Miami, Florida. (Photo: Medical Services, courtesy of Robert Rees)

floors and ceilings and movable partitions, and you will hear technicians wanting to tap electricity from any floor, wall, or ceiling. Those requests betray the domination (first point) of the scientist–technician, who thinks a laboratory should be changed after each experiment. The architect, Louis Kahn, brilliantly designed the Richards Biological Laboratories in Philadelphia to be flexible. But why should long-term patients or members of a continuing care retirement community (CCRC) suffer flexibility or the defects in temporary partitions, which transmit noise and interfere with ventilation systems? Quiet walls with heating and cooling fitted to their permanent space are what they want. Forget plugging into whatever, wherever. The flexibility scientists and technicians ask designers to provide is seldom used.

Above all, hospitable design begs for new imagery. Central is the patient as a whole human being, whose will to be active, creative,

Baptist Hospital of Miami, Miami, Florida. (Photo: Medical Services, courtesy of Robert Rees)

The Gables at Old Farms Forest, Farmington, Connecticut. (Architect: Childs Bertman Tseckares & Casendino Inc./ Photo: Hutchins Photography Inc.)

Waverly Heights, Gladwyne, Pennsylvania. (Architect: Sullivan Associates Inc./Photo: Jim Schafer)

and social wants to be nurtured. Isolation and confinement in stultifying cubicles and 8-foot corridors will not provide that nurture. Rather, nurturing calls for spaces that inspire friendship, love, creativity, and caring. Those are different from mere clinical design, mere efficient design, or superficial decoration. This orange or that yellow does not matter. The scent of toast and biscuits does. Where we can see sunlight, seek stars at night, hear birds, touch and converse, we can *wonder.*

So I invite you to be skeptical about old models, questioning first who is to dominate our healthcare—the technician or patient? What is the program—efficient economical rooms off corridors or rooms that make a life-breathing community? And when you have answered those questions, there will be time to talk about colors, textures, chintzes, velours, and chandeliers. They will matter a lot if we

got things right; but if we did not, they won't matter at all, because we entertained a strategy that failed to put the patient first as a sensitive, dignified member of a community. That strategy has been dramatically and successfully introduced in Miami's Baptist Hospital and the Cleveland Clinic. A rising healthcare institution, the CCRC, has begun to attract profound planners, designers, financiers, and operators inspired by strategies for hospitable design and services.

Considered profoundly, design is the organization of people and services within admirable spatial sequences that support hospitable services. That sort of design has direct therapeutic value, and its dividends to morale, marketing, and finance are bountiful. Such design becomes possible when we rid ourselves of the clinical aesthetic and seek fresh imagery for hospitable healthcare. ■

Caretel®, Peachwood Inn/Borden Court, Rochester Hills, Michigan. Picadilly Lane. (Architect: Hobbs & Black Associates, Inc./Photo: Beth Singer, Photographer, Inc.)

2/Architecture and Healing

Jerry Breakstone

The current revolution in the delivery of healthcare services—a revolution that has focused on management issues such as cost containment, reimbursement formulas, and market share—has further confused and tested healthcare providers' priorities.

One result of this revolution, all too often, is health facility architecture that does little to support the healing process. ∎

3/Healthcare Imagery

Wayne Ruga

The imagery of care is no longer confined to the bed, wheelchairs and meal tray. The new imagery is a total living environment.

The goals of design must be to enhance the quality of life experience through hospitable design. ∎

4/Passage

Lynn Tamarkin Syms

The need for an inviting, hospitable atmosphere is especially essential when serving the geriatric population in nursing homes. Entering a nursing home for the first time as a new resident is a frightening and intimidating experience for an elderly person. Oversized lobbies decorated with large-scale furniture, bright fluorescent lighting, security and information desks made of unyielding surfaces, brightly figured wall coverings, and shiny flooring hardly feel like home. In fact, they tell newcomers that they have entered a new passage of life—one in which familiar surroundings are left forever—in no uncertain terms. ∎

5 / Final Meeting

Carolyn Kizer

Old friend, I dressed in my very best,
  Wore the furs I never wear,
Hair done at Bloomingdales,
Even a manicure; splashed on the good
  perfume
Before I rode the bus up Madison
To the rear entrance of the hospital;
Traversed for miles the corridors
  underground
Where orderlies in green wheeled metal carts
Piled with soiled linen, bottles, pans, and
  tubes.

Then, elevators found, I followed a colored
  line
To the proper nurses' station,
Embraced your wife: pale, having wept for
  weeks,
Worn out with your care.
She led me to your bedside. I swept in with an
  air,
Wrapped you in fur, censed you with my
  perfume.
Jaunty and thin, with the fine eyes and pursy
  lips
Of one of Holbein's Unknown Gentlemen,
You could not speak
Except for some unintelligible grunts
Through the hole they had made in your
  throat;
Impatient with your wife
Who, after years of understanding,
Could not understand.

Months of practice with my dying father
(shamed by his memory lost, he refused to
  speak,
Like Ezra Pound at the last) taught me to
  monologue:
Of our days in Roethke's room so long ago
Far off across a continent in Seattle:
One day when the bell had rung
We stood by the stairs in shabby Parrington
  Hall

As the hordes rushed past us to their classes.
"Oh Carolyn" you said in such a grieving
  tone,
"Beautiful women will never love me."
And I replied, "One day
You're going to be a famous poet,
And you will be pursued by lovely women."
"There! Wasn't I right?" I now say,
And you look up sweetly at the lovely woman
Who stands on the other side of your bed.

Dear one, back then you were so plain!
A pudgy face, a button nose, with a little wen
Right at the tip.
But we all knew, from the moment you spoke
On the first day in class, you were our genius.
Now pain has made you beautiful.
And the black satin domino
To shade your eyes when you nap,
Pushed back on your head, looks like a
  mandarin's cap.
With your shapely thin grey beard
You are phenomenally like Li Po,
A poet you adored.

"Well, dear, there's no Ohio left—except in
  poems";
I keep up a stream of jokes and
  reminiscences.
You scribble notes on your yellow pad,
Nod your mandarin nod.
Grief is not permitted till it's over,
And I'm outside, stunned, standing on Fifth
  Avenue
In the fierce cold of January.
Here I say what I could not say upstairs in
  your room:
A last goodbye. And thank you for the poems
You wrote to me when we were young.
                    Now go in peace, my friend,
Even as I go
Along the soiled pavement of the Avenue
Banked in the gutters with old snow. ■

6 / The Hospitality/Healthcare Marriage

Horace D'Angelo, Jr.

The marriage between hospitality and healthcare is made in heaven. They were born together. The word "hospitality" comes from a Latin word meaning "Inn." In the eleventh century, the Knights of Saint John of Jerusalem cared for the crusaders and pilgrims in the Holy Land. They were known as the Knights Hospitaler or simply Hospitalers. The places where the Hospitalers worked eventually were called hospitals.

From about 800 A.D. onwards, monasteries such as those at St. Gall, Cluny, and Beaune built open wards that usually terminated in a chapel. The cruciform ward emerged in the fifteenth century, and was the prevailing plan until the French architect, Tenon, designed the pavilion plan in 1787.

After the Crimean War, where Florence Nightingale gained the experience that led her to advocate airy, sunlit tent pavilions, the American, John Shaw Billings, in the late 1870s planned the Johns Hopkins Hospital in Baltimore, Maryland, which connected sunny ward pavilions to a northern corridor with nurses stations. In 1905, Dr. Albert Ochsner championed multistory buildings for reasons of efficiency, especially on urban sites.

As modern medicine improved, the hospital became the preferred institution for healthcare. Providers concentrated more and more on the complexities of modern medicine, and emphasis on hospitality lessened.

Fortunately for the elderly, who are the largest consumers of healthcare in our nation, the new models of hospitals, nursing homes, and elderly housing feature hospitality: attractive rooms, elaborate common spaces, and above all a greater selection of services and foods, while healthcare remains professional. The most successful and marketable method of serving the sick and elderly today is to combine hospitality with healthcare. ∎

7 / Integrated Design

Wayne Ruga

The goal of healthcare designers must be to enhance the quality of life through hospitable design. This imperative applies to the full spectrum of healthcare facilities—from the practitioner's office to the general acute-care hospital, special clinics, health centers, adult-care centers, and long-term-care facilities. The design must be fully integrated and extended throughout the entire facility.

The Community Hospital for the Monterey Peninsula is a good example of integrated hospitality design. The design is so effective that it is difficult to know if you are in a hospital or a country club. The lobby is shaped by a large domed skylight over a marble pond with fish. The corridors display art that has been collected from all around the world. The patients' rooms have views of natural settings. All staff are trained to support the commitment to excellence in hospitality. ∎

8/Aging and the Built Environment

George Baker III

How does one grow old in American society today? Certainly not the way our parents do or their parents did. First, a greater percentage of our parents' generation are alive —a larger percentage than their parents', though smaller than the generation ahead. Life expectancy in the United States has virtually doubled in the last century while birth rates have declined. Currently, there are more individuals over age 65 than there are teenagers. The average age is approaching forty! In the year 2020, twice as many individuals will celebrate their 65th birthday as did in 1985; 54 million Americans will be over 65 years of age.

Yet the myriad problems and opportunities arising from our population's age structure are randomly addressed. Today, we debate employment versus retirement, housing choices, the ethics of length versus quality of life, income maintenance, and the enormous costs of both public and private healthcare. Scant attention, however, is directed at what is all around us—"the built environment," where we live, work, and play, the tools and gadgets we use in our everyday lives. How accommodative is that environment toward optimizing our functional capacity as we grow older or are impaired?

Much hardware, many tools, and even instruments such as the thermostat or telephone are ill-shaped for performing regular daily tasks. Yet, our capacities change from the day of our birth until our death. Our abilities to function and use tools improve rapidly during the early decades of life; then almost imperceptibly, we experience decrements in many physiological functions throughout the mid and later decades, even in the absence of disease. Normative biological aging brings declines in visual, auditory, and physical capacities.

Although we can take important steps to reduce the probability of diseases or even retard physiological declines, the process of aging persists. That urges the need for a built environment that is hospitable, where tools, hardware, and equipment are not hostile and doors, faucets, and buttons respond readily even to the arthritic hand. ∎

9/Hospitality: The Future Trend

James E. Eden

During the past several years, healthcare for special populations, especially "the Graying American," has sparked the nation's developers and healthcare providers. For developers who rode the population growth during the postwar decades, the powerful demographics associated with the aging population afford new opportunities to build nursing homes, elders' housing, adult day-care projects, healthcare facilities, and a variety of senior service centers. For hospital administrators with empty beds and expensive overheads, medical services for the aged present the only significant opportunity to utilize excess capacity. Government officials and public policy planners are faced with the challenge of continued and additional funding of the healthcare services that will be increasingly demanded by seniors and those afflicted with illnesses requiring long hospitalization.

Almost void of general strategies, the national response to the rapidly aging American population has been opportunistic and somewhat chaotic growth of senior housing communities and healthcare services. In spite of the Older American Act of 1965, no cohesive or comprehensive national policy exists today. Owners of acute-care facilities are only recently learning that they have to compete for market share; also, in spite of regional, not-for-profit successes, there have also been multimillion-dollar failures because the buying habits of older Americans are not well understood. National, state, and local government agencies have established *barriers to meeting* the needs of seniors.

In the past few years, however, the pressures of competition and the lessons learned from failed efforts have produced the outlines of a general strategy. Healthcare marketing has been elevated to a significant organizational function, and its focus has become service ex-

cellence. Major publicly held nursing home and lodging companies have entered the senior housing markets. Beverly Enterprises and Hillhaven (a division of National Medical Enterprises) are among the top ten operators. Two leaders in hospitality, the Hyatt and Marriott corporations, have recently entered the health and adult-care industry with exceptional results in their early projects. They enjoy respected brand names, strong customer loyalty, and significant expertise in marketing. Further, they are familiar with competing for market share.

The emerging strategy places high value on hospitality for the senior markets. As the concept of service excellence takes hold as a winning strategy, it should lead to the examination of those issues that positively appeal to the various types of elderly. Research will hasten the realization that older persons are very much like any other age group in terms of wanting choice and quality, and there will be a major shift toward service excellence, hospitality, and marketing. ■

Part II

Activity and Membership

What is your image of the patient/resident—passive, isolated and confined; or active, congregate and creative? Can "circumstantial senility" be overcome? What benefits derive from creative engagement—in dance, song, poetry, painting and sculpture? From writing, gardening, dining and a role in governance?

10/Activity and Membership vs. Confinement and Isolation

Albert Bush-Brown

Healthcare, especially in long-term-care institutions, requires a departure from traditional models. Where conventional patterns prescribe patients' isolation, confinement, and disengagement, the preferred program encourages membership, activity, and engagement.

Encouraging intellectual, social, and cultural activity sets special goals for administrators and designers. It proposes that medical care will be more effective when patients feel that they are members of a community that cares. It opens doors to family and friends. It invites parents to stay with the lad who has severely burned his feet. It nurtures friendships for the lonely. It encourages opportunities to work, to create, and to feel useful.

Above all, it fosters stimulating, purposeful engagement within a community. That goal invites social invention and imaginative architecture.

Yet, of all the elements in recent nursing and lifecare communities, the least well designed are the communal spaces. Great effort is spent on private spaces, especially the bedroom and apartment; nursing units are designed admirably; and places for exercise, golf, tennis, and swimming are shaped by experts. Model dining spaces and retail shops increasingly appear in hospitals. But what spaces will stimulate creative engagement? What spaces will nurture a sense of membership? And how shall such spaces be arrayed and connected to develop a sense of community?

Carmel Valley Manor, Carmel Valley, California. (Landscape Architect: The SWA Group/Photo: Dixi Carrillo)

Menorah Park Jewish Home for the Aged, Beachwood, Ohio. (Architect: The Gruzen Partnership/Photo: David Hirsch)

Although Americans were once one of the most socially inventive people, our will to form communities is less evident today. Indeed, the meager communal spaces in our healthcare institutions reveal the loss. Early American creativity built schools, courthouses, churches, temples, and libraries, and set them in villages and towns. America's inventiveness before the Civil War appeared in granges, museums, lyceums, athenaeums, and other gathering places. After that war, American philanthropy and the Morrill Land Grant Act fostered institutes of agriculture and technology and many universities and specialized colleges, including colleges for women. In the 1880s, Baltimore built the Johns Hopkins Hospital and Medical School. By 1890, New Yorkers had organized the Philharmonic Orchestra and Bostonians, their Symphony. The YMCA, YWCA, AFL, CIO and settlement houses were creative responses to the need for membership and social services. Arboretums, parks, and botanical and zoological gardens gave public spaces to tenement dwellers within crowded cities.

Today, our needs for healthcare require a comparable burst of social creativity, but the late twentieth century reveals a decline in social inventiveness. We are not forming new, vital social agencies or renewing obsolete structures. There are exceptions: large performing arts centers in New York, Washington, Los Angeles, and San Francisco; myriad shopping centers; some dramatic waterfront developments, such as those in Boston and New Orleans. All are tokens of energy, organization, and investment at a large urban scale. Where America's social creativity shows marked decline is in urban neighborhoods and new suburban tracts. Except for the shopping strip and the country clubs, the suburb affords few places for congregation. In our cities, a small, old music school, boys or girls club, settlement house, church, or hospital struggles to remain vital. Our social lethargy does not bode well for making hospitable small hospitals, nursing homes, or continuing care retirement communities (CCRCs).

ATOMISM VS. MEMBERSHIP

Moreover, although we pride ourselves on pluralism, Americans have an unrequited hunger for membership. We are separated by our privacies: the freestanding house, the private automobile, and the prestigious, personalized office. We buy clothes, food, and services by paying unnamed people for the transaction. Even in apartment buildings, we do not know our neighbors. If we do, we are not likely to share membership or even congruency of interest with them. The telephone bridges us to distant friends, and work may become a singular preoccupation and source of fellowship. After such a life, we can die at home or leave what family and occupational memberships we have and spend our final days in a hospital or nursing home where concern for our social, intellectual, and cultural life is minimal; we will have gone from atomic motion to isolated confinement, and that is the situation a hospitable healthcare institution can overcome.

Where gaps among people must be bridged by telephone, subway, and highway, relationships and discourse that come easily and daily in the institutions of an urban or rural village are less secure. A singularly possessive affiliation, work in a corporation, then takes on an exaggerated role, and the atomistic American shows a pervasive and unrequited hunger for other memberships. The longing to belong or to champion a cause explains the gang and the fervent followers of rock stars and evangelists. The baseball cap and emblazoned T-shirt proclaim some level of allegiance, but they seldom mean membership. Once family disintegrates or disperses and employment ends, the jobless American who passes from household to institution can be traumatically bereft.

Healthcare leaders who wish to create a caring community must overcome four strong social biases. One is homogeneity and exclusivity. Residential patterns that disperse people in one-generation, single-family households tend to reduce social contact to a shopping mall, school, country club, or church, which separate people by economic level or belief. Some affluent suburban villages, such as those on the privileged north shore of Long Island, zone against those nursing homes and CCRCs that, ironically, their own elder landowners will need.

A second legacy is the simplistic idea of having dedicated districts. We separate place of work from places of residence. We rule out combined uses that would mix shopping centers with nursing homes, colleges with CCRCs, YMCAs and YWCAs with senior housing. That idea is only now being developed—for example, in the region around Minneapolis, and a senior housing project in Lund, Sweden.

A third social movement further diminishes Americans' social creativity in healthcare, namely our reliance on technology and science. That reliance affects healthcare institutions in two ways. Modern transportation and communication contribute to atomism. However beneficial, the highway, telephone, fax machine, radio, television, and electric motor enable us to disperse into isolated social units. They lessen the need for small-scale local institutions where proximity fosters assembly and membership. Furthermore, scientific, medical research further urges healthcare agencies to be remote, specialized, and large. Intent on laboratory analysis, surgical excision, and pharmaceutical drugs, the modern hospital becomes dominated by technicians, and they are not likely to be dedicated to the disabling distress of young or old people who have no supportive social friendships.

The costs and technical specializations of such medical service generate a fourth barrier: the need to consolidate and enlarge each institution, so that it can afford capital investments and become increasingly specialized. Monumental scale races past context or need. The hospital is especially prone to accede to demands for ever more sophisticated instruments and laboratories, and then suffers from the debt consequent upon the cost of a CAT scanner or magnetic resonance imager. Such equipment and overhead may not be wanted at all within a nursing home, clinic, CCRC, or even many hospitals.

Those four social habits affect the infirm and elderly. Dispersed, suburban residence produces an atomistic person for whom communal and institutional life is alien. Technological models are inhospitable. And the aggrandizement of specialized functions makes the institution remote, monumental, and impersonal. The consequent lessened investment in old and new small, local institutions that foster membership and a sense of belonging results in one traumatic moment: the infirm or aged person is lifted from family and local associations and moved to isolation in the remote, specialized, sophisticated, and monumental medical institution. Institutionalized, alone in a facility that is blown out of scale, the patient is truly divested of discourse or membership. That is the final tragic passage.

UTOPIAN COMMUNITIES

Yet, one of the persistent, recurring features of American social invention has been the formation of new communities. The impulse to migrate westward from the American East Coast was often to be rid of distractions, and to found utopian communities where Quakers, Shakers, Amish, Mormons, or Fourians could secure their beliefs in a new and perfect place. Those utopian settlements gained strength from four features. They summoned membership to a belief, often religious, and avowed that their members were special people with a distinct mission. Second, they built common spaces to gather members and strengthen and transmit those beliefs. Third, the utopian communities often celebrated work, especially crafts. Fourth, they were self-governing.

One may well wonder whether utopian communities are possible without a religious cause. Surely, some of the remarkable healthcare foundations and CCRCs today owe their spirit to Moravian, Lutheran, Episcopalian, Roman Catholic, and Hebraic organizations. The Hebrew Home for the Aged in Riverdale, New York, is a model healthcare foundation. The Charlestown CCRC in Baltimore has Roman Catholic origins; others are Moravian, Episcopalian, and Presbyterian.

Reviving the utopian ideal has been the remarkable spirit within several communities founded by Quakers. Among them: Foulkeways at Gwynedd, Pennsylvania; Medford Leas at Medford, New Jersey; Broadmead in Cockeysville near Baltimore, Maryland; and Kendal and Crosslands at Kennett Square near Wilmington, Delaware, and Longwood, Pennsylvania. There, humanistic ideals prevail, and you will hear utopian language. A woman at Crosslands joked, "They call this a retirement center. I have never been more stimulated or active in my life. I'm looking for a place to retire."

SOCIAL INTERACTION

If most of our secular society prefers other than a religious purpose for organizing healthcare and lifecare communities (and if, moreover, public policy and finance will require other purposes), then what shall the organizing purpose be? Some secular models propose a hotel with various levels of housekeeping and contracted medical care. Others propose a country club with golf, cottage residence, and nursing care. Located on an inland waterway in Florida, one successful CCRC features the romantic theme of a luxury cruise on a fine passenger liner. In late 1990, plans were announced for a community in Maryland centered on crafts and agricultural self-sufficiency.

Surveys reinforce the market's need for stimulating communities. Jeffrey H. Los, of Cannon, describes two markets: ". . . Prospective residents emphasize dwelling units' design, size, 'address,' etc., whereas existing residents emphasize social interaction, convenient shopping and an active, stimulating environment." Encouraging the elderly to be

Carleton-Willard Village, Bedford, Massachusetts. (Architect: TRO/Ritchie Organization/Photo: Albert Bush-Brown)

active in the urban setting, even as their mobility decreases, is a declared need. At a nursing home in downtown Baltimore, the most popular event is attendance at trials in the nearby courthouse.

The spirit of a place *depends on the intelligence and creativity of its members.* That cannot be programmed, but it can be nurtured— if the patients or members themselves are encouraged to lead. Some form of self-governance is essential. Helping residents to feel that they can still shape their lives, as they previously managed their household, business, and finances, is the key to eliciting the intelligence and creativity that will vitalize the community's activities.

Activities then will spring from the talents and dedications that characterize many Americans, especially our habitual philanthropy and volunteerism, and our inclination to develop multiple ways of expressing ourselves in writing, crafts, arts, and hobbies. Although the day of "candy striping" in hospitals may be past, volunteerism still attracts the computer literate to help hospitals, libraries, or schools on evenings and weekends, and both flower and entertainment committees still enliven many hospitals and nursing homes. Talents in gardening, painting, music, and writing, now in retirement, can flourish with fewer interruptions, and they can enjoy colleagues' appreciation.

Activities take four forms: personal services, public culture, passive entertainment, and active creativity. *Personal services* are predictably concerned with basic needs: dining, physical therapy, exercise, banking, hairdressing, and shops offering basic toiletries and household items. *Public cultural spaces* and those for *passive entertainment* typically include a living room, library, art exhibition area, and an auditorium, which provides a place for film, lectures, and music. Spaces for *creative activities* are usually confined to rooms for arts and crafts, but a greenhouse is also popular.

It is a great mistake to assume that there is one perfect activities program that will not change and will be right for all locations. Rather, such a program's shape and vitality will reflect the intelligence and creativity its participants bring to it. It must change as they change. While there are basic elements, such

as musical performance and cinema, the most spirited reflect the presence of leaders who are avid for theater and dance, or excited to travel, or to publish a weekly newspaper, and their spirited efforts may last only as long as the leaders are active. Encouraging new initiative is essential.

Equally important is the need to think horizontally, not merely down the lines of administrative responsibility. The book clubs should meet over luncheon if they wish; the library can be set for tea. The choral group can sing in the assisted-living areas, and that hall or this lobby can be a stage for exhibitions. Cooperation among administrators should cross territorial lines and make it easy and natural to mix events and use spaces in multiple, even unorthodox ways.

While many activities programs are strong on passive entertainment and physical exercise, few engage the mind. Lifecare communities provide time to learn. Even passive entertainment can be enriched by film clubs, book clubs, and art discussion groups. Local colleges and schools can offer courses. A library can be a vital center if it is designed to be more than a collection of books; for example,

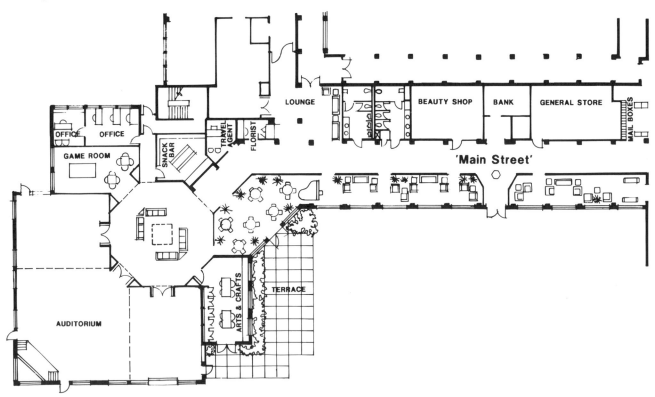

Carleton-Willard Village, Bedford, Massachusetts. (Courtesy of TRO/Ritchie Organization)

Medford Leas, Medford, New Jersey. (Photo: Albert Bush-Brown)

it can be a verbal and graphics communications center.

A fourth comment is directed at the passive nature of most activities programs. The planned event has its place. The auditorium, cinema, music room, and exhibition space are regularly booked. But what activities promote active engagement with intellectual, social, and aesthetic challenges? Most "libraries" are merely a few shelves containing random books, but no one is expected to work there.

Few studios are places for serious creative work. Labeled "Arts and Crafts," the rooms and their tables are not meant for real industry. They look deserted and feel dead because nothing truly engaging and creative can happen there.

Creative activities flourish best where the residents themselves are encouraged to exercise their talents. A woodworking shop succeeds here; there, lathes and radial-arm saws gather dust. Even with 85 percent women in residence, an active sewing room is not guaranteed. Several rooms so designated are deserted except by Singer machines. However, an undesignated area at one side of a general studio where painters and sculptors are working, can resemble a quilting bee, with laughter, stories, and banter abounding. Such studios generate friendships, pride, and membership.

Horticulture clearly summons social invention and membership. Whether a rose garden or vegetables, perennials or annuals, each has adherents. Some communities have avid, even competing rose, daffodil, and tulip clubs; several have libraries, lectures, garden tours, and midwinter planning committees for summer-

Broadmead, Cockeysville, Maryland. Shop. (Architect: Cochran, Stephenson & Donkervoet, Inc./Photo: Courtesy of Cochran, Stephenson & Donkervoet, Inc.)

time splendor. Tying garlands of dried flowers and mixing aromatic potpourri can draw a merry gathering. Walkways and wheelchair paths through woodlands planted with trees and shrubs to attract birds elicit sharing of in-interest. Those who walk the park or woodland often carry binoculars, and their ornithological fervor starts friendships.

Music, poetry, short stories, newsletters, and painting have active practitioners in many CCRCs. At others, such as North Hill, lectures and book discussion clubs seem to be more popular. In 1990, the alumni notes for the Bryn Mawr College class of 1925 quotes one graduate in "a splendid retirement home" as reporting that "many, delightful, congenial people (and) stimulating lectures, art shows, music" give her only one complaint, ". . . days go by too fast."

A recent study ranking patients' choices assigns overwhelming importance to communication; telephones and mail; freedom to walk, shop, and see; and choice of roommate. Those lead the list, well above food and mealtimes, well above access to banks and control of funds, and, much to the amazement of staff members, high above guests and visitors, whom patients, perhaps inured to institutional living, enigmatically ranked last out of ten. Communication lies at the heart of eliciting membership: the activities board, sign-up sheets, and announcements; the newspaper and bulletin; the switchboard; and personal greetings by name. The community newspaper can make newcomers welcome and can herald coming events and meetings.

So much more is possible. Mixing generations can occur in day-care centers for children, such as the one within the Medford Leas Retirement Center. A CCRC located on a college campus would have endless benefits: music and theater, writing, enrollment in courses, teaching, reading for the blind, companionship, even hospital service and a department with intern training for administrative personnel, who are greatly needed.

Nor should the solace of animals be forgotten: one woman with a cat seeks a retirement home that admits animals. She, like others, might enjoy a small farm with calves, ponies, goats, and sheep, and their vital rhythms of

Brookhaven, Lexington, Massachusetts. Library. (Interior Designer: Arthur Shuster, Inc./Photo: Courtesy of Arthur Shuster, Inc.)

feeding, growing, and birthing might make a destination for a walk. One healthcare center makes a spectacle of colorful fish in tanks.

Several organize craft making toward holidays, when sales of quilts, furniture, pots, and paintings enrich the residents' discretionary or activities fund.

Stimulating creativity and membership requires two special attitudes: one is receptiveness to new initiatives; the second is horizontal integration. If managers invent the activities program, it is likely to become rigid and exclude new talents. If managers think of clubs and dining as two separate supervisory activities, the book club's discussion is not so likely to carry into the dining rooms, and afternoon tea is less likely to occur in the art exhibition. Social imagination can salve the wounds of atomism and break the stereotypes of isolation and confinement imbedded in much current healthcare imagery. Creative activities within a community contribute to a sense of vitality and to a sense of belonging, and their nurture should be the goal of healthcare designers and administrators. ■

11/Life-Enhancement Program Reverses Circumstantial Senility

Richard T. Conard

As our bodies age and grow frail, we lose our ability to cope and to make decisions. To compensate for losses, we become more selective in our activities, slowing our world down and making it smaller. We begin to withdraw and exhibit signs of mental confusion, disorientation, and "senility," when in fact there is no physiological reason for such behavior. I call this condition *circumstantial senility*. Without appropriate intervention, a person suffering from it eventually just "goes to bed" and finally dies, often having spent years in depression and isolation.

Circumstantial senility is a needless tragedy, because given proper care and environment, I have found that it is almost always reversible.

Designers of living space and hospitality services for older citizens can promote that reversal by providing smaller, more service-rich environments. Because senescence decreases our ability to integrate as much information as when we were younger, we have to cut down on the number of activities we undertake. When just "getting through the day" (taking care of meals, personal hygiene, and housekeeping) taxes all of our mental and physical

Waverly Heights, Gladwyne, Pennsylvania. (Architect: Sullivan Associates, Inc./Interior Designer: Merlino Interior Design Assoc./Photo: Jim Schafer)

resources, we have no energy left to participate in more mentally stimulating activities. We begin the dangerous journey to withdrawal and circumstantial senility.

But when the more mundane demands are handled by someone else, such as the staff of a senior living residence, our minds and bodies are freed to enjoy a movie, go to a concert, or take a walk. Our world is smaller, easier for us to cope with, but still filled with mentally enriching activities that are the most effective antidote to circumstantial senility.

I call this a *life-enhancement program*. It includes a physical layout that allows ease of movement, smaller but well-appointed living spaces, inviting and pleasant dining areas, and congregate areas for social activities. Services include such aspects of the hospitality industry as housekeeping, food service, environmental security, and transportation. Social activities and healthcare services are important segments of the well-planned senior living community as well.

In my experience with hundreds of elderly patients over the years, I have seen remarkable reversals of circumstantial senility within 90 to 120 days of a patient's moving into a residence that offers a life-enhancement program. When older people move into a smaller environment that provides services that meet their daily needs without requiring much decision making on their part, a place that encourages social interaction between residents, the majority of them "blossoms."

First, they feel better physically because they receive regular and nourishing meals. A physical activity program exercises their bodies, and their intake of harmful substances, such as drugs, alcohol and tobacco, is usually better controlled. Secondly, since they no longer have to cope with decisions about their daily activities, they are able to use their mental capacities in activities that are of greater interest—gardening, reading, visiting with friends, art, music, even volunteer work.

With more and more Americans entering their senior years, it is extremely important that those who design and develop living facilities for the elderly incorporate the life-enhancement program in their designs, for it is crucial to the elder person's maintenance of mental health and quality of life. ∎

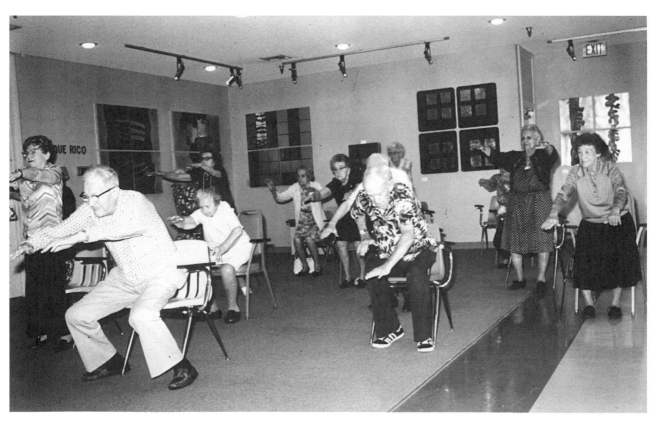

Palmcrest-Senior Eye Gallery, Long Beach, California. (Photo: Courtesy of Julian Feingold)

11A / Avoid Stereotypes in Activities

Jeffrey H. Los

Common facilities for . . . activities can be very positive attributes, but too often they are the result of how we stereotype older adults. In fact, older adults are especially careful to maintain as much independence as possible and the most diverse activities imaginable. Buildings are often programmed and designed to be overly prescriptive about what older adults need, and they resent it!

Interview in *Contemporary Long-Term Care*
September 1987

12 / Rhythms, Melodies, Poems, and Palettes

Albert Bush-Brown

Art summons consciousness. Only the cruelest and most insensitive of minds would cut a person off from conversation, offer no chance for expression, and then wonder at the withdrawal and dependency such deprivation brings. See, instead, what dancing does. Hear the joy in singing. A person creating or experiencing art is far less likely to retreat or to fall victim to old age's self-fulfilling prophecy· deterioration and decline.

Art records engagement. It marks an encounter with fact. It arrests a moment in transitory experience and evokes an urge to hold it, isolate it, caress it, and celebrate it in song or image. The fact may be present and insistent, but the fact rising from memory is equally if not more compelling.

To write, as to paint, in one artist's words, is "to hold up shapes against chaos." Art gives meaning to the formless and accidental parade of incident and event. It is an act of affirmation. It declares that an otherwise fleeting word, laugh, sound, shadow, color, or scent, even those recalled or drifting in from memory, is worth savoring and cherishing.

As acts of affirmation, the painting and poem burst old people's confines. It is mean

Crosslands, Kennett square, Pennsylvania. (Architect: Ewing Cole Cherry Parsky Architects/Photo: Albert Bush-Brown)

and absurd to think that their creativity is ended and their minds quiescent. Given little to do but move between chair and bed, or wander a hall, the aged conform to society's dismal prediction of their future. Expected to be dormant, deprived of productive engagement, the patient, possibly withdrawn into depression, counts the steps toward lessening agility, visual and auditory failure, and other functional debilities. In *Southern Family*, Gail Godwin has one of her characters wonder, ". . . how I will look to others in that waiting room between uselessness and death?"

Prolonging life without deepening its meaning is a vicious trick on the elderly. Yet, that duplicity is enacted everyday where nursing homes and other healthcare agents confine their patients to bedroom, corridor, dining area, and television lounge. A man in Portsmouth, New Hampshire, visiting nursing homes to find a place for his mother, described them as "warehouses for the undertaker."

Immersal of self in artistic expression, outward gesture, is art's reward. Even when all else goes, rhythm stays. The aged Yeats spoke of such immersal in "Among School Children":

O body swayed to music,
O brightening glance,
How can we know the dancer from the dance?

Behold the hand! What a marvelous instrument it is. How it grips, opens, twists, closes, ripples, and taps! What exquisite form, even at rest!

Yes, behold the hand: the hands Dürer drew in prayer, the finger Rembrandt haloed by candlelight, the hand Adam raised to Michelangelo's Creator. Even paralyzed and strapped to a stick, it pointed where Matisse wanted scissored shapes glued.

Shall it now in age and infirmity no longer gesture the heroic tales some blind Homer wishes to tell? Shall it never again weave into warp and woof stories of birth, marriage, and death? Shall it shape no more images of tenderness or terror? Nor again finger a flute nor pluck a harp?

Or shall it carve, shall it weld, shall it tell in print; shall it paint, draw, sketch, even hint at what it remembers of plow, of needle, of chisel, saw, stove, office, and shop? Shall it strike notes, bow strings, mark time, ring bells, this wondrous hand that records and foretells?

Flex nimble, hand. Dance on keys; feel silks; shape woods; swing a line in graceful arc. Touch and respond again! Creativity waits in you.

Crosslands, Kennett Square, Pennsylvania. (Architect: Ewing Cole Cherry Parsky Architects/Photo: Albert Bush-Brown)

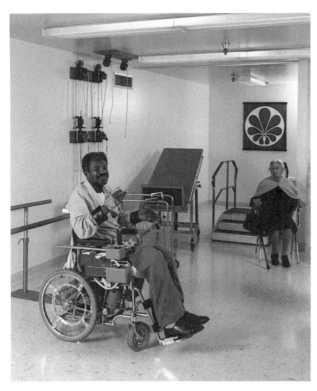

Palmcrest House North, Long Beach, California.
(Photo: Courtesy of Julian Feingold)

In the decade since arts for the elderly was the subject of a congressional hearing in February 1980, followed by the 1981 White House Conference on Aging, all aspects of older Americans' participation in the arts have been discussed in an extensive and growing bibliography. Anyone seeking guidance to that literature should start with John B. Balkema's *The Creative Spirit*, an annotated bibliography published in 1986 by the National Council on Aging, with generous help from the National Endowment for the Arts and the National Endowment for the Humanities. That bibliography introduces the chief themes: adult education, art therapy, crafts, drama, writing, dance, dance therapy, exhibitions, museums, music, photography, poetry, reading, reminiscence, and theater.

For our purposes—the role of the arts in hospitable design—we offer a few observations about nurturing artistic engagement:

1. A successful arts program depends upon recognizing that the ill and elderly are creative. Contrary to our youth culture, creativity does not reside solely with the young.

When encouraged and not stifled, the old also are creative.

2. While we know too little about mature or postmature creativity, we observe that it is different from a revolutionary quest for innovation and originality. Critics and artists alike testify to a greater delight in form itself, a more lyrical flow in Matisse's line, a selective concentration and bolder calligraphy in Rembrandt's and Hals's portraits. The later buildings of Palladio and Frank Lloyd Wright reveal preoccupation with geometric form, in Wright's case the helix, even where it cost functional disservice. That has some implications for the kind of art and the sort of instruction that should be offered. There is, for example, only frustration and discouragement to be gained by forcing a systematic exploration of anatomy and perspective upon an older person fascinated by the grace of a lyrical line or the rhythms, accents, and contrasts within abstract patterns. Elicit a person's native interest rather than impose a program.

3. The elder artist's fascination with exhibiting the medium itself suggests restraint on the part of those who applaud innovation and originality even when expressed crudely. Instead, the creative intent of the elder artist may be refinement, even perfecting the traditional. That, too, requires patient, sensitive responses.

4. Contrary to that observation is the recognized interest of the ill and aged in narration. So urgent and intriguing is the telling that the story presses forward through naive and primitive expression. The story invents its own symbols, defines its own space, flourishes its own color or anecdote. The elderly painter Grandma Moses found a lucrative market for such expression. Much of the value of the reminiscence group rests on the urge to recall and tell.

But, necessary as such observations are for eliciting the creative insight of the aged and infirm, they are sophisticated, when what is needed are practical conditions for stimulating artistic activity in hospitals, nursing homes, and continuing care retirement communities (CCRCs) today.

Cooperative Care Center, New York University Medical Center, New York. (Architect: Perkins and Wills/Photo: Al Giese, courtesy of NYU Medical Center)

Where the creative spirit flourishes, as at Medford Leas and Crosslands, there are resident artists whose skill and enthusiasm inspire beginners and amateurs. Without such resident leadership, attempts at formal, periodic classroom instruction seem stilted and pedantic, but the visiting instructor who is sensitive to elders' special creativity can generate a creative response and sustain courage. Even to the young, a blank page or canvas can be an awesome challenge. A leader helps. In one woodworking shop, three men assembling cabinets spoke admiringly of the physician (absent the day I visited) who had taught them to use the saws, routers, moulders, and planes he had donated to the CCRC. In another studio, a woman intent on refinishing a chair had enlisted her husband to sand and scrape. The guest she had invited for luncheon, she said, was expected to arrive early and join the sanding team!

Music is one of the great bonding experiences. The piano in the living room offers multiple opportunities for concerts and singing. In Baltimore, residents of a nursing home look forward all week long to the Thursday "sing along." Some communities have their own choral and instrumental groups. Gospel choruses in Tennessee and Missouri have been recorded. One pianist who voluntarily gives her Saturday mornings to play popular music in nursing homes comments: "The Alzheimer patient may not remember his name,

but he never loses rhythm. The sense of rhythm is the last to go." And that observation raises the importance of dance, perhaps the most ancient ritual of bonding.

Even the bedridden and frail, the bereft widow, and the elderly have tales to tell. Writing, as an art, needs to be encouraged. A members' literary magazine can be a lively forum; its poems, essays, and short stories stimulate discussion and meetings, much like members' exhibitions. Telling stories can be therapeutic. A reminiscence group recalling memorable life episodes gives continuity and meaning, completing life's circle. Recorders and typewriters are wanted but are seldom provided. One arthritic widow wants to correct a recent sensational biography about her famous late husband, but is unable to find in her CCRC a room with writing equipment or recorders she can use. Members may need help with letters, addresses, and mailing, and responses will be rewarding. For the word is basic to friendship and membership. Poets and writers who read in healthcare centers know that.

When asked how he would prefer to live in retirement, an English architect who is also a sculptor said that he and his wife, who is a painter, would like to buy a farm in Burgundy, convert its barns, sheds, and other outbuildings to studios, build some simple cottages, have a library and dining room in the farmhouse, and invite six couples active in writing, music, drama, and the visual arts to join them. "Wouldn't it be wonderful," my Aunt Lydia asked at 87, "simply to add medical and nursing care to the McDowell Colony and work there the rest of our lives?" A master of batik, she had spent several summers in that idyllic artists' retreat in the New Hampshire woods. Those elderly members of the Century Association in Manhattan who enjoy its concerts, exhibitions, library, and fellowship sometimes dream of an adjacent apartment hotel connected to the Century's grand rooms.

Artistic creativity vitalizes. It channels senses and intellect in communication, which lies at the heart of health for both persons and their community. Art contributes to identity and membership, and its nurture should be the goal of healthcare designers and administrators. ∎

13/Vistas for Communication

Dianne Davis

The personal handwritten letter delivered by a friendly mail carrier is quickly becoming history. Today, a mere push of buttons establishes instant communication: the phone, fax machine, word processor, and dictating machine create our communication links.

A CENTER FOR MAIL

Though the writing and receiving of personal letters are important events, and should be, they are not easily started or sustained. Even when there is the will to write a letter, getting paper, pen, envelope, address, and stamp together is a task. The ill, tired, or recently relocated person finds letter writing difficult. How helpful it would be if the hospital or continuing care retirement community (CCRC) printed basic stationery. At the Healthcare International Medical Center of Tustin in California, a patient need only add his or her name to the envelope. The return address might simply be to a street, without mentioning the hospital or CCRC.

The mailroom should be a natural hub for communication, a meeting place where residents can exchange spontaneous news and greetings. It is not merely a waystop with a trash can! Located near elevators and a reception desk in the lobby, a mailroom can be more than a bank of cubby holes for letters in a "grand central station." A pleasant place for residents to receive mail requires a table and armchairs, perhaps arranged in a small alcove off "Main Street," with end tables and good light. Privacy should be possible but, when desired, conversation should be encouraged.

CREATING "WRITERS"

Nothing is sadder than to see wheelchaired patients sit for hours to watch television. Certainly, there is more to communication than that!

Cedars Medical Center, Miami, Florida. (Photo: Bob Siegel, courtesy of Natalie Schanker)

What can be done with memories of family and personal histories? The attic's trunks of letters and photographs, once a treasury of memories sought by children on a rainy day, no longer exist. Yet, the desire to transmit family lore persists. Writing, taping, and video recording should be encouraged. Videotaping a family album with stories and recorded comment on identities, deepens family roots. A new software program, "Memories?," suggests more than 1200 questions for stimulating writers to prepare their histories.

Anticipating a generation of residents who will feel at ease with computers and word processors, designers are fitting apartments and studios with terminals. Though perhaps not "button-oriented," today's residents can enjoy the new technology. Those who were secretaries can type! Almost all can talk into a recorder to "write" letters, family histories, short stories, and newsletters. Like playing the piano, typing exercises aging fingers.

A communications center can offer private areas and individual locked cabinets for safe storage of personal papers. Equipped with high-intensity reading lamps, desks, carrels, simple dictating machines, and personal computers with large keyboards, a communications center should also include friendly assistance. Even a wary resident might wander into an inviting user-friendly communication center. A helpful assistant can excite residents with a desire to compose poems, compile a biography, or write letters to children, grandchildren, and friends. To stay in touch is a basic human need. New friends make reasons to communicate. Writing family members about a new friend or festivity in the dining room opens vistas for the family; in return, letters received generate "news," which, imparted to new neighbors and friends, increases bonds and enjoyment.

HOSPITAL "OFFICE"

Today, hospitals market communication centers as "catered business services." Offering

secretarial help, computers, fax machines, dictation, and photocopiers, they even supply stamps and Express Mail services. Thus, executives confined in hospitals have an office away from their own! Many private suites include a desk and computer terminal. Rental of fax is now a normal service, as is the phone and TV. Some facilities are installing the Stop 'N Fax Public Fax System, designed for wall or tabletop use in limited-space locations, where a standard modular phone jack is available.

THE TELEPHONE

Public telephones are often installed inside lounge areas, where strangers disturb the privacy that is especially needed at stressful times. In a retirement center, comfortable chairs should be placed near public telephones, and these phones should also be accessible by wheelchairs and, where possible, placed in an acoustically padded alcove. Pen and paper are a convenience, if a way can be devised to keep them available. Though often forgotten or poorly installed as an afterthought, good lighting and ventilation are essential.

A central telephone system may raise con-

The Hebrew Home for the Aged at Riverdale, New York. (Photo: Dianne Davis)

cerns about privacy. Residents may be suspicious of switchboard operators screening callers or remaining on the line to monitor conversations. Such fears are reduced by the explanation that the operator protects patients and guests from unwanted calls, and that there is complete privacy after a call is accepted.

The pleasing tone and friendly "smile" in a receptionist's voice sets the institution's image. It should be welcoming, informative, reassuring, and concerned but not prying. The caller should feel a positive response. Managers should establish simple messages for the receptionist and set standards for communicating information. They should train receptionists to be brief and cordial. Then everyone will benefit from clear facts, less stress, and helpful answers.

ELECTRONIC BULLETIN BOARD

"You Are Here" maps in healthcare lobbies are helpful. Electronic bulletin boards and cablegrams inform patients and visitors about available services such as the location of bank machines, the chaplain's telephone number, restaurant locations, and menu specials. Cultural and educational events can be broadcast easily, including information about outside restaurants and their menus. Transportation schedules can be displayed. In fact, electronic "Concierge Programs" are labor-saving devices, which free receptionists for more urgent tasks.

In patients' rooms, closed-circuit TV systems can offer menu selection, and a Patient Information Network can also carry information about general health and medical topics. Such programs can be selected from a television directory by the guest or can be shown at a physician's request.

At Duke University Medical Center, artists design cablegram posters. In exchange for their creative talent, the artists learn the new medium of computer graphics. Their work is stored on a computer disk and transmitted on the patient TV channel as a video art gallery program.

The location of the TV and the selection of programs are important. When I went with a friend to visit the friend's 86-year-old mother who was confined to a state-of-the-art ICU, I encountered two problems. First, the TV was installed high on the opposite wall and proved difficult to see, which added to her distress. "The patient is demented," the nurse informed

The Mount Sinai Medical Center, Cleveland, Ohio. (Architect: URS Inc. (formerly Dalton, Dalton, Newport)/Photo: Media Services Department)

us. My friend replied, "No way. That woman just asked me the stock market's closing figure and told me about the Berlin Wall! What makes you think she's demented?" The nurse replied, "Well, she doesn't watch TV." Only then did I perceive the second problem. My friend asked, "What programs do you have?" "Soaps," the nurse replied. "Well, she never watched soaps at home. What makes you think she will now? How about 'Night Line,' the news, or a videotape for use with a VCR?" "To think that a diagnosis was made by a misinformed, poorly trained staff member!" my friend later commented.

Renting a VCR should be made easier. Also, vending machines with VCR tapes can be located near a main lobby entrance; some machines accept credit cards or dollar bills.

Rolling carts fitted with tape libraries and offering VCR rental can be successful and appreciated by guests. The vendor or library monitors the delivery, collects the payment, and gains revenues for the facility. Videotapes provide entertainment as well as learning experiences for patients, residents, and visitors.

A five-minute videotape about a special family event can be viewed at leisure. Unlike a phone conversation, it can be rerun for renewed pleasure. Furthermore, such "shorts" can be played for friends in the community.

The possibilities for encouraging communication are endless. Anticipating the need for electrical cables and outlets is a wise precaution. Today's technology with its easy, convenient operation can make communication centers become vital activity areas. ■

14/The Poet and Writer: Art Saves Lives

Shaun T. Griffin

On July 23 my grandmother died of complications arising from Alzheimer's disease. For five years I watched as her once vital body turned to less and less a flesh. My mother could breathe at last, and we children, though relieved, could not name our sadness at the funeral. She lay in an open casket, face painted and calm, calm I think because she could once again see light, paint light, weave, and dream. In the kitchen, on the canvas, in the family, she was an artist.

Six weeks before her death, my second son was born. It may have been the last thing she waited for. The strands of life braid, then knot, and we stand by watching as they unravel again.

Lately, all of the poems I read call to mind her face and others like it. Frita, my grandmother's roommate in the nursing home, at 84, reading to my first son as if he were her own. And the chocolates, all over their eating trays, their faces, with grandma, chewing for what seemed an eternity. Kids, like poetry, can take people, especially seniors, where we in the

middle cannot go. We have no way in, only the outside of their lives, to share.

My mother was very good about walking with and, later, pushing her mother, Mildred Tholl, in sunlight, feeling that sunlight was vital to being alive. I am reminded of the poet Stanley Kunitz in his garden with the worms and trees and the frogs, all giving life to a man now in his eighties, writing still, writing words like these: "Anyone who forsakes the child he was is already too old for poetry."

But the late Kenneth Patchen reminds us that no one is too old for poetry—"Caring is the only daring/ oh you know it." He implores us to do more than sit by and watch. Rather, this poem-painting says, "take heart, join hands, let us say these lines together. Write new ones! Take chalk and make words that dance. Play with them like clay. Feel the rhythms for the first time. Then let them go . . . pass the chalk to a friend."

Keep the poems fresh and tasty:

This is just to say
I have eaten
the plums
that were in
the icebox
. . .
forgive me
they were delicious
so sweet
and so cold

(William Carlos Williams)

Few can write like that, but all of us can experience the sensation of biting into a loved one's plum.

Poetry is vital to all people—mothers and fathers spinning out their years in a convalescent hospital; my neighbor's husband screaming like an eight-year-old, Alzheimer's again; a friend and former student and poet for over 84 years who can barely write for all the pills and pains she has to endure. Yet her words are more vibrant than fifteen students still running to class:

At the moment of awakening
the guilt of my frailties,
like the pointed finger
of the village gossip,
overwhelms me:
I think I am quietly going mad.

(Helen "Zeke" Modarelli)

Poetry plops in your lap like a child. It awakens, it startles, it frees us from the ordinary green room of the day to day. I told my grandmother at the last visit she should put pictures on the ceiling for the times she lies in bed waiting. Why not look up to color? She was a painter. My mother paints because of her, my sister, too. All trace their roots of color on canvas to her. Now we have the colors she has left to redeem.

Just the other day these lines came hauntingly in a magazine: "Oh, don't prettify decrepitude,"/She demands. "Don't lie!/Don't make old age seem so *ornamental!*" For there is nothing ornamental about aging: "Sometimes I'd wear no hat, in fact, would go/ naked, nameless and numb, a breathing stone" (Vassar Miller). But nothing crass either. So long

as breath courses from Ms. Miller's mouth she will be alive and we, the benefactors of her poetry. Now in her mid-sixties, this Houston poet spends her days in the county library, reading, researching, and writing her autobiography. She has battled cerebral palsy since birth, and today she is "disgustingly healthy" (her words), a tribute to the voice of a writer who will not give up.

These anecdotes, really notes on a life of feeling, come directly to us from those, who in our culture, remain outside the mainstream of things. If poetry is to be anything at all, it must have a passionate link to the wellspring of their lives. There are countless such examples of success with other art forms. In San Francisco, a painting project, Pleasure Endeavors, for seniors and shut-ins. Young people teaching old people how to paint and painting with them! Their paintings, more powerful than words can convey. Why art? at this time in their lives? *Why art?*

Of all the media to transmit feeling, art transcends the futility of barren existence. Art uplifts, better still, these words printed on a dollar bill I received in change at the grocery store: Art Saves Lives (anonymous). What more clear expression of the need for poetry among the disabled and the aging? They have to have a way out of their surroundings; they have to be able to express themselves. You take away the human, and you take away the pulse, the need to carry on. Without poetry and literature, they are little more than vines anchored to a past that diminishes daily. We, of all the developed countries, cannot afford to lose their word, their thoughts, their myriad expressions of doubt, hope, and joy.

The joy of a five year old feeding chocolate to an 84 year old whom he has just met. The joy of discovery in her eyes when he kissed her cheek. The joy of movement in her limbs when he held her hand. The joy of letting go in a room of loved ones. All of this potent feeling must not be lost on people too busy, or unwilling to settle and chat a bit, and wonder out loud, just how their lives will journey forth, now that they have time to enjoy them.

When I think of gifts to share, I think of intangible ones. What greater place to start than with poetry and stories that each can partake of? Not the dreary kind, but literature that leaps with every line. Literature that saves lives:

when your belly
is swoln. when your
belly is full. when there is a child.
never in this situation
words like peaches.
to bite into. savor.
peel the skin
with your teeth.
bit of a peach. sweet.
flavor

(Joel Oppenheimer)

Words like peaches to bite into—that is what we need. All of us, not just those at the ends or edges of their lives, but all of us. To have any less, would be a half-life, a life with little more than seeds never grown.

The young and the old travel the road of the imagination naturally. It is only when we make literature a dark work that it betrays us. Children love to read, seniors love to tell stories, and write them, too. Come sample the thoughts that escape them: pure, clear lines like these from my son while working in the garden—"Daddy, you spilled the rose!" Or these, from 83-year-old poet Mildred Weston —"happy are the words/ that speak with voice." Give of them, give of them freely to those who so desperately want to be a part of our lives. That is all. A free and healthy sample of peaches to bite into. Not the straight road, or the wicked road; there are enough of those, but the blue road, the blue road that poets and writers call home. ∎

15/Music is More Than a Piano

Richard Somerset-Ward

Providing music is not difficult. All of us, as individuals, have our own sources within the home—radio, records, tapes, compact discs, and television. And we will surely take them with us to retirement homes. It's important that we should, because there is an essential element of our music listening which is personal and private. Why should we be bombarded by other people's taste in music? We may put up with it, under protest, in Central Park, but not in our own homes. So most of us will have our private collections of recorded music, just as we have our books and mementos. They belong wherever it is that we live. They provide memories and nostalgia for some, intellectual excitement for others, just plain entertainment for most of us.

But there's another dimension to music that is not available to many people, be they young or old. It's the *experience* of music. Those who make their living in music, those who play an instrument or belong to a choral society, those with money and access to go to "live" concerts and "gigs"—all of them can experience music at first hand. Those of us without these advantages have had to make do with the second hand (and a very good second hand it has been), records and tapes.

Technology has changed all this in the last few years. Stereo hi-fi was startling enough four decades ago, but now here's quadrophony, there's digital stereo, there's the incredible clarity and fidelity of the compact disc. . . . And there's vision to add to the sound: there are stereo VCRs and compact videodisc players . . . and soon there will be high-definition television and whole new generations of reproduction systems, each one more startling than the last.

With every technological breakthrough, the experience of music is augmented for the home listener. Yes, it is still second hand (nothing can quite take the place of actually being there), but it is infinitely more thrilling and more rewarding than anything we have known in our homes in the past. And, truth to tell, not many of us are *ever* going to experience these things in our own homes. They are too expensive for most of us, and they take up too much space for the average family home. But within organized communities—within senior living communities, for instance—they can become a reality. And they should.

What does it take? A comfortable "auditorium," not a theater, more like a living room, with movable easy chairs and probably sofas, too: with mobile audio boxes so that those who prefer headphones can use them: with several video monitors, as well as a large screen for high-definition pictures to be projected: with a competent technician in charge of the control room. Sometimes people will go there for a communal screening of, say, an opera or ballet on compact videodisc. Sometimes they will go

there to listen privately, on headphones, to their own choice of music on disc or tape—many people in the same room, all listening to different music without interrupting each other. And a facility like this would be planned in such a way that it could also serve those members of the community who are not mobile, or who are ill and confined to their own rooms, by wheeling mobile equipment on trolleys out of the "auditorium," wherever necessary. It might even be practical to wire the whole facility so that equipment never has to be moved.

The technology is available to provide the experiences, and, for most of us, to add an entirely new dimension to our experience of music (whether it be classical, folk, or pop) at a time in our lives when we will perhaps value it more than we ever could have done in middle life. ∎

Whitney Center, Hamden, Connecticut. (Architect: Engelbrecht & Griffin Architects/Photo: Farshid Assassi)

16 / Sculptural Presences

Joseph A. McDonnell

Sculpture may be as big as the Statue of Liberty (and even Mt. Rushmore) or as small as an amulet. A penny is sculpture; so is a giant bulldozer. Many formerly useful objects, such as a scythe or millstone, continue life as sculptural form. The flowing lines and intersecting shapes we admire in a chair or automobile have been modeled sculpturally, that is, to express function gracefully in three dimensions.

Whether poured in bronze, welded or riveted in steel, woven in yarns and hemps, chiseled in stone, or carved in wood, sculpture

Red Zinger, Bradley International Airport, Windsor Locks, Connecticut. (Sculptor: Tim Prentice/Photo: Nicholas Jacobs)

is first and foremost an object in space. It may convey mythological, religious, or political messages, like so much of earlier heroic statuary, but its enduring aesthetic worth is sculptural: form that visually enhances a special location in a plaza, park, corporate lobby, or shopping mall.

Of all the visual arts, sculpture is the most protean. As relief or plaque, it performs painting's role of enlivening walls, adding depth to a room, or diminishing a plaza's scale. As three-dimensional, self-standing form, sculpture creates spaces, much as those we enjoy within architectural vaults and around columns and obelisks. But sculpture's variety does not end with planear or architectural delights; a high ceiling may become a dramatic setting for a mobile, such as those airy compositions Timothy Prentice delicately floats with whimsey.

Sculpture distinctively marks a place. Whether it becomes a symbol or merely a sign depends on the sculptor's art. While clearly identifying and thereby signifying an urban address, one of Charles Perry's intricately voluted spheres surely also symbolizes the fascination we have with geometric calculation. A fountain may become more than a place to watch weaving rivulets, sparkling spray, and glistening flow; it may become a place to meet.

In healthcare settings and in senior communities, sculpture can be a true presence.

Ethuria. Station Plaza, Trenton, New Jersey. (Sculptor: Joseph A. McDonnell/Photo: Joseph A. McDonnell)

Properly placed and lighted, its shapes, spaces, edges, modeling, and colored, textured materials will enliven many spaces, mark entrances, create themes and moods, and give distinction to ordinary paths and corridors and to rooms that would be dull but for sculpture's presence. ∎

17 / Liberty to Paint

Joseph B. Breed IV

"Art is quite useless," wrote Oscar Wilde, years ago. How wrong he was! Recent experiences have pointed up that art (here meaning painting and drawing) is not only useful, but can become a rewarding creative experience and meaningful focal point in one's life, regardless of ego.

The older adult often labors under the false impression that one must have acquired experience and training at an early age and that at some unidentified point in one's life it becomes "too late" to pick up a brush or pencil. It's not necessary to have had any experience, or the slightest bit of drawing ability. What the elderly do bring to the canvas is a wealth of insight that younger painters cannot possess.

Young people have trouble learning to express themselves while painting. The elderly have few such inhibitions. They are open and ready to accept things, to employ self-criticism, to improve. The older painter generally is able to communicate his or her thoughts and insights without much provocation from an instructor.

Beginners can do fantastic things. People think natural talent is required to paint. It's not necessary—one needs only desire. Most begin painting with an oil sketch of a photograph or print, which provides a certain degree of security. With gentle support and guidance, however, these artists will soon go into their own worlds. The work of art begins to identify more with the individual painter than with the original source.

The instructor's challenge is to assist each student to express an inner vision about life. A natural approach is to explore the student's feelings and to aid in the projection of those thoughts onto the canvas, rather than just painting "things."

Abstract painting can be the perfect form for the beginner. It does away with all the naturalistic terms we traditionally wrestle with. Abstract art allows the artist to deal with form as pure form, color as pure color.

Painting develops one's creativity and imagination. It should be fun. It can also be difficult, for many friends will not always understand the work. Through art, many have learned a new way to look at life more closely, finding new things, objects and events around them. In a real sense, they have come to view the world with artists' eyes.

The older artist expresses a certain awareness of life in painting, which is absent in the younger artist's work. The elderly are contemplating their whole lives, and much of this comes in focus in their work. The older artist rapidly acquires the ability to manipulate images in an idiosyncratic way. This represents a freedom not often experienced by people of this age. The liberty to paint completely free, when discovered by these artists, is truly a joy.

However, the older artist also faces challenges that come with age. Failing eyesight, a common problem, should not slow a student down. Use of broad areas of color, and the exclusion of detail will expand the scope of the artist's work, while effectively diminishing visual problems.

Tremors and shaking hands, another common complaint, can be overcome through the use of short brush strokes and layering techniques. The eventual realization that one needn't draw a straight line, and that indeed straight lines don't exist in nature, is usually a great relief.

Most important is the discovery that there are no rules about how something should look on canvas, or in clay, or whatever the medium. The knowledgeable instructor will prepare his or her class for the revelation that the final product being attempted will never meet the expectations of the creator, and that's all right.

The following are tips for the older artist:

- Forget that you are inexperienced—that's unimportant.
- If you must buy or borrow books, go directly to the masters: Monet, Cezanne, etc.
- Use acrylic paints. They are inexpensive, clean up with water, and can be worked in a manner similar to that of oils and watercolor. They can be used on most surfaces: try cardboards. Large sheets cost very little, and results can be surprising.
- You don't need an easel. Set your canvas or paper pad against the back of a chair on a stack of heavy books.
- Do not hesitate to copy a painting, photo, or magazine illustration as a beginning step. Other artists' work should be studied. It's the easiest way to learn.
- Try painting a view from your window or a familiar object from your room. This can be the most difficult challenge, and if you need to build up to it, that's fine.
- Work with colors; don't try to draw an object exactly.
- Don't attempt portraits, at least in the beginning. They require a great deal of technical training and can be too frustrating at first.
- Always look at the scene as though for the first time. Force yourself to experience your own reactions to what you see. Recognize

shapes and colors as you walk through the streets, and experience them. This new awareness will be a resource at the canvas.

- Don't let poor eyesight or shaking hands deter you. Your work will still be an expression of you, and you will have the pleasure of creating.

The older artist is common throughout history. Rembrandt, Picasso, and O'Keefe all painted in their eighties and nineties. The most famous beginner in late life was Grandma Moses. This is good company.

Like those great artists, the older painter may also discover that living with art brings untold joy to the art of living. ∎

18 / Landscape Settings

Albert Richard Lamb

A colleague recently moved from her suburban Boston home of nearly twenty years to a high-rise condominium on the edge of the city. When asked if she missed her gardens and Victorian house, she responded, "Not in the least—thanks to Frederick Law Olmsted's vision years ago." Her new home on the eleventh floor looks over a majestic view of Leverett Pond, one of the links of the "Emerald Necklace." What excites her is this glittering image of trees, pond, and bridges. Brilliant sun illuminates the trees; mist and rain shroud the scene; and, almost always, shadows play on the water. The new landscape became a companion as well as therapy. More than Manhattan enjoys Central Park.

Where a healthcare or senior living community is located fixes its character. A rural site may become a village with a green as the residents' focus and rolling hills and meadows their setting. Walkways and small front yards with porches and flower gardens are part of the village environment. If protected, older trees will offer shade and a sense of maturity. A village green easily accepts central facilities, such as small shops, offices, and places of worship, and a public garden engenders pride.

A suburban property challenges us to knit the healthcare community into an existing town. Extending the town's traditions of flowering trees, white fencing, or regional architecture helps integrate the new community. Landscape can reduce isolation and unnatural segregation by incorporating a park or garden

needed by the town or a school. A garden club can link the new senior residents with the existing community.

A recently widowed neighbor has entered a senior community where she continues to garden. She transplanted some of her favorite plants and shared others with her new neighbors. Thinking that her first year would be difficult without her garden, she organized a group to revive an empty greenhouse. Nurturing seedlings and cuttings, the group now is adding flowers and plants to the landscape. Plans for next year include guest speakers and a garden tour. Gardening remains the focus of her life, with a varied calendar of anticipation.

An urban, inner-city site may suggest themes such as Boston's brick sidewalks, attractive lighting, and trees, but urban land also suggests interior atriums and roof gardens. Even a city garden can be cherished, recalling memories of cattails and ferns, hummingbirds probing flowers, and a cardinal singing high in a maple tree.

Each location has its own sense of place. The climates of California or Florida allow landscape to grow year-round, while northern landscapes mature through distinct seasons.

Working with nature is rewarding. Working against nature is fraught with problems. To gain a site's greatest potential, professional studies should include a thorough site analysis, comprising topography, drainage, trees and vegetation, soils access, adjacent land uses, and sun exposure. Topography can be modi-

Central Park. (Artist: Albert Bush-Brown)

fied; berms and valleys may enhance privacy and character.

A beautiful landscape is a bond that transcends social differences. At Bloomfield, Connecticut, the Duncaster Continuing Care Retirement Community has a small greenhouse on the south side of the passageway leading from social rooms to the dining room. There, a newly arrived couple moved an extensive collection of orchids. How they are tended and when they blossom are matters of daily moment for the entire community. ∎

19/Dining as Social and Cultural Experience

Dianne Davis

Dining can be a social and cultural event with intellectual and aesthetic rewards. Regrettably, the prospect of dining in hospitals, nursing homes, and retirement centers often conveys a contrary experience: diets, dull foods, belated service, cold fare, unappetizing presentations, and dreary places. The food may be nutritious, even good for one's body, but it is not often good for one's soul.

How often great conversations and friendships start where a hostess has orchestrated candlelight, flowers, linen, silver, china, food and wine, placed dinner partners, and come to the table with hair done and earrings on, of course, but also ready with two good topics, several good questions, and one good joke!

Think of an Italian family gathered twenty-four strong for mother's birthday. Think of the banter and laughter when southern blacks meet. Can you imagine an Irish celebration without stories, song, and dance? Dining then is a happy experience. However fine the food, its abundance is incidental, a foil for the enjoyment that satiates a deeper hunger.

Feeding is different from dining. Today, some hospital administrators recognize that foodservice must offer more than nutritious meals. Drawing notably from the travel and hospitality industries, their initiatives demonstrate success in five directions: *extending the time* when foodservice is available, as in 24-hour cafeteria and room service; *increasing the food choices offered*, as in a range from pre-pared sandwiches, salads, and hot meals to take-out foods, à la carte menus, and "suite" service complete with waiter, wine, fruit baskets, and flowers; *increased variety of foodservice locations*, all the way from vending machines, "deli cafes" and "coffee shops" to formal, elegant, "white table cloth" restaurants; and *providing festive themes* through ethnic foods, holiday specialties, picnic fare, and parties for family celebrations, hospital events, and conferences.

Perhaps the most significant initiative is the fifth: *elegant dining rooms and service within healthcare institutions.* Unthinkable as it was a decade ago, we now can meet at a major urban museum, such as the Metropolitan in New York City, for cocktails, dinner, and an exhibition, and, increasingly, we can also go to hospitals and nursing homes for a Sunday brunch, leisurely dinner, or a catered affair. To compete for patients, hospitals have lifted the cafeteria out of the basement and, transformed into a fine restaurant, hospital foodservice attracts guests to lobbies and corridors that are convenient and congenial locations for dining.

"What we are doing is trying to influence potential customers to come to us versus going to someone else," admits one foodservice executive. "We realize that memories regarding food and dining are retained long after patients have forgotten the medical condition and pain that created the reason for being in a healthcare setting; and we are trying to communicate the message, 'We care about you.' "

THEME EXPERIENCES

Themes help create atmosphere and festivity. The entrance and servery can be decorated to mark holidays or special celebrations. A Caribbean theme, for example, will greet guests with island music, cuisine, and costumed staff members. Each holiday or anniversary can be the cause for a celebration. Visiting the Medford Leas continuing care retirement community (CCRC) at Halloween, I was greeted by a smiling pumpkin, scarecrow, and corn shock at the entrance to the formal dining room. Preparation for Seder at Jewish homes for the aged involves community participation. At Broadmead, a newly engaged grandson proudly presented his fiancée during luncheon in a private dining room, which his grandmother had set with her heirloom china and silver. Christmas, birthdays, and the Fourth of July offer obvious reasons for special themes, as does St. Patrick's Day. Some festivities may be organized by the residents themselves. They may feature the holiday in their newsletter, they may draw or paint decorations, and they may make gifts to exchange with the other residents.

May Day might be celebrated at a picnic highlighted by planting a tree or flowering shrub. Even though it may then be too cold for an ice cream truck to roll by, perhaps a horse-drawn carriage or vendor cart, with pennants and flags flying, might deliver hot bouillon, cider, and tea with croissants and soft cheese, while the local school band welcomes the Spring. Wouldn't you like an oompha band, flags, hot dogs, and hamburgers on the Fourth of July? The long terrace and balcony would be filled for that event, followed by a showing of *Yankee Doodle Dandy* or *The Music Man* in the auditorium.

Developing a "calendar of table drama," scheduling the year's special events, and setting the themes help to simplify their organization and ensure participation and success. By popular demand, the residents of North Hill CCRC in Massachusetts organize a party

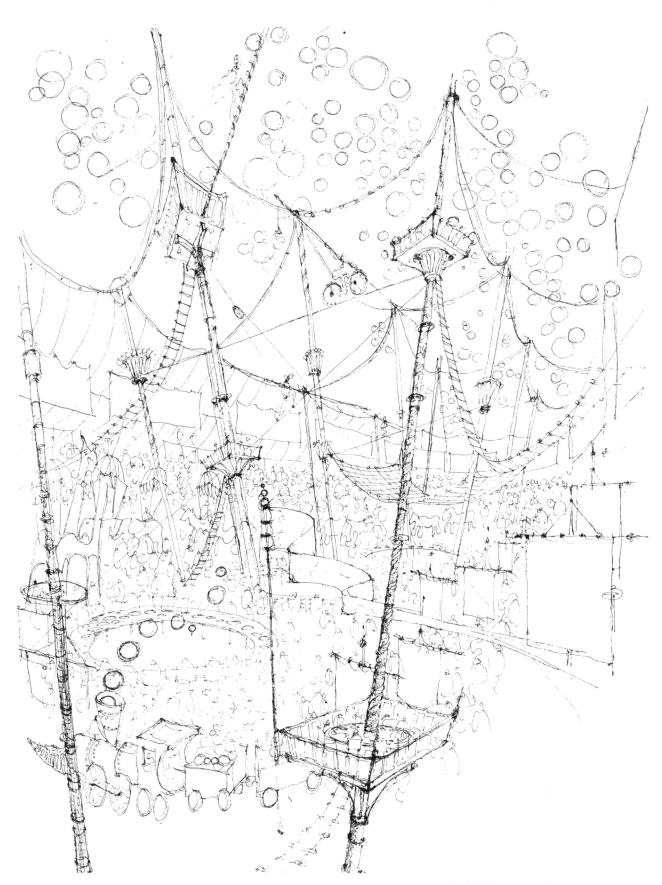

I dreamt we dined one night under the BIG TENT! (Artist: Byron Bell, AIA, Farrell, Bell & Leonard)

on April 15th to celebrate IRS filing, and the CCRC director shows up as a striped jailbird. California's Palmcrest Hospitals and Retirement Center's Annual Fantasy Cruise has "traveled" to Greece, Italy, Brazil, India, and down the Mississippi River. These festive cruises involve passports, decorating the healthcare center, the staff authentically costumed, ship bell ringing, native cuisine, music, and dance; the cruise ends with the Captain's Ball.

Taking instant photographs of such events is a sure crowd-pleaser. Photographs and creating "photo buttons" of special occasions, birthdays, or anniversaries remind guests of their celebration and the fun they had.

TEATIME

Teatime, which is regaining popularity as a "pause that refreshes," is fast becoming a highlight of the day. Anticipated as a chance to exchange the day's "happenings," teatime should be attractive, and the place for tea must be accessible. In a library, exhibit area, or alcove adjacent to the lobby or dining area, a table or cart strikingly set with fine china, silver and white linens is the ideal. A good tea, well-steeped in a silver or china pot is essential. To dunk a bag in a thick cup of tepid water will kill the event. Delicate sandwiches, scones with cream, jam, and lemon curd; cookies, tea cakes, and fruit tartlettes—these delicacies start conversation! Inviting students to play the piano or strings may add a grace note to the tea.

DINING ROOM ADJACENCIES

In long-term care and senior communities, social dining is encouraged by having a comfortable gathering area—living room, cocktail lounge, or "pub"—near the dining rooms. Transitions from corridor or lobby to dining are imperative. They encourage meeting, bonding, and queuing, and reduce traffic jams. Music and exhibitions ease waiting and encourage interaction. The tape cassette, electronic piano, and compact disk make entertainment easier.

The Gables's living room at Old Farm Forest, Farmington, Connecticut, the lounge at Harbour's Edge, Boca Raton, Florida, and the Atrium Garden Bar at Leisure Technology's Leisure Ridge in New Jersey encourage residents to assemble, exchange experiences, listen to music, and enjoy a drink before dinner.

Eventually, no matter how much patients enjoy social dining, the day comes for feeding the bedridden. How do we make this a social experience? Again, we can learn from the Metropolitan Museum of Art in New York City, which has joyously modified its preoccupation with security, costs, and dry art history by interspersing art galleries with tables for wine, beer, dinner, music, and friends! That experience can be adapted to healthcare hallways, lobbies, and clusters, where exhibitions and foodservice in alcoves will encourage visitors to dine with patients.

Buffets are a welcome change from table service, even in nursing homes. They appeal to the sense of independence craved by residents, who can select what they want or, if frail, can be walked to the buffet where "waitstaff" carry selections to the table. Wheeling dessert carts to the tables helps to redress the chief complaint about long-term food service: that residents have no choice about the food they eat. By offering modified "restaurant-style" services—informal snack areas, services on terraces and in gardens, ice cream parlors, lobby teatime, popcorn carts, and theme box-lunches—long-term facilities increase residents' satisfaction.

ALTERNATIVE DINING OPPORTUNITIES

The old-fashioned fruit cart or stand placed near restaurant registers, or freestanding in lobby corridors, has become a popular gathering point. Espresso carts topped with bright, colorful bottles of flavorings for Italian ices; hot dog and popcorn stands; candy and cookie jars—all provide variety. Separately, they may not seem important; together, incidental, amusing points of foodservice make an impact through their "psychological contribution to the whole." The authors of *Successful Restaurant Design*, Regina Baraban and Joseph Durocher, urge us to recognize that almost every design element and environmental condition in the restaurant works as a psychological tool:

> From lighting to color to texture to temperature, the nuances that influence people's feelings and behavior number in the hundreds. Design choices, therefore, should reflect careful consideration of their psychological impact. Customers can be encouraged to leave or linger, feel exuberant or mellow, feel like part of the action or secure in an intimate enclave—all as a result of design applications.

Excitement grows when it is announced that a local celebrity chef will visit. When the chef leaves the kitchen to speak with guests in the dining room, perhaps signing "signature recipes," the event will be appreciated and long remembered. Incorporating the chef's specialties into the regular menu cycle extends the experience.

The experience of dining is enhanced by four conditions: first, *the human element:* trained staff, cheerful greetings, attentive serv-ers, and attractive personal appearance, possibly with hotel-style uniforms; second, *cuisine:* food that pleases both the eye and palate; third, *social:* opportunities to converse with fellow residents and visitors; and fourth and most important, *variety:* a choice of fare, cheerful on-site restaurants, and informal settings for dining.

Since youth, dining has enriched our lives socially and culturally. "Let's meet and have a bite" is a social invitation that conveys more than nourishment by food. The kitchen table is a symbol of family, roots, belonging, customs, ethnic cooking, discussions, and decisions. Hospitable design enriches that symbol. Resting with a cup of coffee after shopping, gathering for luncheon before a museum trip by bus, meeting over dinner to discuss the book chosen by the book club, or assembling at tea to hear about gardening or to see an exhibit will foster new bonds, stimulate minds, overcome lonely isolation, and contribute to individual and collective well-being. ∎

20/Participation and Governance

Donald L. Moon

Whenever a resident enters a continuing care retirement community (CCRC) there is an inevitable feeling of loss. The resident has probably been in a decision-making position most of his or her working life. Now the resident, entering an institution to live with other people, is subject to the rules of congregate living. Others now make decisions that formerly were self-determined. For some, the sense of powerlessness and loss of control are almost overwhelming.

Recognizing that feeling, the administrators and trustees of a CCRC must help the residents have a role in deciding issues that affect the community. Somehow the community must assure a large measure of personal independence and self-determination. Certainly, the type of issue where decisions are made by residents differs from those made by the board

Broadmead, Cockeysville, Maryland. (Architect: Cochran, Stephenson & Donkervoet, Inc./Photo: Courtesy of Cochran, Stephenson & Donkervoet, Inc.)

Broadmead, Cockeysville, Maryland. (Architect: Cochran, Stephenson & Donkervoet, Inc./Photo: Courtesy of Cochran, Stephenson & Donkervoet, Inc.)

of directors and the administration. They are, however, no less important.

Most decisions that directly affect the ongoing residents' activities can best be handled by the residents themselves. That is the chief function of residents' associations. They are vitally important both in maintaining residents' morale and in organizing many activities, which could not be sustained otherwise.

Open and friendly relationships between the residents' association and the administration and board of directors are critically important. The residents' association acts as a sounding board for various decisions, and the administration can benefit from its viewpoint and knowledge of the residents' thinking. On the other hand, the officers of the residents' association can approach the administration with suggestions for advancing the concerns of the community as a whole. If the Senior Administrator enjoys good rapport with the head of the residents' association, there is no end to cooperative initiatives.

The residents' association of Foulkeways has over forty-five committees. Most deal with activities (e.g., art classes, book reviews, current issues, field trips, games, orchestra trips, programs, sewing, swimming, woodworking shop); others perform practical functions (e.g., emergency assistance, buddy system, dinner announcements, fire brigade, flower arrangements, gardens, grounds, library, art exhibits, volunteer alert, welcome to new residents). Whatever the need, a committee probably exists to meet it. There also are committees that are advisory to the administration, such as the economic study committee, the calendar clearance committee, and the health center advisory council.

Of more importance than any governmental organization is the spirit of mutual concern for community life. If all three sectors of the governance triad wish to foster individual freedom within a healthy, active community, cooperation is essential.

One example should suffice to show the benefits of mutual cooperation on a matter of resident life. Several years ago, a group of Foulkeway's residents approached the corporate board to ask that an indoor swimming pool be built on campus; after much discussion, the board informed the residents that such a facility could be built if the residents raised funds to build it and endow its operations as well. The residents named a "swimming pool" committee, and the committee and administration started to raise funds. Shortly, they raised enough to fulfill the board's conditions. Then the committee began to work with administrators to design the natatorium. Surveys were taken, and design questions were sent to residents, administration, and the board of directors. Various philosophical and practical issues were addressed. It was a joyous day when the natatorium was opened and all three members of the governance triad were able to point to it with pride as a community project. ∎

Part **III**

Membership and Communal Spaces

Having advocated the therapeutic value of activity and membership, we devote Part III to their architectural setting: their nurture through hospitable design. What public and activity spaces are needed, and how shall those communal spaces be shaped, connected and organized?

21/Main Street: Activities and Communal Space

Albert Bush-Brown

While exemplary designs for the individual or shared room and the one- or two-bedroom apartment are well documented, architects and interior designers have few models to guide their design of communal spaces. True, they can look to hotels for examples of lobbies and dining rooms, and they can study some boarding schools and small residential colleges for ideas about libraries, classrooms, and studios. Princeton's Graduate College, Harvard's Lowell and Eliot Houses, and Yale's Stiles and Morse Colleges offer models of communal spaces, all modern versions of an English collegiate and monastic heritage. But nursing homes, continuing care retirement communities (CCRCs), and other long-term care communities are neither hotels nor colleges: their residents are older, more diverse in their needs, confined to a single environment, and often more sophisticated in their expectations.

Failure to recognize those characteristics of older active and infirm residents accounts for the lifeless, arid aspect of most healthcare communities. First, the common spaces are few because the activities program is thin. Second, the spaces are polite; they are meant for passive, seated reception, not active engagement whether in dance or woodcarving. The rough workshops, the messy greenhouse, and the greasy mechanic's bench are ruled out. Third, they are programmed. Each space is

Kendal at Longwood, Kennett Square, Pennsylvania. (Architect: Ewing Cole Cherry Parsky Architects/Photo: Peter Olson)

Kendal at Longwood, Kennett Square, Pennsylvania. (Architect: Ewing Cole Cherry Parsky Architects/Photo: Peter Olson)

labeled: a place to read, a place to receive mail, a place to eat. Having separated each activity, most designers then box each space with walls, floor, and ceiling. A name is affixed to its door, and the door is locked. Having made it uninviting and inaccessible, architects then array such boxes along the sides of corridors. And, compounding those mistakes, the designer then puts the collection of activity boxes in a basement or wing remote from the central paths within the community.

MAIN STREET

Experience demonstrates that communal spaces must be designed as a group, not as separate entities, nor added as afterthoughts. Designing them to be a sequence or group of incidents on a major traffic path is essential. "Main Street" may be a sequence of areas along a wide corridor, radiate from a crossing at an intersection, or surround an atrium. In any case, Main Street should never be in a basement, unless a sloped site allows the basement to emerge at ground level with significant glazed width. Rather, the proper level for Main Street is that level which is the most

densely occupied concourse. It may be several levels above ground.

Moreover, the concourse should be a wide path instead of a corridor lined by locked doors and boxlike rooms. It should open vistas to wide and varied areas. Some areas will be living rooms, meeting rooms, libraries, and sitting areas. Smaller ones will be mailrooms, stores, music rooms, and places to meet guests. The concourse is then a path with no confining walls or ceilings. Open areas will flow together. Where a boundary is wanted, glass doors and internal windows will still provide transparencies.

A corridor or bridge is not merely a way to walk or wheel from here to there. It can be a path through activities. Crossing a bridge can resemble the experience of a motion picture film, a panorama, unreeling views, right and left, of shops, meetings, and libraries. It can be a place for music, dining, or a greenhouse. Each vista is then an invitation; each intersection is an opportunity for chance encounter, greeting, or discourse.

A successful living room will be located on the main traffic artery, letting into an adjacent dining room. To separate a living room from dining, either by locating it on a different floor or at a distance, is fatal to the vitality of each. Greeting, assembly, conversation, and grouping occur in the living room before and after dining, which is a social and cultural event.

To encourage that sort of discourse, the living room should have generous width and height, but, while lofty, it should also suggest small islands for reading and conversation. A tall room with a central, freestanding chimney and two or more fireplaces is a proven success, as at Medford Leas. Intimacy within a large space is also nurtured by having adjacent, lower sitting areas, such as a library or tea room, that are lesser spaces. Wide passageways and a lack of doors encourage people to move easily among large and small spaces, from Main Street into the living room and off to a library, tea room, or reading area, where paintings, art, and sculpture may be displayed.

The common error of thinking of Main Street as a sequence of separate activities, each boxed into its own room with a closed door, neglects the virtues of combining activities and clustering them around the principal public space, a generous living room. An attractive reception room may be part of a library; an art gallery is a fine place for tea. Gathering reception, switchboard, bulletin board, sign-up sheets, and mailroom in one area does wonders for communication, however much it may tax the skills of receptionists!

Contrary advice must quell the temptation to build a "multipurpose room" and assign film, television, music, crafts, dance, lectures, and theater to one hall. Such spaces seldom serve well. They invite bothersome technical gadgetry such as accordion walls and rolling stages, and their sightlines and acoustics are apt to be defective. Far better is a flat-floored, movable-seat auditorium with a raised stage and projection booth.

In dining rooms, offer variety both in place

Kendal at Longwood, Kennett Square, Pennsylvania. (Architect: Ewing Cole Cherry Parsky Architects/Photo: Peter Olson)

Kendal at Longwood, Kennett Square, Pennsylvania. (Architect: Ewing Cole Cherry Parsky Architects/Photo: Peter Olson)

and type of service. Within the larger dining room, smaller areas defined by screens and openings will still remain visually and functionally connected to the main space, as at the Willows.

It cannot be stated too often: It is folly to designate specific artistic functions, separate them, and assign each to a boxlike room behind a locked door. They do not entice and will not long be used as designated. Creators are organized but messy. Creators like rough, open space; they want light, air, and action. A single studio will serve painting, sewing, quilting, and drawing, all worked together.

A large, high studio with several lower alcoves is even better. Fellowship and camaraderie develop: A brush is lent, a technique is borrowed, a date is set to visit an exhibition. The liveliest CCRC studio I have seen has a large platform covered with mountains, lakes,

bridges, and villages where "Fred" runs four miniature electric trains, while bantering with nearby residents, who chat and embroider while he repairs switches, tests track, and helps a sculptor mend a tool. Meanwhile, two painters and a potter work in the distance. There is no "program;" all are self-motivated; all respect each other's fantasy.

Of course, some artistic activities must be separated and need special provisions: a floor sprung for dance; a shop fitted with dust collectors for cabinet-making and carving; an area with sinks that will survive sculptors' plaster; kilns and wheels for potters; ventilation and presses for etchers; and darkrooms for photographers. Instrumentalists will want to practice the piano, violin, or clarinet without disturbing a choral group. Keeping all such areas gathered, visible, accessible, and as inviting as possible is the goal.

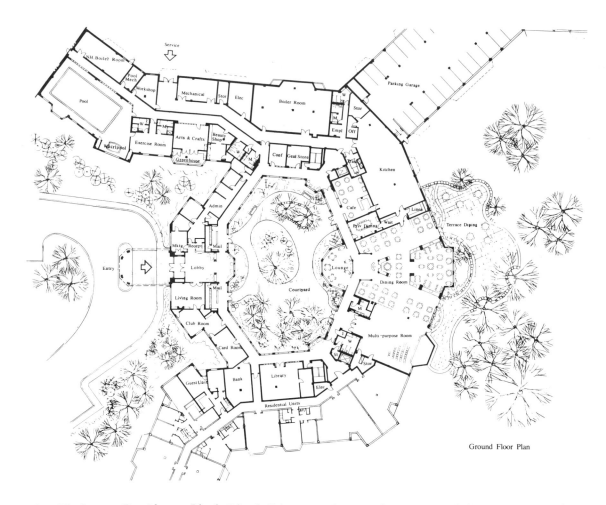

Homecroft at Blackstone, Providence, Rhode Island. Schematic plan. (Architect: CBT/Childs Bertman Tseckares & Casendino Inc.)

While writers like privacy and quiet, painters and sculptors enjoy group studio life. Arts and crafts thrive when done together in large windowed studios. Personal areas within a common studio are readily claimed and territories established. Being together generates exchanges and cooperation. Yet, absorbed in making images, the painter creates an island of privacy that neither the weaver's shuttle nor sculptor's mallet invades.

Such studios nurture membership, friendship, and pride. One studio works all Fall to create quilts, rugs, garden baskets, book shelves, paintings, and sculpture to be sold at Halloween, Thanksgiving, and Christmas to benefit the CCRC's activities fund. Exhibitions of members' photographs, paintings, drawings, and sculpture appear regularly, and it is noteworthy that the best galleries are not some remote or dedicated room that requires a direct visit but, rather, occur along the Main Street or concourse and in areas where mail is picked up and library or banking services are natural destinations. That stimulates conversation and pride. One painter at Medford Leas is willing to have their studio compete against Foulkeways' and Broadmead's—"not in field hockey, mind you, but in art." ∎

22/Commonsense Common Space

Mary Harrison and Barbara Proven

People may retire from a career but not a lifestyle. Long-standing traditions, preferences, and values still guide the elderly.

The ideal community not only provides opportunity for involvement, it motivates. Strategically designed common areas provide multiple opportunities for involvement. Then staff initiative can set the tone for motivating residents to continue an active lifestyle. In fact, a lifecare community can foster a social lifestyle that is richer than most people enjoyed, even in the most palatial single-family home.

Spatial design creates the potential for involvement; staff members foster the motivation to enjoy an active lifestyle.

Two lifecare communities currently under management by Life Care Services Corporation make the point. Abbey Delray South, Florida, an 8-year-old community with 286 units housing 361 residents, represents typical and fairly universal features. Harbour's Edge, a 3-year old community with 276 units housing 400 residents, illustrates some unique adaptations for socioeconomic and lifestyle characteristics of special retiree populations.

THE OWNERSHIP FACTOR

A key motivational factor, ownership, will urge the resident to become involved in the life of the community. A sense of ownership, combined with residents' participation in planning and decision making, will foster community involvement.

1. Avoid over-planning the social programs. Sometimes new communities overplan the activity program. This creates two problems. First, the preplanned activities may not fit the needs, values, and habits of the residents. Second, overplanning leaves little room for input from residents.

   (a) Avoid a preestablished program. Let the residents design it.
   (b) Avoid a spoon-fed approach that can trigger an irreversible trend toward resident noninvolvement and dependency.

2. Allow residents to contribute. Residents lend paintings to be hung in the library or dining room, enhancing the "ownership" theme. A resident may wish to donate a piano to keep this treasured possession nearby, rather than sold off to an antique dealer or stranger. Also, a partly stocked library invites residents' contributions. Budget for everything, but don't provide everything until the residents have an opportunity to contribute.

   Also learn how to say "no" to items that are not useful to the community. Rechannel the resident's energy. For example, help the resident donate some unwanted furnishings to the needy via local thrift shops.

3. Dynamic programming. As a resident population ages, turnover is inevitable. Constantly adapt the program to aging residents and new entries. This underscores the importance of residents' input in program planning. As the residents age, common areas like banks and shops or stores may not be convenient, and other ways must be developed to provide services.

4. Avoid an institutional approach to programming. Residents typically come to the retirement facility from the local community. Programming should respect their community ties. In-house programs should not compete with those outside activities that the resident may wish to continue. Otherwise, the residents become institutionalized, limiting their social world to the confines of the retirement community. In short, the in-house program should:

   (a) Complement outside activities and encourage continuation of historic relationships that were established over a lifetime.

(b) Provide for support services (transportation, escort, help with reservations) that foster continued involvement with the community.

THE DESIGN FACTOR

1. Design common areas for both group and individual activity. There is a time to be with others and a time to be alone for reflection.

2. Design common areas for active and passive roles. Participation is not an absolute but a matter of degree. Residents should have choices for the level of involvement they desire.

3. Design things to be "along the way." If it's not along the way, then it's "out of the way." Let residents "discover" new programs on their way to routine stops.

4. Design to encourage continuation of everyday activities. For example, parking spaces adjacent to the dining room enable residents to drive to dinner after an excursion or from an outlying villa.

5. Design for visibility throughout the community. The greater the resident's vista, the greater his or her sense of belonging and ownership.

6. Common areas should be less central and more dispersed in order to draw people to walk past other residents' apartments and crisscross the community. That design also widens the residents' sense of personal space and ownership.

COMMON AREAS IN THE LIFECARE COMMUNITY

Interior Cultural Spaces

Provision should be made for interior spaces that provide cultural and intellectual stimulation, such as an auditorium/theater, library, game rooms, and lounges.

1. *Auditorium/theater.* The auditorium/theater calls for special planning because of its many uses. Room capacity must accommodate at least 50 percent of the resident population in formal auditorium seating style. Furnishings such as chairs and tables must lend themselves to easy moving, stacking, and storage to allow for the many transitions from formal presentations, such as lectures and plays, to entertainment formats.

2. *Library.* Libraries offer many opportunities. First, there's intellectual stimulation, volunteer opportunities, and the chance to contribute to the library collection. Libraries offer residents a quiet place to read and reflect. In addition, portable libraries can be brought to residents who are temporarily ill in their apartments or in the nursing center.

3. *Game Rooms.* The game rooms provide more than a space for favorite activities—they are places for entertaining friends or inviting outside clubs and groups. Refreshments provided by the food and beverage department allow residents to entertain with minimum effort.

4. *Lounges.* Lounges extend the personal living space for people in apartments that have less square footage than their previous homes. Lounges come in all types: entrance lounges, floor lounges, building lounges. Entrance lounges foster community interaction. Floor lounges foster interaction and identity for each floor. Cocktail receptions and family celebrations are often conducted in lounge areas.

Interior Active Spaces

Interior activity spaces include arts and crafts and hobby rooms, billiards room, exercise room or spa, party room, bingo room, classroom, meeting room, boardroom, mailroom, corridors, and lobbies.

Arts and crafts rooms are truly multipurpose, reflecting the multiplicity of activities residents wish to pursue. The arts and crafts room should accommodate sewing, needle work, painting, ceramics, floral arrangements, and a decorations committee for holidays. Residents often contribute their time and talents. One resident group makes clothing for underprivileged children. While enjoying a favorite hobby, they feel needed. The well-stocked arts

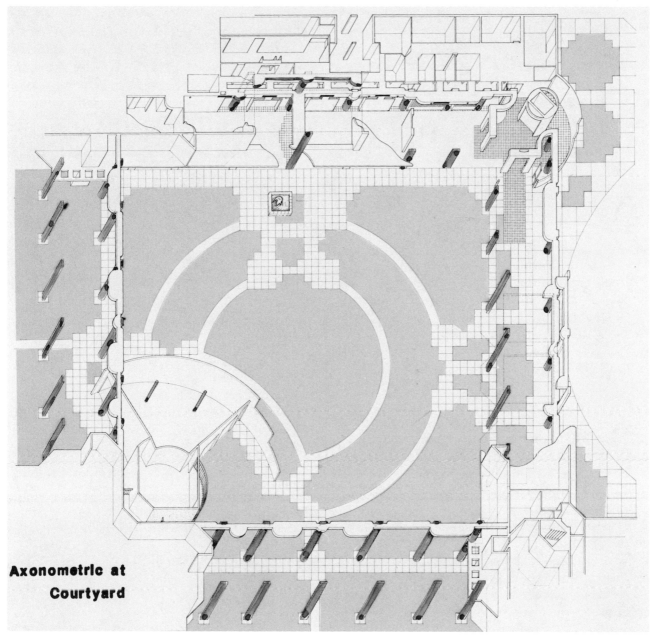

Axonometric at Courtyard

Abbey Delray South Life Care Community, Delray Beach, Florida. Axonometric at the courtyard. (Architect: Engelbrecht & Griffin Architects)

and crafts room should include direct and natural light for painting, storage for supplies, sewing machines, kiln, shelves for ceramics, and tables and chairs for group activities.

Exterior Active Spaces

Opportunities for physical activity are offered through the swimming pool, exercise rooms, shuffleboard courts, putting green, lawn bowling, croquet, picnic areas, barbecues, walkways and bike paths, and courtyards and patios. The Vita-park, conceived as a woodland or scenic trail with simple stretching apparatus located at intervals, is a popular, healthy outdoor diversion.

Exterior Cultural and Informal Spaces

Lakes, fountains, reflection pools, scenic spots, and sun decks provide settings for outdoor concerts, presentations, holiday celebrations, and special events.

Abbey Delray South Life Care Community, Delray Beach, Florida. (Architect: Engelbrecht & Griffin Architects/ Photo: Courtesy of Life Care Services)

The Health Center

The health center is part of the common space. Well residents need to be encouraged to seek the support offered them. Policies that "hide" the infirmary may actually be anxiety producing. Suddenly, someone in the next apartment isn't there anymore (gone to the health center). The resident wonders where his or her neighbor has gone and what is happening to him or her. The health center needs to remain "connected" with the rest of the community. Yet, the well resident's entry into this area can be buffered. Architect Kevin Donahue proposes a "transitional gallery," a common area that both separates and connects. This common area between well and frail allows residents to "come to terms" with the transition.

Since "life goes on" in the health center, we should expect a full complement of common spaces to allow the frail to continue with their adapted lifestyle. The following areas should be found in the health center: (a) dining room, (b) resident activity room, (c) lounge for family visits, (d) private meeting room for consultation with trust officer, clergy, attorney, counselor, (e) porch/patio/solarium, and (f) courtyard.

SPECIAL FEATURES:
HARBOUR'S EDGE

We offer special observations from our experience with Harbour's Edge. This new community suggests a luxurious cruise on a fine passenger liner. Built for autonomous individuals who are well-traveled, accustomed to the best of everything, and likely to entertain friends frequently, Harbour's Edge has unique characteristics.

1. Visitors must enter the community through a gatehouse to arrive at the luxurious waterside facility.
2. Inside the main lobby, the visitor is greeted by a spectacular fountain overlooking the intracoastal waterway.
3. Lounge areas are plush, yet comfortable and intimate.
4. The receptionist is replaced by a concierge.
5. Game rooms have a sleek, contemporary look.
6. The main dining area rivals the best in formal dining.
7. For dinner parties, there is private dining for residents and guests.

Abbey Delray South Life Care Community, Delray Beach, Florida. (Architect: Engelbrecht & Griffin Architects/Photo: Courtesy of Life Care Services)

Abbey Delray South Life Care Community, Delray Beach, Florida. (Architect: Engelbrecht & Griffin Architects/Photo: Courtesy of Life Care Services)

8. Most residents are accustomed to entertaining a party of 10 to 12 guests. Staff is prepared to cater dinner parties.
9. The worldly resident will be acquainted with the latest developments in the wellness movement. Fitness opportunities such as a fully equipped spa and tennis courts are vital.
10. Cultural events—plays, dramatic readings, piano recitals, lectures, and the like—require state-of-the-art theater facilities.
11. Perhaps because the community emphasizes socialization and active lifestyles, areas for solitude and reflection become even more important. Include opportunities for gardening and sitting areas that allow casual observation of the community activities.

SUMMARY

While Abbey Delray South suggests the universal activities to be incorporated in retirement living communities, Harbour's Edge demonstrates how these universal features can be adapted to meet the unique needs of an exclusive clientele. In each case, the resident is surrounded by an environment that seems natural because it reflects personal traditions, preferences, and values established over a lifetime. ∎

23/Vital Extensions of the Living Unit

Stephen R. Roizen

A retirement community should reflect the philosophy of its sponsors. At The Willows in Westborough, Massachusetts, the philosophy is "to provide a retirement community which fosters continued independence and self-determination for its residents." The Willows's residents govern their activities and determine policies that affect their lives.

This is exemplified most dramatically in community spaces like the library, greenhouse, general store, and woodworking shop. The Willows's sponsors built those spaces and furnished them. The books in the library, however, were donated by residents. With minimal involvement of a Resident Services Coordinator, committees of residents manage the library, store, greenhouse, craft show, and woodworking shop. The coordinator helps them schedule activities and entertainment, but only recommends and does not decide on programming.

Generally, the resident population of continuing care retirement communities and fine nursing homes comes from single-family homes that are well-furnished and well-appointed. These appointments reflect a family's interests and activities and are not readily discarded. Even though aging often means loss of flexibility, diminution of sight and hearing, and a greater tendency to suffer from fractures and falls due to osteoporosis and the spine's curvature, the elderly don't want to give anything up. In fact, the prospective clients' fear of loss is the most difficult aspect of marketing retirement communities. In their minds, the single-family home is a symbol of self-sufficiency, independence, and active engagement. When they do decide to move, they want a domestic, noninstitutional environment that feels comfortable and maybe even resembles their former home.

Beyond the facts of age and debility, design-

ing retirement communities differs from hotel design in that the elderly are not a short-term population. Residents live in retirement communities for years, not days. They eat in the same dining room every day, play cards in the same lounge, walk the same corridors, and go to the same activities rooms.

Further, a retirement community is not a collection of rooms or apartments. Even the most comfortable and spacious apartments, with adequate closet space, safe and convenient bathrooms, and large kitchens, are secondary. *Community space is the important extension to the apartment.*

Residents generally come to a retirement community from private homes where they had a den, a basement, a yard, and rooms for various activities. When they move into three rooms in a retirement community, they don't want to give up puttering in the garden or potting plants or getting together with friends. The retirement community's greenhouse, craft room, woodworking shop, library, lounges, exercise room, auditorium, and lobby become the extensions to the apartment. *They make apartment living tolerable, even*

Willows at Westborough, Westborough, Massachusetts. (Designer: DiLeonardo International, Inc./Photo: Warren Jagger Photography Inc.)

enjoyable. Residents can pot plants in the greenhouse, spilling dirt on the floor, or saw lumber in the woodworking shop, making a mess, all the while not having to care about cleaning up.

As heavily used extensions to apartment living, common activity spaces must be accessible, inviting, and serviceable. The challenge is to design an environment that is attractive and, at the same time, functional and safe for the user. Seating, lighting, floor covering, distances, door handles, position of electrical outlets, air conditioning, all take on a new dimension.

How will the aging person use the environment? Meeting codes and making the facility beautiful are not enough. Attention to detail is imperative.

A greenhouse or woodworking shop cannot be so "picture perfect" as to make a resident reluctant to enter or afraid to make a mess. Furnishing and equipment must be of a design the older adult can easily use. Table height is important, as are lighting and ease of access (location), safety features, and type of equipment. A universal gym is not likely to be used in a retirement community by those in their second stage of retirement, ages 79 and up, but a treadmill, stationary bicycles, and possibly a rowing machine will get occasional use. Likewise, a greenhouse must be furnished with basic potting tables, display areas, storage areas for soil, pots and tools, a source of water, proper drainage, and, of course, light and con-trolled ventilation. The woodworking shop needs a good assortment of hand and power tools, but they need not be cabinetmaker's quality.

Auditoriums work best if they have a raised stage, level floor, and movable seating. Fixed seating diminishes movement, especially in a darkened auditorium, and when an elderly person uses a cane or walker, sloping aisles can obstruct. Having to exit during a performance to use a rest room can be dangerous and frightening for an elderly person whose footing is slightly unsure and whose sight is starting to fail.

Banking on premises is a very desirable feature. The Westborough Savings Bank, a century-old mutual savings bank, studied retirement community banks before designing their branch bank at the Willows. They noted that the elderly are not comfortable with automated-teller machines and did not like waiting in line at a teller's window. The branch has two bank representatives who sit at desks, and the customers sit across from them when doing business. Open three days each week, the branch is very successful, and its elderly customers in the Willows community find it inviting, reliable, and discreet.

Building for the elderly and infirm requires special sensitivity to their abilities and needs. That sensitivity is especially wanted in all the common spaces that are vital extensions of the living or nursing units. ∎

24/Dining as Spatial Experience

Dianne Davis

Joie de vivre describes the vital spirit created by healthcare institutions that have adopted some of the successful foodservice settings found at fine restaurants, shopping malls, airports, and revived seaports, such as Quincy Market in Boston. Gone is the imagery of traditional inpatient trays, old-fashioned vending machines, and dreary, linoleum cafeterias. Now there are fine restaurants in hospitals, and attractive cafes, special dining areas, and mobile hot and cold carts are conveniently stationed near ambulatory care and clinic areas. Even microwave/vending machines can provide an enjoyable eleventh-hour snack.

"SIDEWALK" CAFES AND MINI-FOOD COURTS

"Bright, cheerful and relaxing, it makes me forget I'm in a hospital," says a customer about one of the coffee shops and mini-food courts. Designed as on-site retail kiosks, they have become favorite sites for dining, meeting relatives, or awaiting medical appointments. Their convenience, comfort, design, and fare have improved hospitals' image and strengthened public loyalty.

Riding up Madison Avenue in a crowded bus, I remarked on the large flower baskets an elderly couple had bought to plant on their terrace and soon learned that the couple, who live near Manhattan's Mount Sinai Medical Center, eat daily in the hospital's cafeteria, which they raved about. In large dining space, they said, "You never feel crowded; anyway, we go for dinner at 4:30 P.M. and everything is so fresh and beautifully presented. There is such a large selection. The staff in clean white uniforms and high hats treat us so nicely. Where else can you have a complete meal for $3.00? . . . and their soups are better than homemade! You help yourself at the soup bar. You must go!" After completing my errand, I followed their instructions and found the Plaza cafeteria. New, opened two weeks before, it already had become a neighborhood eatery. Its inviting large, square mini-court stands within an L-shaped dining room, with huge picture-frame windows that create a gracious, "noninstitutional" feeling.

HOSPITAL RESTAURANTS

The lobby "sidewalk cafe" was a revolutionary and controversial idea when the Lobby Café at Hackensack Medical Center, New Jersey, was designed in 1984. It success reflects the strong belief of Robert Shakno, the center's former president, in adapting hotel-oriented services and restaurant models. Even though prices are slightly higher than in the employee's cafeteria, the Lobby Café has become the favorite eating spot of both staff and visitors.

The Ground Restaurant at Roanoke Memorial Hospital is a prototype of the popular, upscale, mini-food-court cafeteria. Its quick service and scatter design give staff and visitors

Hackensack Medical Center, Hackensack, New Jersey. (Architect: NBBJRosenfield, New York Studio/Joint Venture: The Gruzen Partnership/Photo: John Hill)

a wide selection of popular fare. Rather than having a straight serving line, which creates bottlenecks, the restaurant has take-out stations, which include a "Deli and Bakery," "Hot Fare" counter for hot food and grill items, and self-service "Fresh Fare," a salad bar, and beverage areas. By removing a central corridor between the former cafeteria and snack area, the dining area was enlarged, and mirrors expand the space even more. A counter in the dining room provides a convenient place for the "quick bite" diner, and microwave ovens at the condiment stands accommodate those wishing to take food out or brown-bag it.

The Mountainside Hospital's Bayberry Cafe in New Jersey is located directly off the hospital's main entrance. Visible through segmented glass windows, the cafe opens to an outdoor dining terrace. Two distinct dining areas, separated by a series of planter walls that also define the seated bar/grille area, divide

Roanoke Memorial Hospital, Roanoke, Virginia. Ground Floor Restaurant. (Interior Designer: Cini-Little International/Photo: Ed Hamilton)

Roanoke Memorial Hospital, Roanoke, Virginia. (Interior Designer: Cini-Little International/Photo: Ed Hamilton)

staff and the general public. Indirect lighting in cove ceilings creates a warm ambiance as waiters provide tableside service.

Recently, fast-food chains have expanded into hospitals. Marriott's contract-feeding division has programmed 1000 Pizza Hut Express Kiosks. Little Caesar, McDonald's, and Burger King are also opening outlets in hospitals. Many hospitals are designing their own kiosks to offer similar fare and regional themes.

WHITE TABLECLOTH RESTAURANTS

Within medical centers fine restaurants now attract the general public. Offering choice dishes, service, and decor, these restaurants are located either adjacent to the lobby, such as Classics at the Cleveland Clinic, or on a roof offering vistas, as at the Atrium Dining Room in the University of Iowa Medical Center. The Atrium also has a terrace. Designed to compete with successful local restaurants, the hospital restaurants often offer valet parking, coat checking, reserved tables, and à la carte menus featuring both gourmet and "lite" healthy fare. Some medical centers have imported an existing successful restaurant. This is the origin of Grisanti's Courtyard within Methodist Medical Center in Memphis, Tennessee. Assured of John Grisanti's reputation as a restaurateur, the Medical Center anticipated a dividend to their own image as a hospitable institution.

INFORMAL SPACES

Many healthcare facilities are developing a variety of informal dining places: corridor nooks with cafe canopy, attractive "coffee shop" counters, or "front porch" cafes, where one can sip coffee and watch the world go by. High tea in the lobby or an anteroom encourages informal meeting. Such informal dining "places" help single diners to participate in a social environment rather than eating alone in an apartment. The informal setting plays to the desire to see and be seen—an important psychological need—and helps the solitary diner gain community membership.

University of Iowa Medical Center, Ames, Iowa. (Architect: Hansen Lind Meyer, Inc./Photo: Don DuBroff)

Willows at Westborough, Westborough, Massachusetts.
(Designer: DiLeonardo International, Inc./Photo:
Warren Jagger Photography Inc.)

MAIN DINING SPACES

Spatial design can achieve choice and variety
within a single dining space. Even without dispersed locations, where only a main dining
area is wanted for reasons of economy, the experience can be varied. A high central space
can be furnished for formal dining, while its
periphery can be developed as lower small
rooms or alcoves screened from the main
space. Thus, variety, including different
themes, can exist within unity. Between master space and alcoves, divisions should be implied; any separations should be subtle, to
reduce any sense of isolation and containment. Dividers can be glazed walls, lighting,
terraces, shutters, and low walls topped by
flowers and shrubs. Columns, lattice ceilings,
alcoves, staircases, and mezzanines subdivide
large spatial areas. In The Willows at Westborough, Massachusetts, the main dining room
offers views to its private rooms through shut-
tered windows.

Peninsula Regent, San Mateo, California. (Architect:
Backen, Arrigoni & Rossi/Photo: Charles S. White)

Dining at Harbour's Edge, Florida, is intended to convey the experience of being on a cruise ship docked to give an unobstructed view of the intercostal waterway. High above Tucson, the dining room at La Posada offers views of the distant city, and the dining room's centerpiece is a buffet for salads and desserts.

Dining room entrances should be inviting. Direct access to an outdoor terrace, preferably with a shaded area and bordered by gardens, enlarges dining spaces and provides variety. The indoor Courtyard at San Marcos, California, and the terraces in Peninsula Regent and Park Lane Retirement Suites encourage informal gathering and easy access into dining rooms. Flowers, posters, glass partitions, low walls, and plants create welcoming entrances. Some restaurants display appetizers and desserts that stimulate conversation, as do theme murals and displays of artifacts.

Plan ahead for the mobile buffet unit. Introduced into a formal dining room as an afterthought, it can ruin the effect. Given staffing problems today, it is shortsighted to plan an elegant dining room only for service at tables, without anticipating the possible need for steam tables and either buffet or waitress-assisted service. Why ruin a formal dining room by rolling in some protruding marble or metal unit?

Whether to centralize dining rooms or to disperse them is often debated. Consolidation has the obvious advantages of proximity to kitchen and ease of management. Dispersed and varied dining locations, however, have the advantages of variety and encouraging residents to walk, plan, and make choices. Whether consolidated or dispersed, the dining location must be clearly related to a spatial concourse, Main Street.

Table size and spacing can encourage a sense of privacy. A square table permits easy exchange with a small group planning a gallery trip; a round table, for no more than ten, is perfect for a birthday celebration; and an 8-foot rectangle makes swapping ideas easy. Adjacent meeting rooms or small dining rooms equipped with spot or track lighting and serving pantries or kitchenettes encourage space for club meetings with lectures and demonstrations. Combining intimate meeting areas

Willows at Westborough, Westborough, Massachusetts. (Designer: DiLeonardo International, Inc./Photo: Warren Jagger Photography Inc.)

with dining facilities fosters friendships. More relaxed dining and a greater sense of privacy are possible when tables are widely spaced and arranged at angles to eliminate visual distractions.

Dining is made more enjoyable by comfortable chairs. However, beautiful and colorful, deep-cushioned, armless chairs are foolish. Chairs must be easily movable, supportive, appropriately scaled, and comfortably suited to table height. In carpeted dining rooms chairs with front leg casters work well. Some tables should have wheelchair extensions that prevent isolation and enable impaired residents to dine comfortably with friends. Finding a table that will both admit wheelchairs and provide a height that is also comfortable for diners in chairs is not easy. Unable to find a manufactured table, the staff of a large teaching nursing home in St. Louis, under the direction of its administrator, Miner L. Brown, designed a model now produced by Guild Craftsman, Inc., in St. Louis. Four drop-leaf ledges, which fit between the wheelchair's arms, rise from the sides of a 36-by-36-inch tabletop that is supported by a central column. The table accommodates four diners in combinations of chairs and wheelchairs.

Use of soft materials, as well as acoustical ceilings, shutters, panels, or banners, even sound-catching corners, shapes, and spaces, can significantly diminish uncomfortable "buzz" noise.

Setting the stage and mood is important. Tabletop ornaments, colorful cloth surfaces, woven placemats on wooden tabletops, textured napkins, cut glassware, well-balanced flatware, attractively color-rimmed china, and other table accoutrements all influence dining satisfaction. Coordinated colors and contrasted textures add surprise and interest.

Often forgotten, especially in senior communities, is the need for independence. For women that may mean, "I can cook what I want, when I want." Being served three times a day with food prepared by someone else may seem luxurious, but to some older women whose kitchens were part of their demonstrable independence not having a kitchen is traumatic. The kitchen can be the heart of any community, the hospitable component of sociability and gracious living. Most continuing care retirement communities provide a kitchen in each apartment, but shared kitchens and a convenient take-out store may offer alternatives in other long-term care communities.

Dining is the one activity in healthcare and senior communities that people feel secure to judge. Their judgment regarding their dining's quality, service, and atmosphere often colors their evaluation of an entire facility. ∎

25 / Saving the Mansion

Glen Tipton

Restored mansions, hotels, and even remodeled factories and warehouses may provide fine dining spaces and other rooms for a community center.

The earliest form of continuing care retirement community (CCRC), sponsored by the Quakers in suburban Philadelphia, was built on the campus plan, with clusters of connected cottages linked by covered walkways to a distinct community center. This plan appeared in Foulkeways in the mid-1960s at Gwynedd, Pennsylvania. It has since been repeated in many variations, such as Broadmead, in Cockeysville, Maryland.

More recent communities are more compact: a series of mid-rise (two or more stories) residential buildings are connected to a community center, as in Duncater in Hartford, Connecticut, and Charlestown, in Baltimore, Maryland. Each has a distinct community center. In high-rise construction, however, the community center does not dominate the plan. There, it is an integral part of the architectural statement, as in Marriott's twin-tower Jefferson in Arlington, Virginia.

THE COMMUNITY CENTER

The components of a community center vary, depending upon the size of the community, the philosophy of its developer/sponsor, and the demands of the marketplace, but a typical community center houses a main dining room or rooms, a common living room, a flat-floor auditorium or multipurpose room, and a mail and message center. More elaborate centers contain card rooms, libraries, craft rooms, conference rooms, recreation rooms, coffee shops, gift shops, club rooms, music rooms, and exercise rooms. Some centers offer private dining rooms, guest rooms, even swimming pools, greenhouses, banks, chapels, stockbrokers, travel agents, and variations of all these. A community center typically also houses the community's administration and services such as kitchen, housekeeping, and laundry.

HOTELS AND MANSIONS

Since the community center demands a combination of grand scale and elegance, the mansions and hotels of yesteryear have often been saved and adapted to new uses. As architectural fashion and public sentiment now favor historic preservation, the abandoned or "useless" hotel, mansion, or school can find new life as the community center of a CCRC.

Beaumont

On the Main Line, northwest of Philadelphia, long home to the socially elite, some mansions have fallen into disrepair, as was the case with Beaumont, the former home of locomotive tycoon William Austin. Built in 1912 on a 50-acre estate in Bryn Mawr, Pennsylvania, this imposing Edwardian graystone mansion is now the centerpiece of a 200-unit retirement community. Developer Arthur Wheeler saw its potential, and local authorities agreed, granting the necessary zoning and building permits. Today, Beaumont, a full-service lifecare community managed by American Retirement Corporation, provides 132 apartments in a three-story building linked to the mansion. Also provided are 68-unit, private, individual "villas" with garages, a 22-unit assisted-living wing, and a 28-unit skilled-nursing center.

At its center is the 30-room mansion, whose elaborately detailed interior offers eight dining rooms, with lounges, a bar, a club room, and a grand music room—the showplace of the mansion, with its magnificent Aeolian organ. The room's ornately gilded and painted vaulted ceiling was created by an Austrian court painter and has been restored by Philadelphia artist Brian Cesaria. Architect Ann Capran and interior designers Arthur Schuster, Inc., collaborated to create a functional community center that integrates the mansion's wonderful detail and painted friezes with new details, colors, and finishes.

Beaumont at Bryn Mawr, Bryn Mawr, Pennsylvania. View of the music room, showing the Aeolian organ. (Architectural Restoration: Arthur Shuster, Inc./Photo: Tom Crane, courtesy of *Restaurant/Hotel Design International*)

Park Village

In the mid-1800s, in Williamsport, Pennsylvania, lumber baron Peter Herdic created a neighborhood now known as Millionaires Row. Among these elaborately detailed Victorian mansions, predominantly Italianate in style, the centerpiece is the former Herdic Hotel. Built in 1865, this four-story stucco and brick Italianate building adjoined the railroad station and fronted on a wonderful open space known as Deer Park. Until the Depression, it served travelers in an elegant style.

At some point, its top two floors were removed, and in 1940 the hotel became the Park Home, a home for elderly women. Now a study is underway to adapt the once magnificent hotel to a new use. Architects Cochran, Stephenson & Donkervoet, Inc., have designed its conversion to a community center and residential component for a new CCRC. If the study proves it feasible, Park Village will

provide 150 apartments, 30 assisted-living facilities and 30 skilled-nursing beds, and an array of community services in the old home/hotel.

Sunrise

Not every project can literally "save" an existing mansion. In Arlington, Virginia, however, one developer of assisted-living facilities, Paul Klaassen, believes that the ideal image for his developments is the "mansion." His brand-new 47-unit facility on Glebe Road in Arlington is a modern-day mansion. The "Victorian" edifice has received favorable publicity and marketing success. Indeed, there are many ways to "save the mansion." ∎

James Steam Mill, Newburyport, Massachusetts. (Architectural Restoration: CBT/Childs Bertman Tseckares & Casendino Inc./Photo: Nick Wheeler, Wheeler Photographics)

Leonard Hotel and Park Village, Williamsport, Pennsylvania. (Architect: Cochran, Stephenson & Donkervoet, Inc.)

25A/Sunshine Villa

Precia Harthcock

When he purchased the property in 1885, James Phillip Smith, a leader in the international food business, wanted to create a lavish estate, with Sunshine Villa a diamond for Santa Cruz's sparkling Monterey Bay. The villa became a social hub for both Santa Cruz and the San Francisco bay area, attracting public servants and presidents to a Venetian Water Carnival where a dammed San Lorenzo River floated gondolas with musicians playing.

Today, the restored mansion is the centerpiece for senior residences within a 75,000-square-foot addition that embraces the Victo-rian mansion. The mansion's lower floor features a parlor, chapel, and museum, while the upper floors, approached by a grand staircase, are residential apartments. An intimate courtyard is the focus for the main dining room, library, lounge, and activity areas.

Overall, the interior is Victorian, with furniture, brocade, satin, and velvet in nooks and crannies. Old and new benefit each other, enhancing the whole, and add yet another chapter to the story of a "grand old lady," continuing her tradition of hospitality, now as a senior living community. ■

Sunshine Villa, Santa Cruz, California. (Architectural Restoration and Design: Treffinger, Walz & MacLeod/Interior Design: PRH Interior Design)

26/Hotel Conversions Into Senior Living Communities

Dianne Davis

One of the most successful directions for providing local assisted-living housing for the elderly is the restoration of small-town hotels. Their conversion is approached enthusiastically (and affectionately) by the Westin Financial Group (WFG), whose founder, Richard Westin of Berkeley, California, says, "There's a wonderful association of old people and old buildings. They're really made for one another; they grew up together." With developer Jesse A. Pitman, Westin has restored more than two dozen small hotels since 1984, and WFG's Evergreen Management, Inc., operates them as assisted-living residences.

The 1890s hotel near the small-town railroad depot on mid–Main Street had a romantic aura: gracious restaurants, spacious guest rooms, grand ballrooms, and elegant staircases and lobbies. Victorian interiors with marble floors, decorative oak panels, ornamental ceilings, and large fireplaces often exist in National Historic Registered buildings. Some have accents of Richardsonian Romanesque arches, windows, and gables.

The Harrington Inn in Port Huron, Michigan, and the Algonquin Hotel in Cumberland, Maryland, fell into decay as travelers took to the highway and motel. Thanks to the restorations by WFG, they now revive memories of the days when travelers danced there. About the Algonquin, Margaret Yantorno, a lifelong resident of Cumberland, recalls: "When my father-in-law came to stay with us, my husband and I would put the kids to bed and say we were going out to walk. We wouldn't tell him where we were going because he didn't believe in spending money, but we'd come here. We had to go in the side door to dance because we couldn't afford to go to the restaurant or the hotel itself. But we'd go in and go clear to the roof and dance on the concrete." Today, Mrs.

Kensington Residential Hotel, Hastings, Nebraska. (Architect: Klick Inter Arch Design/Photo: John Klick)

Yantorno lives in the Algonquin, where, more than 63 years ago, she and her husband danced.

Restoring such hotels to their former glory has inspired neighboring merchants to restore and transform adjacent stores. Located in towns of one- and two-story buildings, the hotels provide public rooms that attract weddings, luncheons, and meetings. Of the more than two dozen hotels WFG has converted, one—the Kensington in Hastings, Nebraska—is illustrated here. ∎

27 / The Agora

Zachary Rosenfield with Janet Hays

Menorah Campus, the new suburban continuing care retirement community (CCRC) of the Rosa Coplon Jewish Home and Infirmary, is designed to create a lively community that is closely tied to people and organizations in greater Buffalo, the former home of most of its residents. The campus has 52 apartments for independent living, an 80-person adult home, a 180-bed nursing home, and an Alzheimer's Wing for 40 people, all centered around the agora—20,000 square feet of enclosed common space that forms the focus of the Campus.

Our design intends to give a residential, not an institutional or medical quality to the space, achieved by appropriate shape, scale, materials, and furnishings. We provide a continuum of living spaces, from private to semiprivate to semipublic to public, in order to provide sensory variety. Compactness, to minimize travel distances for residents, care givers, and foodservice, was a primary goal; so was our intention to support independent behavior. We also varied spaces, making them distinctive in design and purpose, such as libraries and music rooms, rather than amorphous "lounges." To allow varying staff/resident ratios from shift to shift, and to accommodate changing needs of the resident, we tried to provide flexibility.

With a clock tower at the entry and a pool, gazebos, courtyards, and river walks, the Campus provides a graceful, interesting atmosphere that entices visitors and encourages residents to stroll outdoors.

From the courtyard, we enter the agora, where residents of all three housing areas on campus meet casually and comfortably. The apartments, the adult home, and the nursing home all connect to the agora by easy indoor walks (especially important in the harsh Buffalo winters). Residents can watch the action, indoors and out, from several pleasant sitting areas, bay windows, or porches; eat a snack or a meal in one of the dining areas; shop, exercise, or watch the children in the day-care center, read in the library, or entertain guests, all the while moderating their involvement according to their individual capabilities and preferences.

Menorah Campus buildings have no "back door." Every entrance is a front entrance—welcoming, dignified, and leading to useful and interesting spaces. Entrances differ, distinguishing buildings and adding interest to the daily routine. For instance, people in the adult home and the apartments can enter through the agora and pass the shops and activity centers on the way to their apartments. They experience the feeling of living in a hotel or resort.

The agora is not a street or corridor, but rather a series of living rooms with "boutiques" providing goods and services. Windows for the boutiques provide views that make walking interesting, entice people to enter, and help orient those who are memory-impaired. Several rental spaces are leased to multiple renters, making goods and services, which could not be supported full time, available on an affordable part-time basis. Pushcarts with gay umbrellas offer a changing cornucopia of food, drink, flowers, and crafts.

Sometimes facilities for the elderly are unappealing: a sterile atmosphere with antiseptic odors (at best), closed windows, controlled air, and hard surfaces. In those situations, residents are more likely to become depressed and lethargic and lose appetite. Visitors find excuses to stay away.

Menorah Campus is different. At the deli, for instance, the aroma of fresh bread emanates from ovens located in the central serving area. Tables arranged around this central serving area flow into a generous sky-lighted bay window overlooking the courtyard. Nearby,

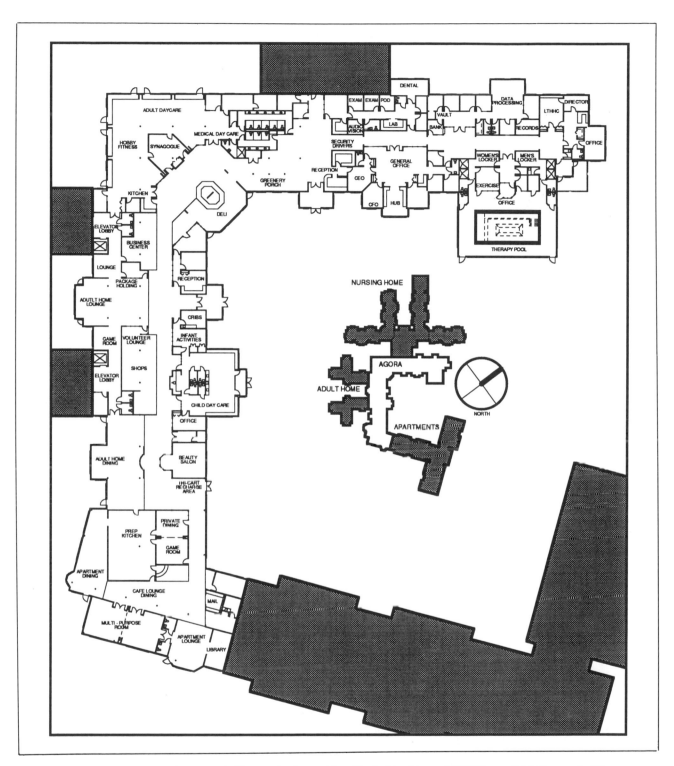

Menorah Campus, Rosa Coplon Jewish Home, Amherst, New York. [Architect: NBBJRosenfield (formerly The Rosenfield Partnership)]

residents come into the fragrant and sunny greenery room every day to see how the plants are growing and which flowers are blooming. All the agora windows open. The entry vestibule has removable glass panels so that summer residents can enjoy fresh air, breezes, and the sounds and smells of the out-of-doors.

It is not easy for a woman to exercise when she is wearing a dress, stockings, garter belt, and conventional shoes. Yet in most nursing homes, women and men come to physical therapy in their regular clothes and are inhibited and awkward in carrying out their routines. Menorah Campus operates its gym, exercise, and rehab rooms like a health club or spa: everyone wears comfortable, appropriate exercise clothing. Interest, participation, and effectiveness are heightened.

The business center, just to the right of the main entrance lobby, has fax machines, computers, and current issues of *The Wall Street Journal* and *Business Week*. By providing useful equipment and information, Menorah Campus encourages residents to continue active management of their financial accounts, investments, and taxes, and to stay abreast of Social Security and Medicare legislation. Multiple renters—banks, tax preparers (at tax time)—and representatives from local social service agencies come in regularly to provide services and information.

The board and administration of Rosa Copplon Home want visitor and community groups on campus, so that the residents can continue their long-standing associations and activities. Components of the agora are designed to serve community needs and make visits pleasant and relaxing to encourage families and friends to come often; restaurant-quality dining rooms provide comfortable and dignified places to entertain guests, while the deli soda fountain and small decentralized sitting areas lend themselves to informal visits. Philanthropic organizations meet in the multipurpose rooms (movable dividers allow for large and small groups), and the synagogue hosts community services. Every day, residents can see the children (and their parents) who come to the day-care center. Some volunteer to read or play with the children; others, who are unable or disinclined to volunteer, enjoy watching the children come and go. On the other side of the lobby, the adult day-care center offers another useful service that draws people from the community and gives residents a chance to see old friends. ∎

28/Goals for Communal Space

Ronald Kollar

When Classic Residence by Hyatt was formed in 1987 to develop senior communities, we believed that our hotel design experience would translate well to our new building type. As we became more involved in the design and operation of our communities, we learned that a resident population, as opposed to one that is transient, and moreover residents who may develop physical limitations as they age, forces us to adjust our planning and design.

The obvious similarities between community space in a hotel and that in a senior living community diverge in scale. While hotel designers seek a sophisticated, grand environment, our challenge in the senior living industry is to create an intimate, residential atmosphere. Adjustments in scale are needed to enable small groups of residents to feel comfortable, rather than overwhelmed, in the community areas. For example, we have introduced the "wintergarden" concept, an intimate version of the hotel atrium. Bright, comfortable, and airy, the wintergarden is the focal point of the community, with all other living areas radiating from it. The wintergarden is not nearly so expansive as a hotel atrium, and furniture groupings and alcoves give it a residential scale where residents can casually interact or entertain friends.

Other community areas that are directly accessible from the wintergarden include a library, card room, art studios, and dining rooms. Again, a residential tone is set, because

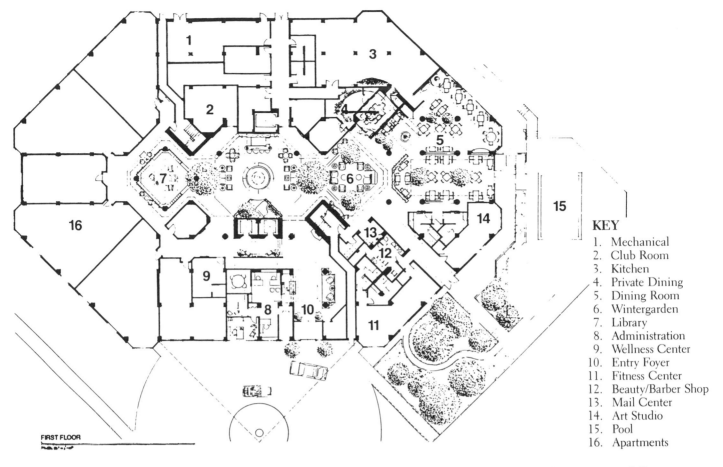

KEY
1. Mechanical
2. Club Room
3. Kitchen
4. Private Dining
5. Dining Room
6. Wintergarden
7. Library
8. Administration
9. Wellness Center
10. Entry Foyer
11. Fitness Center
12. Beauty/Barber Shop
13. Mail Center
14. Art Studio
15. Pool
16. Apartments

FIRST FLOOR

Classic Residence by Hyatt, Dallas, Texas. Floorplan for first floor community areas. (Architect: Culpepper McAuliffe & Meaders)

residents consider these rooms extensions of their private apartments. They want to feel at home in these areas, dress casually, and walk around to see what's going on. Ceiling height and room sizes are comparable to those in a private residence, with bold colors and patterns such as stripes and florals.

Because the wear and tear one finds in a large convention hotel is not an issue, residential-quality fabrics including silk and cotton work well in these settings. Various furniture styles, fabric patterns, finishes, and accessories are introduced throughout the community to create the effect of a "collection" of pieces rather than a totally coordinated design statement. Designs are on the traditional side; in fact, considerable energy is expended incorporating the regional or local traditions, tastes, and styles into each community. Photographs, paintings, and sculptures by local artists, and residents' personal collections personalize the

community spaces. Because our designs impact their daily lives, residents tend to review and judge their surroundings with a much more critical eye—and they're not forgiving about mistakes!

Since it is the most frequented area of a residential community, a thoughtful design for the dining room is essential. Typically, residents will eat at least one meal a day there, if not two, and for many, mealtime represents the most important social activity of the day. The dining room must have an intimate quality at breakfast time, yet meet the seating requirements of the busy dinner hour, and ideally, be flexible enough to be used for non-mealtime activities. Depending upon the size of the community, the dining room may be subdivided into two (or three) sections. The larger section generally has a high ceiling and is visually separated from the smaller section by planters, screens, or a fireplace. This larger room is the more formal of the two areas, and place settings feature linen tablecloths, silver, and fine china. The smaller dining area might have a cafe-like atmosphere—the perfect setting for a breakfast buffet for early risers. In each room, high-back chairs and banquettes are available to accommodate different seating preferences and to further subdivide the space.

Since adults experience physical changes as they age, we utilize redundant cueing to help residents who may have sensory or cognitive impairments. Distinctive furniture groupings in elevator lobbies, differences in color, art, floor coverings, and changes in tactile surfaces from one room to the next act as references as residents move about the community.

To help seniors who have some visual deterioration, we introduce greater light levels, multiple light sources, both incandescent and fluorescent, and both recessed and direct, throughout our communities. Glare is reduced by the use of sheets and tinted glass in community areas. Color and depth perception are also affected by changes in the eye; we compensate by presenting a brighter color palette, with substantial contrast between floors and walls and carpets whose borders will not be mistaken for steps. Tone-on-tone fabrics and wall coverings are difficult for seniors to distinguish, as are busy patterns that sometimes appear to "move." It is best to stay with a graphic scale that is easy to perceive.

Subtle design alterations can improve the acoustics to help people with diminished hearing. Carpets, draperies, wallcoverings, and plants absorb sound, thereby filtering background noise. Furniture groupings are clustered together to facilitate face-to-face communication, enabling conversing residents to pick up visual clues.

Classic Residence by Hyatt, Dallas, Texas. (Architect: Culpepper McAuliffe & Meaders/Photo: Rion C. Rizzo/Creative Sources Photography, Atlanta, Georgia)

Strength, stamina, and flexibility also tend to decrease noticeably in older adults. To accommodate these limitations, we select furniture that can easily be repositioned by our residents. In addition, most chairs and sofas have relatively shallow seats, and their backs have nearly vertical pitch to compensate for reduced flexibility. Almost all have arms, which provide additional support when sitting down or rising. In each corridor, chairs in alcoves offer residents places to rest while waiting for an elevator or in the hallway leading to their apartments. Chair rails that function as handrails enhance the residential appearance of the corridors and also aid residents in keeping their balance. Near the mailboxes, a seating area enables residents to wait for the mail or read their letters in comfort.

In designing senior living communities, the key is to make subtle adjustments that compensate for the physical limitations of our residents, without compromising their dignity or institutionalizing the communities. Although we can generalize about the tastes and preferences of seniors as well as their physical limitations, each senior living community must be fine-tuned to its own resident population. ■

29/Architectural Design Principles for Communal Dwellings

Imre Halasz with Noel J. Brady

Architecture can neither resolve the contradictions nor assuage the cultural injustice implicit in the concept of housing for elderly people. Even the best architecture cannot replace lost family and friends; it cannot erase the stigma of age; it cannot restore to old people their traditional roles as tellers of tales, transmitters of culture, and repositories of wisdom; it cannot make whole the fragmented conduct of modern life that banishes the aged into ghettos.

In her book *Nobody Ever Died of Old Age*, Sharon Curtin observed, "Segregation solves none of the problems of aging; it just improves the packaging. It is a solution without substance and underlines a poverty of imagination." No matter how seductive the green lawn and shaded arbor, the segregated place offers no relief from the tyranny of the managed facility.

So, although it would be flattering to believe otherwise, architecture cannot prevent the depletion of the vast treasury of memory and experience accumulated by society's elders. When they, the aged, are cut off and hidden away in isolation, younger generations are deprived of an important cultural testimony. Architecture cannot combat what contemporary society and its institutions defend: hierarchies of segregation.

Given these powerful limitations, what does architecture actually offer? Architecture is not, after all, entirely helpless. Thoughtful architecture can improve the quality of places. It can provide insights toward a better future if architectural principles of humanism are kept alive.

This discussion rests on the premise that architecture for the elderly should not differ substantially from any built environment for communal dwelling. The qualities of shared residence must not be determined along group lines whether identified by sex, race, religion, or age. Rather, communal residence must meet universal human needs: clarity of space, light, direction, scale, and proportion transcend any artificial boundaries of social typology. Since building codes now dictate the removal of so-called "architectural barriers," there remains no excuse to set different standards for different groups of people.

Architects can therefore concentrate on

providing good architecture grounded in the essentials of communal living. The basic patterns that relate chair to room, to building, to street, to city arise from man's innate impulses and needs, rather than theory. Therefore, it should not be surprising that a successful communal building relies upon the same patterns as those of a successful village, town, or city.

Attention must be paid to the individual as well as the group—in fact to a whole range of group sizes—and to the community itself. We must accommodate the existential forms of behavior that occur in ordinary communities: there must be places for privacy, public participation, spontaneous meetings, small gatherings, large groups, and opportunities for connections to the larger external world. People conduct their singular and social activities in places of sympathetic scale. An integrated series of spatial sizes therefore helps to organize the whole into what Paul Valery called a "wonderfully fitting relationship." The poetic aim is not an empty gesture; rather it sets the complete frame of human existence as the only real reference.

The city designed to speed large volumes of traffic fails its residents by denying them the finer-grain activities of human life. The communal dwelling built for the convenience of managers and custodians fails its residents by efficiency. Yet this "efficiency" is largely illusory. Given responsibility, residents—children, students, or elderly—will take what they can handle and relieve management of many headaches. Human dignity must lie at the heart of an architecture for communal living.

The following diagrams illustrate how durable architectural principles guide the creative process. The objective is not to imply the completeness or a list of easy-to-follow rules, but to call attention to the treasury of collective experiences of form making that help order a coherent whole and aid the effective interpretation of a specific context. The precise "fit" between use and behavior, frequently occupying center stage of project evaluation, is too simplistic. During their lifetime these spaces will have to accommodate different people and a variety of unforeseeable activities. Unpredictable needs occur at different times and places in the built environment.

Architecture would serve the occupants better by adhering to the best and most appropriate use of the timeless attributes of architectural form rather than arcane theoretical models that hope to project a fixed pattern of behavior.

Baker House, M.I.T.'s dormitory in Cambridge, Massachusetts, designed by the Finnish architect Alvar Aalto in 1948, is an excellent example of good communal architecture. Although it was designed as a home for young students, Baker House was conceived as an archetypal place for community living. The selection of an undergraduate dormitory for a discussion on housing for the elderly may provoke expressions of disbelief. But Baker House is a seminal illustration not only for a highly successful place for generations of students— a volatile and ever-changing community—but also of principles of design that embrace the need of the individual and the community, which is the predominant theme of collective dwelling. The following paradigms focus on a few generic aspects of architecture that had a major design role in achieving the resolution in Baker House. ∎

Figure 1. Constructing an Environment. The building volume, conceived as an elastic membrane, recedes as if molded and pressed by the two permanent open spaces: the Charles River basin and the M.I.T. athletic fields. The resulting exchanges form gentle concave edges to embrace extensions of the larger landscape. Two of these spaces (1 and 2) appear to have the appropriate size to house the most important collective uses, including lobby and dining hall, as their volume seems to penetrate the main building form.

Figure 2. Correspondence of Community. The seemingly isolated site is encouraged to become an element of a larger hierarchy by bridging the entrance and related public functions between the Charles River and the domed entrance of the Institute. This direction, the confluence of major uses along the way, was a fundamental design decision which enables all emerging elements of the design to become part of a larger whole.

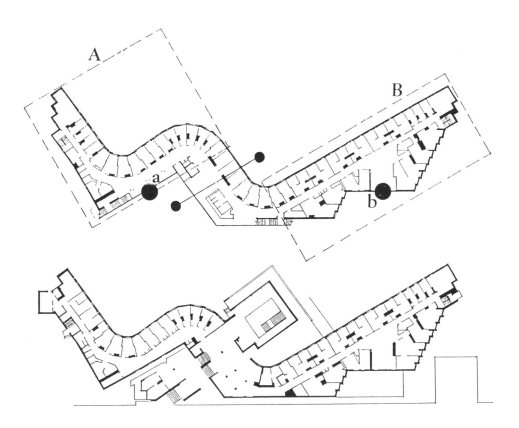

Figure 3. Branching Diagram. Decisions based on the unique aspects of the site as demonstrated above facilitate a clear diagram of two houses (A and B) with their own social areas (a and b) linked to the main community spine (1 and 2).

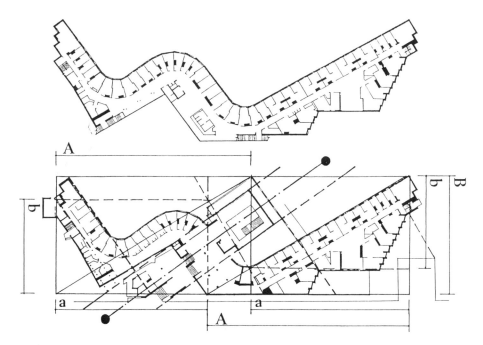

Figure 4. Geometry as an Ordering Device. "Regulating" lines based on the diagonals of rectangle ab and overlapping rectangle AB help organize the place within the orthogonal boundaries of the site in consonance with conceptual constraints of the larger decisions (Fig. 1, 2, and 3), making the built form unique and site specific. It not only "fits" the site but is almost made by it. The building would lose all its essential qualities anywhere else.

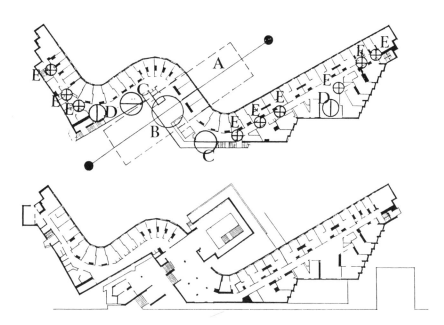

Figure 5. The Hierarchy of Social Spaces. 5a: The fine grain and hierarchical structure offer a range of river views and special configurations for the "units," and concentrate shared zones on the opposite side of the buildings. From A and B the vertical and horizontal shared-space entrance zones, C, open on each floor to the neighborhoods provided with their own social zones, D. Informal nooks, E, are found in the short stretches of double-loaded configuration, associated mostly with entrances to rooms. 5b: The vertical organization in which the two reference levels (1 and 2) integrate the ground and building with the two "houses." The diagonals (3) are spatial replicas of the diagonals found in the plan. They tie the entrance zones (C) to each other without forcing circulation through main shared spaces and thereby masterfully completing the range of social areas from A to E.

This fine example of what could be considered good architecture shows how the essential characteristics of community can be anchored in physical form. Baker House remains the most popular dormitory on the M.I.T. campus because of its ability to provide for the well-being of the individual in a variety of settings within and beyond the building.

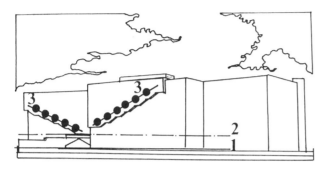

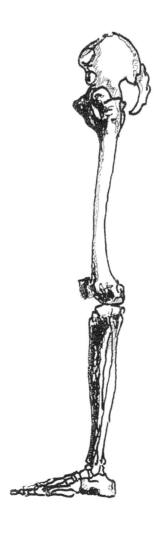

Figure 6. Pages from Paul Klee's "Pedagogical Sketchbook." It will help to consider now how the formal character of shared spaces in Baker House, regardless of scale, will perform their role in the structure of the whole spatial organization. The human skeleton, as a tectonic metaphor, intrigued Paul Klee. In his "Pedagogical Sketchbook," he examines "The natural organism of movement as kinetic will" as a basis for understanding additive growth. Through a similar metaphor we can consider the social spaces not as mere rooms but as key elements in a larger organism.

While the skeleton's marvelous architecture seems endlessly complex and articulated, each bone can be diagrammed identically. The elongated portion (link) of the bone is linear and serves within certain proportional limits as a path that transmits forces from joint to joint. The role of the elongated bone is limited and passive in determining movement. The joints, on the other hand, are responsible for continuity between the elements of structure. Their configuration enables certain kinds of movement from the simplest to the most complex. As places of connection they could be at rest or transient, regulating movement according to their shape and specific functions in harmony with the purpose of the whole. The links (streets, bridges, edges, or corridors in architectural morphology) do not invite choice and are purposefully singular and one-directional. Joints have their architectural equivalents in plazas, lobbies, places for social interaction of different kinds and sizes. They are nondirectional. They invite stopping and orientation, allowing for continued involvement. Since links never connect directly to links, joints are the sole agents for additive growth of an entire system.

Without attempting to over-stress the helpfulness of the metaphor, we could view the social/communal spaces and their hierarchy as formal and functional equivalents of joints and review the five generic categories found in the human skeleton as a taxonomy of their architectural counterparts. This will enable us to ascertain essential features of architectural morphology which can be seen at the heart of good architecture.

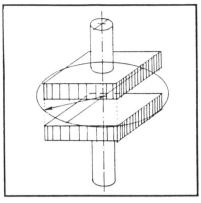

Notation A

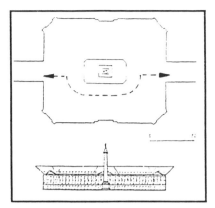

Place Vendome, Paris

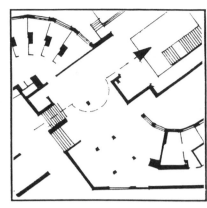

Baker House

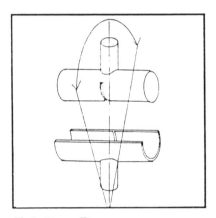

Notation B

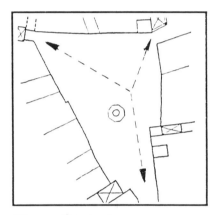

Piazza Cavour,
San Gimignano

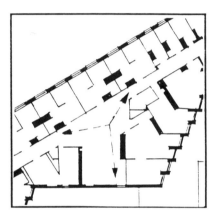

Baker House

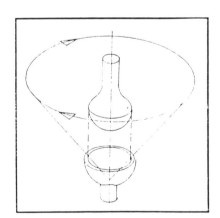

Notation C

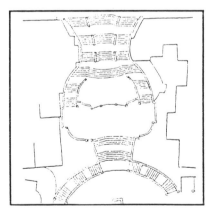

Piazza Di Spagna,
Rome

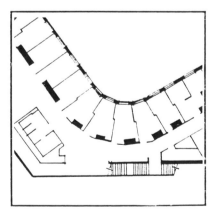

Baker House

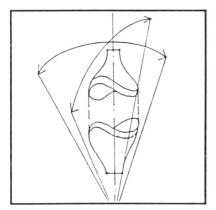

Notation D

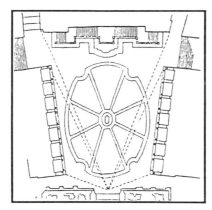

Campidoglio,
Rome

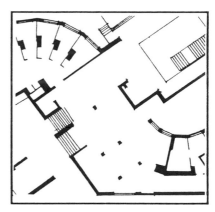

Baker House

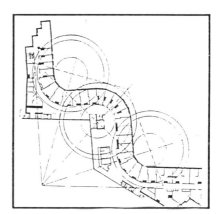

Notation E

S. Filippo Neri,
Guarino Guarini

Baker House

Figure 7. Planar notations of design situations, with architectural examples. Diagram A: The simplest form of movement—entering a room on an axis from a link and having to walk around an element located in the room to continue along the same direction.

Diagram B: A planar direction change is a more complex form of movement, which enables a simple planar direction change such as turning a corner along a path.

Diagram C: A spatial multidirectional rotation with one fixed stem is a more complex form of diagram B, in which the three-dimensional element permits one segment of the joint to rise or fall when its path must turn up or down.

Diagram D: Planar notation combined with multidirectional rotation—a composite of diagrams A and C—invites both three-dimensional upward movement as well as planar rotation.

Diagram E: This three-dimensional double rotation permits all movements, and its sophisticated form reflects sophisticated spatial and structural behavior.

These elements form places, ranging from the small to the large. Obviously this didactic analogue for the compositional attributes of communal spaces does not even begin to describe the rich, sensuous qualities they will incorporate in their developed design. Architecture depends on the active participation brought about by associations with the many polysensory aspects of our experiences.

Architecture cannot guarantee responsibility but good architecture can, with real intent, provide for some physical pattern of existence to guard against isolation and keep our elders at the very heart of our experience. Unlike science, architecture has no rules or inflexible axioms. Its principles, however, are sustained throughout the ages by reaching out for what C. G. Jung called the "typical modes of apprehension," the search and reinterpretation of archetypes.

Part IV

Architectural Design

Starting with interior design—the shaping of lighted spaces and spatial sequences—Part IV discusses the organization of private and public spaces and circulation through spatial sequences. How should the site plan for a healthcare community be arranged?

30/Spatial Composition as the Origin for Hospitable Design

Albert Bush-Brown

Where a healthcare facility prospers, while others languish, look into decisions reflected in its architectural composition. Right design helps good management succeed. If, instead, you find mazes, contorted rooms, and badly located services, you are likely also to find frustrated staff and managers. A lobby that leads nowhere, a garbage compactor beneath an intensive care unit, or a dining room entrance encumbered by parked wheelchairs can interfere as badly as slow elevators and jammed waiting rooms.

If you find unrelieved confinement—small, identical cubicles lined up on two sides of a central corridor, long walls, closed doors, flat ceilings, small windows, congested elevators, and constricted stairwells—and those confinements repeated for as many stories as steel-cage construction and zoning allow, the result is not likely to be welcoming, inspiring, satisfying or, in short, serviceable. Such niggardly architectural composition betrays wrong premises and bad decisions. A lady in a high-rise continuing care retirement community (CCRC) in Stamford, Connecticut, said to me that people do not want to be "stuck in little boxes" and "programmed."

Hospitable, humane design begins with the fundamental architectural element: space. First, last, and foremost, architecture is a spatial experience. Defining space, shaping it, enclosing it, and lighting it is the fundamental architectural service. The boxing of boxes, as in many hospitals and nursing homes, may be building or engineering, but it is not architecture. Architectural space has character, variety, and spirit. Spaces billow, undulate, constrict, expand, and soar. Space is plastic. Think of it as fluid, like water. Channel it and space runs like a canal; twist it, turn it, and space meanders like a river. Let it flow, eddy,

and form pools. Like water, space can cascade over a grand stair or billow like a fountain.

Space serves two practical functions. One is dynamic: as path, space conducts traffic from one point to the next; the other is static: as node, space makes places for rest, meeting, and work. Together, path and node form spatial compositions. They have social and emotional results. They can separate and isolate; they can join and encourage meeting and membership. They can relieve confinement and stress.

SPATIAL COMPOSITION

In healthcare design, as in all architectural design, the choices of paths and nodes are influenced by four conditions: site design and its implications for plan and section; spatial geometry and its lighting; spatial sequences and hierarchies, which affect variety and unity; and spatial linkages, which determine privacies, movement, and congregation.

Those four conditions are crucial for composing effective, admirable sequences of path and node. Do not assume that they will be fully and competently explored and the right answers protected during the long course of planning, financing, design, and construction. Only an architect's talent and a client's vigilance will spare them from compromise and platitude. One architect who insists on serious, uninhibited exploration of compositional choices fights continuously to preserve good spatial sequences: "Prolonged search for capital and twelve-year gestation periods for some CCRCs deflect developers' attention towards economies and banalities. Eliminating architecture only worsens their marketing and operational problems."

To gain effective siting, well-lighted spaces,

Harbour's Edge Life Care Community, Delray Beach, Florida. (Architect: Shepherd Legan Aldrian/Interior Designer: Donald J. Stanzione Associates/Photo: Courtesy of Life Care Services Corp.)

and enjoyable spatial sequences and transitions, clients must recognize that gaining wonderful space and spatial sequences is not mastered by all designers. Those whose expertise lies only in hospital equipment or decorating and furnishing or economical efficiencies are least capable. Do not be seduced by the clinical imperative. Do not be persuaded by architectural practitioners who insist that getting through zoning, building, and environmental regulatory agencies is their expertise. We can hire them, but they have no magic. Above all, recognize that spatial composition is different from style. Avoid being beguiled by Georgian cornices, pediments, and clapboards that decorate ill-proportioned geometry. Fine spaces can occur in all architectural styles. But, while it may establish a structural or decorative language, style alone—whether Georgian, Romanesque, Classical, Gothic,

Victorian or Modern—will not in itself deliver fine space. For spatial composition rests first on geometry and organization of volumes. Thereafter, it rests on balances, proportions, scales, inflections, and rhythms.

CHOICE IN SPATIAL COMPOSITION

Choices in spatial composition are first invoked by the site. On a given acreage, we must arrange a program of healthcare activities and establish points of arrival and departure. How will a flat or hilly site best accommodate medical care, work, rest, dining, and recreation? Shall they be dispersed: distributed in one- and two-story buildings? Or unified: centralized in high buildings? What areas shall be public, communal, or scenic, and which private? Will a linear plan make the best beginning, or a radial plan, or a campus plan that scatters activities in clusters? What shall be done with the automobile? And which site plan will best accept later additions and expansion? Functional performance has much to say about such choices.

An early decision must be made about operative levels. Should we assume that ground level shall be assigned to principal circulation and major traffic generators such as dining rooms and ambulatory patients' clinics? Or shall the base or zero level be higher or lower? Some flat sites suggest that dining rooms and major arteries, especially Main Street may be best located on a high floor, perhaps the top floor, for distant views, or midway in a tier of patients' floors, to reduce vertical circulation. Entered at ground level, a hillside site may permit Main Street to emerge midtier in multiple storeys, where large spaces can overlook the lower slope and valley. Located there, can the high spaces be ramped to connect with the

lower ceilinged patients' floors? Within such high spaces, can mezzanines and galleries be ramped into other floors, thereby enabling the large spaces to be ramped into three or more patients' floors?

A site may suggest further choices in plan and section: below-grade services; bridges over roadways to free pedestrians from vehicular traffic; and atriums, terraces, courts, and gardens at various levels, to create gathering places and relieve the confinement of patients' rooms or apartments. While heavily affected by anticipated practical performance, such choices in spatial composition are imbued with social, aesthetic, and cultural implications, all engendered by space.

Architectural space is generated by two or more planes that suggest or enclose a volume. The simple generators are regular volumes, such as cubes, spheres, hemispheres, triangular prisms, pyramids, parallelepipeds, cylin-

Carolina Village, Hendersonville, North Carolina. (Architect: Engelbrecht & Griffin Architects/Photo: Farshid Assassi)

Arnold Palmer Hospital, Orlando, Florida. (Architect: Hansen Lind Meyer, Inc./Photo: Phil Eschbach)

Whitney Center, Hamden, Connecticut. (Architect: Engelbrecht & Griffin Architects/Photo: Farshid Assassi)

ders, and half-cylinders, which are barrel vaults. A simple generator may stand alone, as an independent cube or triangular prism. More often, it is combined, as in domestic form, a triangular prism over a parallelepiped. Combined geometries are complex: The Byzantines enjoyed a cube covered by a hemispherical dome, and their joining requires pendentives, which are spherical triangles.

The generative geometry establishes spatial directions along major axes. Whether horizontal, as in most paths, oblique, as in stairways, or vertical, as in high nodes, one axis should dominate. Where no axis dominates, neutral spaces are transitional; they are useful as connective links to major spaces. Seeking a sense of distinct place, ready orientation, spatial flow, and clear organization, we emphasize spatial axes. Illustrating that point are spatial compositions where the spatial theme is a half-cylinder.

Between the space and its enclosure, the geometric congruency must be as clear and faithful as construction will allow. All indentations, extrusions, and inflections in plan should be reflected in explicit volumes in section. Floors, walls, roof, and ceiling should shape a volume that reflects the plan. A cylinder climaxed by a flat roof is disappointing. A rectangular plan suggests a triangular prism or vault; but a square enjoys a more vertical form, such as a hip roof or dome. Thus, each space and sequence of spaces will be declared in a corresponding sequence of masses. A high space, for example, with subordinate spaces around it, will be visible in elevations, and its internal spatial organization will be revealed from afar and from the building's entrance inward. Some of the most interesting spatial compositions rely on having a large "master space" entered through tiers of smaller spaces.

Gulf Coast Medical Office Building, Baytown, Texas. (Architect: Earl Swensson Associates, Inc./Photo: Bill LaFevor)

Wexner Institute for Pediatric Research, Children's Hospital, Columbus, Ohio. (Architect: NBBJRosenfield, Columbus, Ohio Studio/Photo: Michael Houghton, STUDIOHIO)

THE LIGHTED SPACE

Light is critical to spatial definition. Whether natural or artificial, light should intensify and celebrate spatial shape, direction, sequence, and flow. Some vertical spaces relish light at roofline climaxes. Horizontal spaces enjoy lateral and terminal light. Like all spaces, they change dramatically when light is admitted to only one wall or is shifted from high to low, from roof to floor, or from lateral to terminal. You may want one of those variants. Light at the floor line or light at the high juncture of wall and ceiling can enliven space as no common pattern of lateral windows can. Particularly important is to light the intersections of the wall, floor, and roof planes. Merely to settle for a set of boxes regularly riddled by patches of lateral light is to invite monotony. Select light: light entering obliquely, light from a transverse source, light bouncing from different origins at different times of day—all can

Casa del Mar, Boca Raton, Florida. (Architect: Mouriz, Salazar & Associates, Inc./Interior Designer: Design 1 Interiors/Photo: Joel Grimes)

North Hill, Needham, Massachusetts. (Architect: Engelbrecht & Griffin Architects/Photo: Farshid Assassi)

give a room multiple dimensions and moods.

To feel the spring of space, its lift, its invitation to enter, to pause and admire, is the desired goal. Entering a high space through a low anterior is dramatic; walking a narrow space to a wide intersection offers anticipation of chance encounter and meeting.

Successful spatial composition joins well-defined, well-lighted whole volumes. These spaces can be connected, subdivided, or placed in sequence. When connecting two or more spaces, each should be a total volume, and one should be prominent, indeed dominant in size and scale. The lesser, connected spaces are then clearly recognizable extensions. Forcing differences between spaces, contrasting long and wide, high and low, light and dark, horizontal and vertical, can achieve lively spatial sequences in an arcade or series of rooms. That is at least part of our interest in spatial transparencies and reciprocities. We look through a screen window upon a garden or terrace, or see a distant part of our own building, and the spatial sequence relates part to whole, clarifies organization, and enhances our sense of location and membership.

SPACE IN HEALTHCARE ARCHITECTURE

Those theoretical observations have vital consequences for healthcare architecture. Spatial composition makes privacies and congregations possible. A sequence and hierarchy of spaces at Kendal at Longwood in Kennett Square, Pennsylvania, permits the assignment of its members to apartments, which are arranged around landscaped courts. Then a spacious spine, a concourse, connects a series of high spaces: the communal library, large meeting rooms, a dining room with an alcove, an auditorium, and a large, high living room with a connecting sitting room behind the massive fireplace. All spaces flow into the concourse, and all are subordinated to the principal gathering place. The areas are volumes, not rooms. Generated by planes and roof forms, they have minimal walls and doors. Space flows. The spatial invitations to enter are easy and compelling, yet the sense of place is strong. Spatial composition furthers congregation, membership, and belonging.

Enjoyable, useful environment originates in

Kendal at Longwood, Kennett Square, Pennsylvania. (Architect: Ewing Cole Cherry Parsky Architects/Photo: Peter Olson)

an orderly, continuous, and rhythmical revelation of spaces that have been organized for use and revealed by light and shade. Where we find successful spatial composition in healthcare architecture today, we also find a vibrant, hospitable environment. No superficial decoration will achieve that delight, nor will it disguise or retrieve errors in spatial composition. The sun does not shine into miserable rooms nor cast welcome shade on poorly oriented terraces and balconies. Moonlight does not dance on dull walls or flat roofs. Nor does rain sing when conducted from eave to cistern in closed pipes that muffle the magical sights and sounds descending water can display. How a building touches the ground, meets the skyline, and rounds a corner can be wondrous acts, encounters of greeting and inflection.

Generous spaces in our healthcare architecture can offer cheer and graciousness. As foundations for hospitable design, spatial sequences and hierarchies give even more: they make privacies possible, and they nurture community. ■

31/Walkways, Corridors, Bridges, and Ramps

Thomas R. Hauck

From my earliest days as an architectural student, I was instilled with the premise that the "efficient" building plan linked all its component rooms by a minimum of circulation space. The higher the ratio of the net area of component rooms to the gross area of plan, the better; circulation space was an undesirable necessity; keep it to less than 20 percent of gross area.

I became increasingly skeptical of that premise. Circulation spaces—the corridors, stairs, ramps, and bridges—are more than traffic lanes, they are also meeting places.

Unfortunately, the building and health codes that establish minimum corridor widths and heights to protect public safety have been misapplied. Driven by budgets, those minimums often became design goals. The result is circulation in tunnels, rather than through parkways, plazas, avenues, and squares. Open areas are as vital to the life of a healthcare facility as to the city.

Circulation is always in contest with privacy. Were it not necessary to protect the occupants in a series of rooms from intrusive traffic, easy circulation could occur merely by opening the dividing walls and letting people flow through them or along one side of them. Preserving privacy while gaining circulation leads to corridors and doors. Economies and efficiencies lead to double-loaded corridors. Then privacies dominate, and the public space requires extraordinary attention if it is not to seem impersonal, inhumane, even antisocial.

Much skillful design has been given to the corridor: variations in shape, size, corners, heights, and views can create better circulation space. Break long corridors into short segments and offset the segments at a window and alcove; floor coverings can be patterned; wall lighting and pilasters make rhythmical divisions. Ceilings become more interesting with panels of patterns and textures, articulated by moldings.

Similar imagination should be applied to the bridge. A bridge over an atrium or between buildings is not merely a path arching us over a road where cars and trucks move. Like all paths, it can be a marvelous experience. It should begin and lead to a significant place, not merely to another corridor. Its origin and destination should be worth the trip, and the passage itself should also be rewarding.

Recall the Ponte Vecchio, at Florence; its central apex is a platform offering views of the River Arno, and its street is lined with open

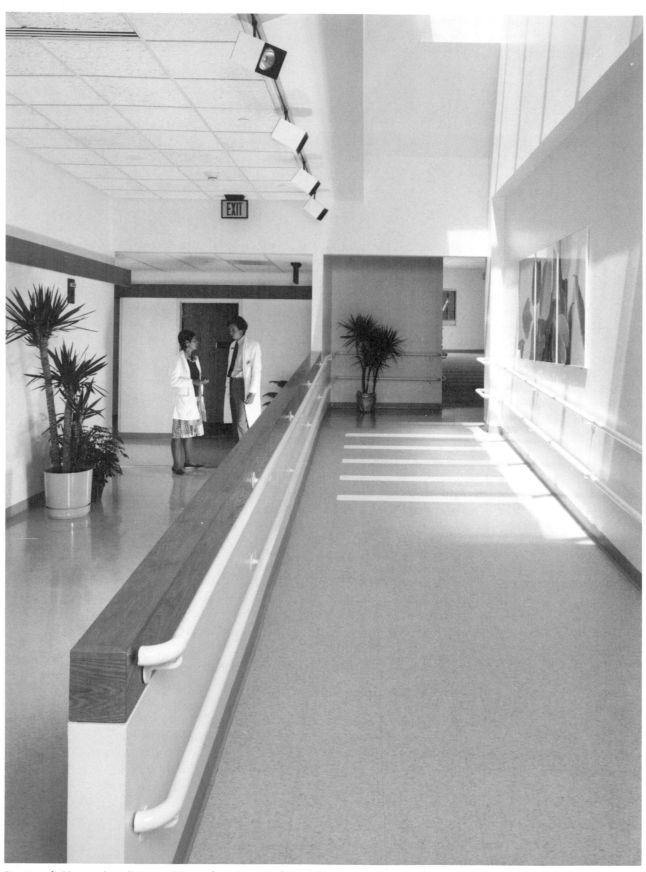

St. Anne's Hospital, Fall River, Massachusetts. (Architect: Hoskins, Scott, Taylor & Partners Inc./Photo: Wayne Soverns, Jr.)

stands and shops. A bridge in a healthcare facility can start at a library with music, end at a dining area and, in between, offer entry into a greenhouse and snack bar or tea room on the bridge itself. The bridge at Linus Oakes in Roseburg, Oregon, suggests such an experience. At the North Hill continuing care retirement community (CCRC) in Wellesley Hills, Massachusetts, a wide bridge containing kitchens stretches from residents' dining room to the skilled-nursing unit. Views outward from such bridges, to gardens or a skyline, will be better appreciated if the bridge is constructed to allow pedestrians to stop at benches and the wheelchaired to see over any bridge structure, sill, or wall. Groups of people should be able to gather in a sitting area in the sun or to watch activity, even if no more than traffic at night. Such alcoves might be places for mobile vendor's carts, especially with changing holiday themes.

Ramps also invite greater architectural attention. The ramp is a wonderful device; it has marvelous architectural potential, as Le Corbusier often demonstrated. Yet, most ramps are afterthoughts, merely expedient answers to the legal requirement to have barrier-free handicapped access. To meet that requirement at the library of Long Island University's C.W. Post College campus, I designed a ramp that rises to an outdoor stage before it ascends to the library. There, students play guitars, study, and take the sun. The ramp I designed to connect the Bush-Brown Concert Theater (now Tilles Center) to its parking lots, flows downward through a switchback to reveal multiple views of the sculpture court below. At St. Anne's Hospital in Fall River, Massachusetts, Hoskins, Taylor designed a ramp that is coordinated with skylight, railings, and art.

A concourse rather than a corridor links the freestanding concessions and boutiques at airports. They are often designed to be islands in a lake. Having the concourse act as an activity spine works magically in the J. E. Moss Elementary School in Nashville, Tennessee. The forecourts joining classrooms invite exhibits and informal groupings for instruction. A variation occurs in the Carleton-Willard CCRC in Bedford, Massachusetts. Its wide concourse offers a series of open sitting and game areas along the southern wall, which admits abun-

Quinco Community Mental Health Center, Columbus, Indiana. (Architect: James Stewart Polshek and Partners/ Photo: Courtesy of James Stewart Polshek and Partners)

Linus Oakes at Mercy Medical Center, Roseburg, Oregon. (Architect: Soderstrom Architects)

dant sunlight. The opposite wall is a long row of cheerfully colored entrances to a bank, shop, auditorium, dining room, and other activities. The dining rooms at Medford Leas, Medford, New Jersey, open from a corridor along four sides of a landscaped atrium. In the better corridors, as in the Quadrangle, at Haverford, Pennsylvania, lights, ceilings, floors, and walls are coordinated with indented entries, where occupants' personal treasures are exhibited. The result can be an effective expression of privacy within public circulation space.

No other building areas are as capable of handling spontaneous changes in use as are the circulation spaces. A long east-windowed corridor can be a promenade in the morning sun after breakfast; a quiet, bright alcove can draw a cluster of wheelchaired residents for lunch; an elevator lobby can become a vantage point, like the bow of a ship. The corner beside a bedroom door can be as dynamic as a stoop in the city or as cozy as a front porch in a village. The most obvious delight is a view. Dropping window sills for the wheelchair's lowered perspective will make a view more accessible. Lowering the paintings or sculpture will enhance their impact.

Occupants in an extended care facility require a reassuring familiarity with their environment, but not dreariness. Circulation spaces can be full of little delights and surprises, rewarding enough to entice occupants to seek them out. ∎

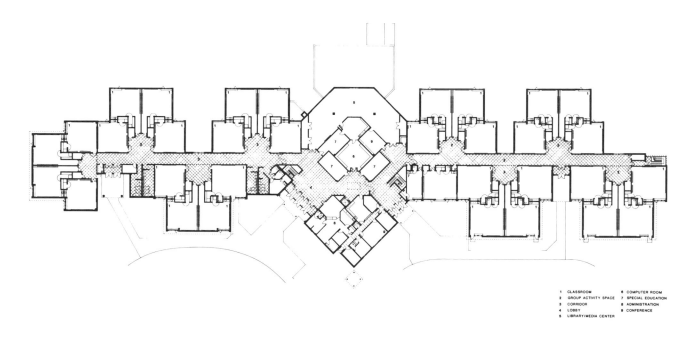

1	CLASSROOM	6	COMPUTER ROOM
2	GROUP ACTIVITY SPACE	7	SPECIAL EDUCATION
3	CORRIDOR	8	ADMINISTRATION
4	LOBBY	9	CONFERENCE
5	LIBRARY/MEDIA CENTER		

J. E. Moss Elementary School, Nashville, Tennessee. Upper-level plan. (Architect: Earl Swensson Associates, Inc.)

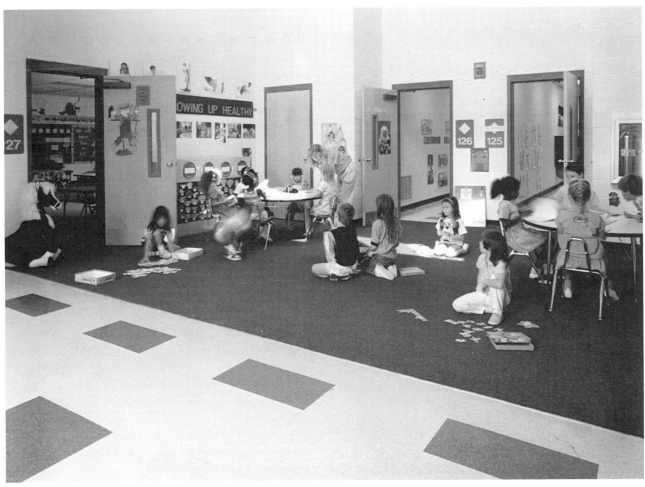

J. E. Moss Elementary School, Nashville, Tennessee. Classroom. (Architect: Earl Swensson Associates, Inc./Photo: Anthony Lathrop)

32 / Basic Design Decisions

Albert Bush-Brown

Introduced about 1725, the corridor or hallway rapidly became a standard connector, especially in wide buildings. As a spatial diagram, it has some virtues, but it is also a source of defective planning. Four errors in basic circulatory design mar many nursing homes and other healthcare centers.

Two of the most pernicious, inadequate corridors and elevators, directly affect circulation because they impede the movement of people, goods, and services. Mistakes in lateral and vertical circulation and interchanges reveal failures to anticipate internal transportation through time–density–motion studies. Moving wheelchairs, beds, and other large equipment crowds even large lobbies and slows elevator doors' operation. Throughout a 24-hour day, when will corridors be encumbered by patients, cleaners, equipment, medical staff, food, and laundry? When will elevators and their lobbies be packed? Will a larger size or more elevators help? Will stairs combined with dedicated or skip-stop elevators ease the loads and speed staff members' travel? Will some different arrangement sort out competing uses? Studies of density, cargos, and schedules will reveal the need to design large junctures where lateral directions meet and also where they intersect vertical directions. The interchange is a critical design problem.

A third error also affects circulation: major traffic generators are separated and assigned to the wrong floor levels. When dining rooms, living rooms, studios, and exercise rooms are placed on a single floor, the flow can work well. The medical and social advantages of their consolidation, or their dispersal, will be debated, but, whether compact or dispersed, public spaces distributed on several levels add operating expenses and tax circulation. A basement kitchen serving several higher levels of dining rooms, patients' rooms, and other food-distribution points increases circulatory problems. A study of the points for the origin and destination for food, garbage, and soiled dishes may indicate that better service would result from having kitchens and dining rooms together on a high floor. Similar origin and destination studies are wanted for laundry, furniture, and medical equipment.

The traffic generated by dining rooms, auditoriums, and mailrooms should raise questions about which is the best level for dense, frequent flows of people. In low buildings, public spaces on the ground floor work well, offer easy access to walkways, gardens, and roads, and do not burden vertical circulation. But the high-rise building and the multistory building on a sloped site suggest that Main Street might best be a high or middle floor.

The fourth error in circulation—beyond inadequate lateral and vertical circulation and misplaced traffic generators—is what I call "spatial enumeration." Each function is named, numbered, and assigned to a box: a partitioned room. The building then is a collection of boxes, each walled in on all six sides. The boxes are then punctured by doors and windows and peppered with carpets, chairs, lights, sprinklers, and grilles. Corridors connect the boxes. Such rooms and corridors are confining. Could they be flowing areas and liberating concourses—paths bordered by floor-to-ceiling windows displaying gardens or terraces opposite wide openings into living rooms, library, gallery or music room? Are all the corridors and closed doors necessary? Could any have greater height and lighting to become less confining?

Those four errors cause untold damage. They give many nursing homes a bad reputation. So prevalent and baleful are the errors that, reneging on our resolve to demonstrate only the good and beautiful that are possible, rather than the bad and ugly that are probable, we recite the faults in two examples.

A NEW NURSING HOME

I still cannot believe the basic design errors I saw in a new nursing home in Hawaii. You will not appreciate their lesson unless you know how I came upon that collection of fundamentally flawed decisions.

No sooner had I ended my presentation in a symposium in Honolulu than a vigorous man in his mid-thirties approached me, asking "How can I gain hospitable space and open a view at my new nursing home?"

My questions revealed that this enlightened and dedicated administrator was attempting to manage the delivery of expensive, first-class care in a building that fought against him and his staff. It is a private nursing home, and the staff, I was told, is excellent. I decided to visit the facility and did so the next day.

Opened six months before my visit, the nursing home is a three-story building on a sloped site. It rises from the site's lower edge, and the upper slope is reserved for parked cars and a driveway. Entering the middle story on grade, one passes offices to approach a nurses'

station, which stands at the juncture of two wings containing patients' rooms on long, dreary cinder block, double-loaded corridors. The third floor is virtually identical to the second floor. At the nurses' station, the floors are connected vertically by a stairwell and a pair of elevators, which descend to the lowest of the three stories. There, partly below ground level, are the dining room, kitchen, laundry, disposal, and maintenance areas, all abutted downhill by a service road.

The problems are readily predictable. Three times a day most of the 110 patients are wheeled to the nurses' station, congesting that area while they wait for the two elevators, which electrical failures irregularly cut out.

Once aboard, the patients descend one or two floors to the ground floor. There they wait again, squeezed into a small vestibule, next to the laundry, which blows damp heat, odors, and noise into the vestibule. Ultimately, the patients are wheeled to tables in a low-ceilinged room with one exterior view, the service road.

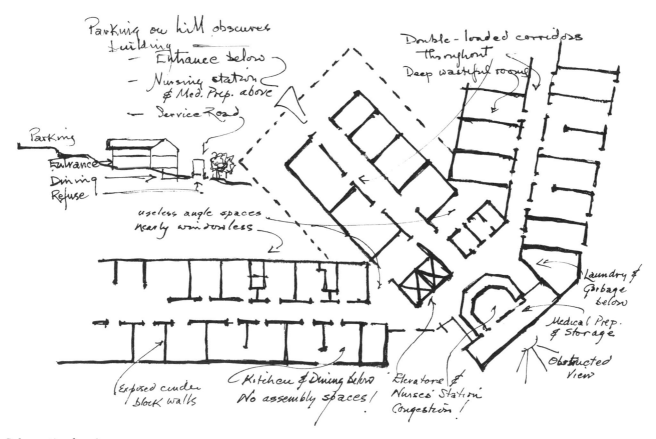

Schematic plan A.

One might suppose that this depressing scene had been conjured by a malevolent builder, but, in fact, I was assured, it was designed by an architect, and his plans were shown to me. "Who decided that it was easier, cheaper, better to move people rather than labeled trays of food?" I asked. "Who decided on long double-loaded corridors, nurses' stations at elevators, and blank walls where there should be windows, and other blank walls where there could be doors opening on terraces?" "Who decided to put the dining room in the basement?" "Who chose to reserve the best, high part of this site for parked automobiles?"

The manager and his excellent activities director shook their heads in dismay, "It was all built before we arrived." We then threaded our way past wheelchairs, kitchen entrance, and laundry, amid patients waiting for an elevator to return to their cell-like, cinder-blocked rooms, each on a cheerless corridor. No amount of good food, medical care, flowers, and festivity could relieve the sense of oppressive confinement, nor could the staff's morale long sustain such basically flawed design.

DESIGN THAT NEGATES GOALS

In March 1990 the newly arrived director for a nursing home under construction in Maryland unrolled its architectural plans. With opening scheduled for October 1990, following six years of land analysis, zoning discussions, and engineering and architectural planning, the sponsor, a national corporation that owns many nursing homes, pressed the director to move forward. Walls, floors, and roofs were up. The plans astonished the director: completed as designed, the building would nullify the best efforts of his staff to realize the corporation's objective—a nursing home, with Medicare/Medicaid patients, that would also appeal to the private patient.

What did the plans reveal? What, at this moment of advanced commitment in construction, could be changed?

Virtually nothing. It would be obsolete before it opened. Its faults would block realization of the goal.

Essentially L-shaped, the three-story building would have multiple entrances, and cars, buses, and trucks would circle the site. At the corner of the ell, the chief entrance intro-

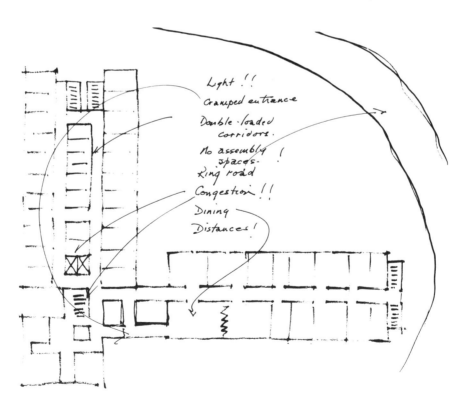

Schematic plan B.

duced a maze of cut-up rooms on each floor. Two elevators and a stairwell would not carry the impact of moving wheelchaired patients, food, medical equipment, staff, and visitors through any 24-hour period. Lateral circulation was similarly defective: double-loaded corridors ending in cramped waiting areas at the elevators. No one had envisioned those corridors when rooms were being cleaned and patients, by state regulation, were lined up in already encumbered corridors.

Sitting areas and dining rooms were no less mean. Boxing small boxes, the Medicare mentality prevented any sunlighted lobby or terrace, any vista to flowing space. There was to be no chance to burst the confinement. Though fitted with a large window, each patient's double room would offer a single closet, a single fixed arrangement of beds, and a ste-

rility that would deny personal expression.

Advice at this moment of construction? Glaze some interior walls to open vistas into dining rooms; sacrifice a patient's room here and there to make an internal garden, aquarium, library, or game and music room; add a windscreen and balcony facing south; improve the choice of furniture; expand the lobbies at elevators; provide some murals, tapestries, lighting, and colors to identify each wing; and retain a graphics designer to clarify circulation and identity of patients' rooms. Later, perhaps, by tying into the corridors, a new wing could be built to provide hospitable areas that would ease the staff's work and improve patients' experience.

Serious improvement, all possible, but still not enough to overcome the mean thinking that permitted flawed design. ∎

33 / Wayfinding Designs: Navigating with Ease

Janet R. Carpman

Designing a facility that enables unfamiliar users to find their way with ease is a complex undertaking. Too often signs are thought to be the cure-all for mazelike buildings, but orientation is more complex than the simplistic, product-oriented term, "signage," implies.

"Wayfinding" is a better term. It refers to what people see, think, and do to find their way. It involves five deceptively simple ideas: knowing where you are, knowing your destination, knowing and following the best routes, recognizing your destination upon arrival, and finding your way back.

Floor numbering.

* Excerpted and edited with permission from Carpman, J., Grant, M., and Simmons, D. *Designs that Care: Planning Health Facilities for Patients and Visitors*, published by American Hospital Publishing, Inc., copyright 1986.

Wayfinding is a *system*, coordinating *numerous* factors, not merely signs. Environmental design, operational policies or practices, and individual design making all play a part. Accurate, consistent, and carefully coordinated wayfinding systems can help people find their way: these include site and building layout, visual access, circulation systems (roads, paths, corridors, stairs, elevators, escalators), terminology, exterior and interior signs, directories, floor numbering, room numbering, "You Are Here" maps, emergency exit information, interior and exterior "landmarks" (such as sculpture, paintings, a fountain, or pavilion), hand-held maps, color coding, and environmental features.

Operational policies and practices should support the system, especially wayfinding staff training programs, spoken directions, previsit information, and wayfinding system maintenance. The keys to a successful wayfinding system are well-designed, mutually supportive elements that provide accurate and consistent information on an ongoing basis.

It is one thing to cope with large, intimidating, labyrinthine sites and facilities when we are in a normal frame of mind. But patients and visitors, especially elderly ones, experience stress simply by being in the healthcare setting. They may not be able to concentrate on spoken directions, they may not notice landmarks, and they may misread or disregard signs.

Having a wayfinding system is more than a nicety. Patients who have trouble finding their way may experience emotional stress from being lost and worrying about being late for their appointments. Weak or disabled patients may suffer fatigue from walking the wrong way and getting lost.

Wayfinding is also a concern for staff. Serious medical and legal consequences can result from the ambulance driver's not finding the emergency room, a code blue team slowed by taking the wrong turn, or critical lab specimens delayed by a confused messenger.

Wayfinding must be considered from the

Cedars Medical Center, Miami, Florida. (Photo: Bob Siegel, courtesy of Natalie Schanker, Cedars Medical Center)

outset of a building project and *throughout* the design process. Decisions at every stage of the planning process have a profound impact on how easy it will be to navigate the resulting building. Since the wayfinding system must be able to be changed often and quickly, each wayfinding element requires periodic updating, checking for wear and tear, and assessment of its accuracy and consistency with other components. ■

34 / Individualized Cluster

David M. Dunkelman

While the corridor is a critical but over-looked source of hospitable welcome, care, and entertainment, its traditional form is obsolete and counterproductive to hospitality.

Merely a highway, the traditional corridor enables residents to walk or wheel to centralized destinations. Yet, few chronically ill residents can walk independently; most are wheelchair-bound, and their sensory and physical decrements make distant travel a major barrier.

Nor can patients' transport rely on volunteers or aides. Volunteers' decreasing availability and aides' involvement with prophylactic and debilitative interventions for the chronically ill leave them no time to transport patients or leave the unit.

Even were help sufficient, most physical plants do not have the elevators needed to transport an assemblage of 30 to 40 wheelchairs on a timely basis. Assembled, the extremely ill patients have sensory and attentional losses that make large gatherings inappropriate.

Those facts converted the corridor, really a hallway-highway, to a different purpose. Residents often live in lineups along it, lined up "to go," but in fact going nowhere. Instead, they live in long isolating queues where the corridor's narrow width and concerns over fire hazards force them to sit front-to-back or side-to-side, locked in isolation by lost peripheral vision, failed hearing, and inflexible necks. Conversation with neighbors is impossible. Lacking sufficient windows and adequate air transfer, most highway-hallways are wretched, a lineup of isolated, lonely, old people, disoriented by absence of stimulation, light, and relief from disagreeable odors.

The resulting "deindividualizing" increases restlessness and "acting out," and repels any visitor. Getting off the elevator to walk that highway of misery discourages visits. Such an invasion of privacy makes both parties, visitor and resident, feel scrutinized. The result is fewer visits, increasing isolation, and more guilt-laden exchanges between the resident, family member, and staff.

The aide also toils in the highway to care for the stranded, deindividualized residents. Daily routines are oriented around batch processing. Residents arranged in an assembly line suggest batch treatment. Residents line up in queues waiting for 10:00 A.M. toileting, 11:15 A.M. nutrition, and 12:00 P.M. lunch. Gang or batch processing denies individualized attention; residents cannot eat, snack, read, toilet, or socialize within their own personal rhythms.

The growing recognition that the traditional corridor is not appropriate for the new nursing home clientele has led to a new concept. Because residents are, in fact, going nowhere, the corridor is eliminated. In its place, there is a cluster, consisting of a den/living room or activities space, surrounded by residents' rooms. This cluster accepts and encourages the individualized tasks required for residents in that space. An atmosphere of individualization replaces group processing. By enabling wheelchairs to be grouped near private bedrooms, the cluster allows residents to arrange seating configurations that foster socialization. Windows, ventilation, and noise-reduction devices eliminate distracting, disorienting stimuli, and the cluster's scale encourages interchange.

Placing the aide within the cluster individually tailors each resident's day. The living room's proximity to each resident's bed and bathroom enables one resident to toilet while another eats, and still another converses in a social group. Proximity allows the aide to respond promptly to individual needs. Such response is critical, for the debilitated resident's activity time no longer clocks in at regular times that can be anticipated; rather, activity

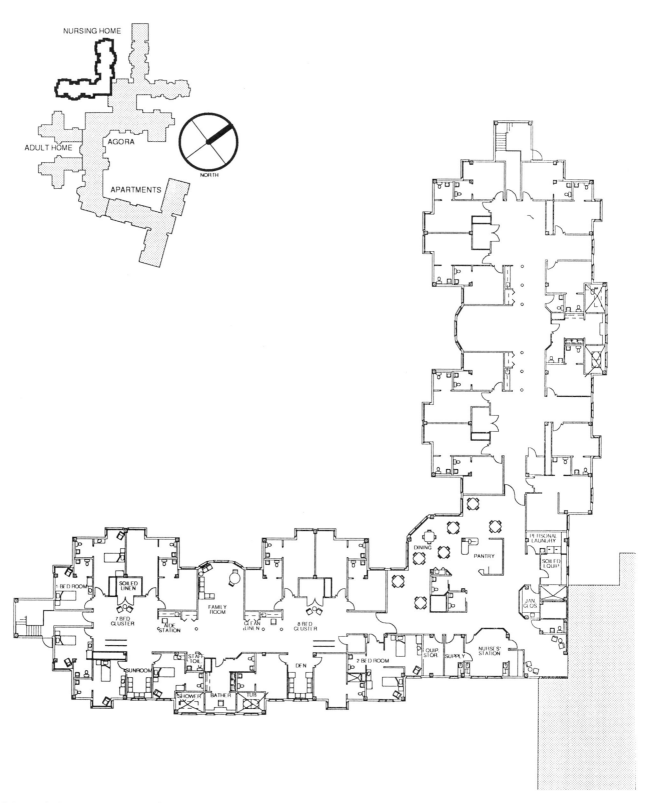

Menorah Campus, Rosa Coplon Jewish Home, Amherst, New York. (Architect: NBBJRosenfield, New York Studio/ Design: Mary Bissett, with consultant Lorraine G. Hiatt)

time occurs in short bursts that must be recognized and snatched quickly and informally.

The transformation from a centralized, corridor-based facility to a decentralized, living-room-based facility has profound consequences. To keep aides consistently within the cluster, functions traditionally centralized must now be decentralized. For the aides' convenience, clean and dirty linen, laundry, and food must be placed within the cluster. Rather than transporting residents to the nursing station, dining room, and clinic, therapists, social workers, physicians, and medications must now travel to the cluster. That calls for reforming those systems with new technologies and new roles for various paraprofessionals.

All spaces must be designed to be hospitable, quiet, and residential. The cluster gives the resident his or her own bedroom, bathroom, and living room. Sense of the larger institution is suppressed. The resident's life is normalized and is much more consistent with his or her preinstitutionalized years. People, services, and stimulation come to residents and, to whatever degree possible, they are able to shape the timing and sequence of their day.

The aide's role shifts from that of an assembly-line mechanic, turning a bolt on each car, to a craftsperson who puts whole cars together. The aide sees the whole resident and participates in therapies and activities. By modeling paraprofessionals' behavior and interventions, the aide learns skills that are not easily transferred in the classroom. Individualization encourages more frequent and more appropriate family visits and normalizes the lives of those who live and work in the nursing home. ■

35 / The Cluster Nursing Unit

Herbert Bienstock with Janet Hays

The design of the cluster nursing unit, a nursing unit without corridors and without conventional nursing stations, was pioneered by NBBJRosenfield. Nurse work areas are decentralized, with each nurse near the patient rooms and supplies and medications. The cluster nursing units in the Link Pavilion at Hackensack Medical Center in Hackensack, New Jersey, were designed in intensive work sessions with nurses and representatives of the various services supporting inpatient care.

Cluster nursing units have received widespread attention for the improvement they foster in patient care and in nurses' performance. Because the nurses and patients can see each other easily and nurses can respond swiftly to a patient's needs, both are reassured. In the cluster nursing units at Hackensack, length of patient stay has come down (compared to a matched group in traditional units in the same hospital), sleeping medication is used less frequently, and patients fall from their beds less frequently.

The nurses report that their relationship with the physicians has become smoother and more congenial, probably because attending physicians entering the unit on rounds see the nurses immediately and can get the help they need without frustrating delays. Resident physicians find the layout encourages them to stop at the nurses' work station and talk over patient problems with the nurses. This easy interchange raises the quality of care and the understanding, professional capabilities, and mutual respect of all parties. Physicians now invite nurses to their conferences and nurses participate.

Since 1982, when Link Pavilion opened,

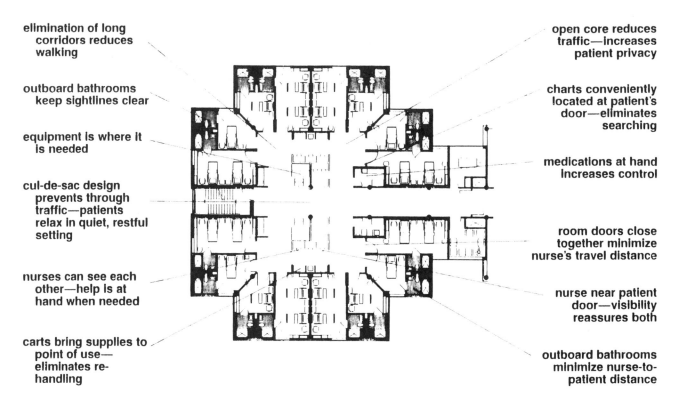

elimination of long corridors reduces walking

outboard bathrooms keep sightlines clear

equipment is where it is needed

cul-de-sac design prevents through traffic—patients relax in quiet, restful setting

nurses can see each other—help is at hand when needed

carts bring supplies to point of use—eliminates re-handling

open core reduces traffic—increases patient privacy

charts conveniently located at patient's door—eliminates searching

medications at hand increases control

room doors close together minimize nurse's travel distance

nurse near patient door—visibility reassures both

outboard bathrooms minimize nurse-to-patient distance

Hackensack Medical Center, Hackensack, New Jersey. Twenty-four-bed cluster. (NBBJRosenfield, New York Studio/ Joint Venture: The Gruzen Partnership)

Hackensack Medical Center has enjoyed an improved market position, with high occupancy. The hospital is fully staffed and less troubled by nurse shortages, nurse "burn-out," and nurse turnover than are other hospitals in the region. Because it is fully staffed, transfers are made for medical reasons only. ∎

36/Room Configuration, Privacy, and Personalization

Dianne Davis

To offer companionship with privacy, including some sense of control over personal time, space, and belongings, is easier in a continuing care retirement community (CCRC) or medhotel than in a hospital or nursing home. In the latter, the single-room isolates and conventional double rooms offer little privacy. Neither affords companionship or much opportunity for personalization.

For that reason, there is growing interest in the L-shaped bedroom for two beds and other configurations that combine two or more sleeping alcoves with an area furnished for sitting and dining. The L-shaped room, the T-shaped room, and other extruded shapes permit sequestered bed locations, proximity to toilets and baths, and varied views through windows. They produce interesting spaces where territories are defined, but also blended, and the exterior walls can be shaped as bays or

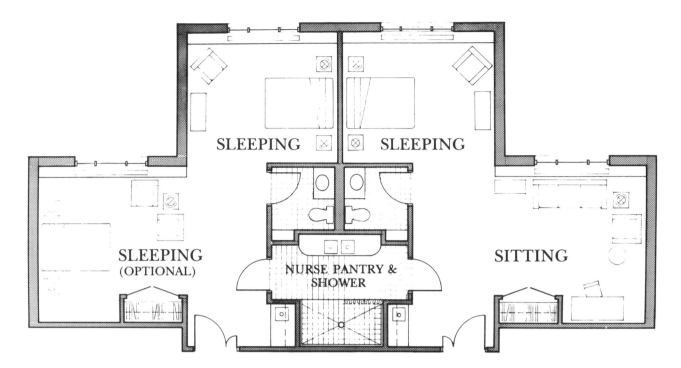

SLEEPING

SLEEPING

SLEEPING
(OPTIONAL)

NURSE PANTRY &
SHOWER

SITTING

Orchard Cove Continuing Care Retirement Community, Canton Massachusetts. (Sponsors: Hebrew Rehabilitation Center for Aged, Roslindale, MA, and Terence G. Lewis, Sr., Senior Vice President, New Ventures/Architect: Huygens DiMella Shaffer and Associates, Inc., in association with Korsunsky Krank Erickson and Associates Architects, Inc./Consultants: Martin H. Cohen, FAIA, Armonk, NY, and Lorraine G. Hiatt, PhD, Innovage, Inc., NY.)

sawtooth windows to further enliven the space, views and light.

Such rooms offer many places for personal expression. Indented entries can be fitted with shelves and locked cabinets for displays of occupants' mementos and treasures. Interior walls can hold paintings, quilts, and tapestries. Spatial efficiencies may suggest closets and built-in shelves, but the L-shaped room can provide space for a personal desk and wardrobe or bureau and dressing table.

Carrying the idea of gaining both privacy and companionship a further step, clustering can gather groups of L-shaped rooms around an enclosed atrium or living space. Such clustered units help to achieve small, cohesive social groups. ∎

Duncaster, Bloomfield, Connecticut. (Photo: Dianne Davis)

37/Emerging Trends in Long-Term-Care Design

David A. Frank

The underlying concept of residentially based nursing homes should be "design from the inside out," starting with the basic building block of the bedroom with attached bathroom, in efficient and interesting configurations. Since 1984, the evolution of our approach to design can be followed in the cluster plans of several homes: the River Garden He-

brew Home for the Aged in Jacksonville, Florida, a 180-bed skilled-nursing facility, occupied in December 1989; The Sholom Home West in Minneapolis, Minnesota, a 160-bed skilled-nursing facility, scheduled for occupancy in January 1991; The Orchard Cove Project in Canton, Massachusetts, sponsored by the Hebrew Rehabilitation Center for Aged in Bos-

LEGEND

1 Nurses' Station   8 CNA Station
2 Med Room   9 Soiled Utility
3 Office   10 Linen
4 Conference Room   11 O2 Closet
5 Clean Utility

6 Dining   12 Lounge
7 Pantry

Sholom Home West Inc., Minneapolis, Minnesota. Cluster plan. (Architect: Korsunsky Krank Erickson and Associates Architects, Inc.)

ton, Massachusetts, a 227-housing-unit continuing care retirement community with an integrated 48-bed skilled-nursing facility, scheduled for a construction start in early 1991; the B'nai B'rith Home in Memphis, Tennessee, a 144-bed skilled-nursing facility, scheduled for construction in late 1990.

The chief objectives of cluster design include minimizing walking distance and the typical double-loaded-corridor image, thus improving staff efficiency. Most designs have more than 70 percent private rooms, with the bedrooms designed for several bed placements. Interior finishes are planned to be changed periodically. Supplies and equipment are localized at the cluster level, with some at the bedroom level. Each cluster unit of 24 to 40 residents provides decentralized dining.

The cluster unit is designed with the capability of being adapted to different staffing modules. We design for residents, staff, family, visitors, housekeeping, and foodservice. The cluster design decentralizes several services: dining, bathing–grooming, and restorative services, with some flexible office and conference space provided. The cluster designs strive for more staff efficiency by utilizing the team approach, and increasing the job responsibility and self-esteem of the nursing assistant.

In cluster design, the selection of structural systems, structural bay size, and mechanical and electrical systems must allow for future program changes, cluster room mix, and change in configurations. We also try to give the cluster and unit a residential scale.

Acoustical control is especially important in the cluster configuration and its surface materials. Internal noise is generated by unruly

Sholom Home West Inc., Minneapolis, Minnesota. (Architect: Korsunsky Krank Erickson and Associates Architects, Inc.)

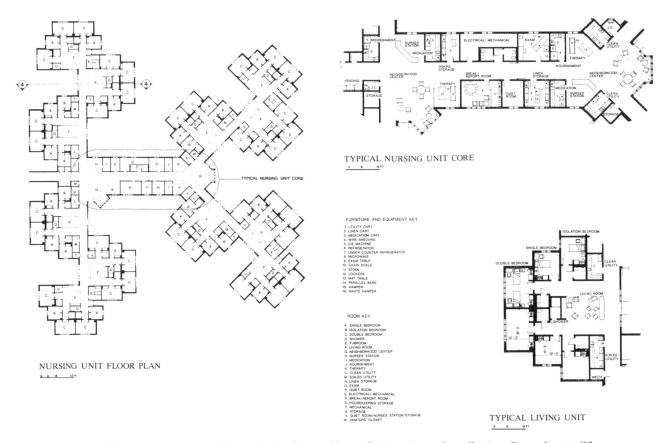

TYPICAL NURSING UNIT CORE

NURSING UNIT FLOOR PLAN

FURNITURE AND EQUIPMENT KEY
1. UTILITY CART
2. LINEN CART
3. MEDICATION CART
4. WIRE SHELVING
5. ICE MACHINE
6. REFRIGERATOR
7. UNDER COUNTER REFRIGERATOR
8. MICROWAVE
9. EXAM TABLE
10. CHAIR SCALE
11. STOOL
12. LOCKERS
13. MAT TABLE
14. PARALLEL BARS
15. HAMPER
16. WASTE HAMPER

ROOM KEY
A. SINGLE BEDROOM
B. ISOLATION BEDROOM
C. DOUBLE BEDROOM
D. SHOWER
E. TUBROOM
F. LIVING ROOM
G. NEIGHBORHOOD CENTER
H. NURSES' STATION
I. MEDICATION
J. NOURISHMENT
K. THERAPY
L. CLEAN UTILITY
M. SOILED UTILITY
N. LINEN STORAGE
O. STORAGE
P. QUIET ROOM
Q. ELECTRICAL/ MECHANICAL
R. BREAK/REPORT ROOM
S. HOUSEKEEPING STORAGE
T. MECHANICAL
U. STORAGE
V. QUIET ROOM/NURSES' STATION/STORAGE
W. JANITORS' CLOSET

TYPICAL LIVING UNIT

Missouri Veteran's Home, St. Louis, Missouri. (Architect: Kennedy Associates, Inc./Design Consultants: The Christner Partnership, Inc.)

residents, and heating, ventilating, and air-conditioning (HVAC). Gaining natural light without glare is also a key design objective.

The cluster/neighborhood should have distinct character and provide choice in social interaction. The design also provides for a hierarchy of spaces from small group to assembly. These areas should have images that induce residents to enjoy mental vacations.

The bedrooms should be designed so they can be personalized by residents. For example, the bedroom plan should provide flexibility in furniture placement so that residents can use some of their own furnishings. Also, we try to provide the resident some level of choice in the selection of some custom furnishings, such as window coverings and bed spreads.

We give the bather/spa much attention because the typical bather configurations in existing homes are degrading and uncomfortable. In our homes—the River Garden Home, for example—the baths are designed to create a positive, warm, familiar, and residential experience through the equipment, color, pattern, and natural lighting. Also, the bather has appropriate and convenient clean and soiled storage areas and an easily used large shower. The bath should be located near a lounge or passive activity area and near a nursing assistant desk.

Waste and odor control are real and perceived problems at the cluster and unit level. We have been using new materials and waste product storage and handling systems. The control of waste products and odor might be the most important factor in minimizing the typical institutional image. ■

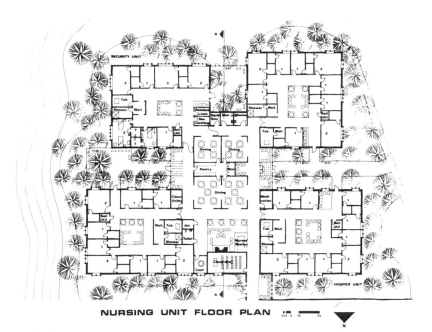

NURSING UNIT FLOOR PLAN

Jewish Home for the Aged, St. Louis, Missouri. Floor plan. (Architect: JRB Architects, Inc.)

38/The Architecture of Retirement Communities

Mark Engelbrecht

Retirement communities are complex, discrete social and physical entities. A retirement community does not come to exist simply by adding a nursing facility and large dining room to an apartment complex. Rather, it requires sophisticated integration of various components into a larger architectural system —a special community. Even when a mansion, hotel, or hospital preexists, which is frequently the case, integration must guide both sponsors and architects if a properly functioning retirement community is the desired result.

This is a new architectural form generated by a new way of life. It does not yet fit easily into codes and ordinances. Planning officials, for example, are notorious for insisting that retirement communities must conform as either apartment projects or as nursing facilities. Burdened by simplistic regulations and a casual attitude toward the elderly's welfare,

officials frequently fail to recognize in the lifecare retirement community a new reality integrating diverse components.

We frequently use the metaphor of the village to explain that point. A village combines many diverse public and private uses. Their combination produces a larger order, the "village." On another level, "village life" is the ebb and the flow within the private and public environments. A retirement community is analogous: a village with community life. Some master plans developed by our office elaborate this metaphor, incorporating neighborhoods, parks, streets, and public squares.

This village—the modern, lifecare-based retirement community—is an integrated, institutional response to the continuing lifelong needs of retired citizens, a fresh social reality that evokes a unique architecture. It has three essential components, which are shown in Figure 1: (1) dwelling units, (2) commons, and (3) healthcare facility. Their critically important interconnections in plan and their significance in site planning require architectural integration to achieve a village with community life.

THE DWELLING UNIT

The residential unit clearly differs from the standard commercial apartment. Its design poses unique, seemingly contradictory goals.

1. Reasons of cost and efficiency require that the dwelling unit be compact, yet its resident, more likely than not, will enter directly from a commodious house or generous apartment.
2. Each unit must support fully independent living, but each unit must also be connected to a network of services and associations that the resident will increasingly require.
3. The dwelling unit must gracefully accommodate diminishing physical capacities, yet it must support the resident's will to remain active as a vital member of the community.

Many other criteria affect the design of the residential unit, but those three seemingly contradictory considerations return again and again as the central issues for design.

In designs for over 8000 dwelling units, our office has witnessed significant changes. Twenty years ago, our prototypical designs included a standard array of studio, alcove, one- and two-bedroom apartment types. Recently, only two types, the one-bedroom and two-bedroom models, are common. The studio and so-called alcove unit do not meet residents' need for space. Except for unusually affluent markets, the one- and two-bedroom types now constitute nearly 100 percent of the units in our retirement communities. The smaller units are reserved for specialized roles such as assisted living. Our experience suggests, then, that a 600- and 750-square-foot one-bedroom dwelling unit, and a two-bedroom design of 900 to 1050 square feet, optimally satisfy the current requirements. The ratio of those two basic types within a particular community varies, but increasingly favors a mix of half and half.

The enlarged plan (Fig. 2) shows a typical

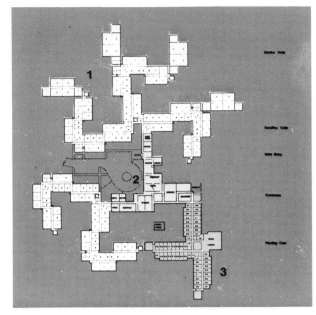

Figure 1. Plan (Architect: Engelbrecht & Griffin Architects/Photo: Farshid Assassi)

one-bedroom unit for a retirement community we recently designed. Since the dwelling unit must accommodate residents accustomed to life in single-family residences, their new quarters offer clearly defined entryways, both from the corridor and within. No matter how small, a discrete kitchen is a necessity, and a dining place must be clearly implied by the plan. Since visitors should not invade private rooms, a half or second bath is often provided. Finally, for each unit, we achieve a strong relationship with the outdoors, in this plan by a large balcony, accessible from both primary rooms.

Since most lifecare-based retirement communities will contain at least 200 dwelling units, integration of each unit into the whole requires special strategies. At Engelbrecht & Griffin, we pursue the concept of the "neighborhood." In this example (Fig. 3), our one-bedroom unit joins thirteen other apartments, all centered about a vertical circulation core, with an attendant lounge and service area. Three such neighborhoods are arranged in each structure, which is then joined by three similar buildings linked one to the other. Thus, twelve neighborhoods define a community, with units interrelated laterally and vertically. The concept of the neighborhood can take many different forms, but it is a graceful

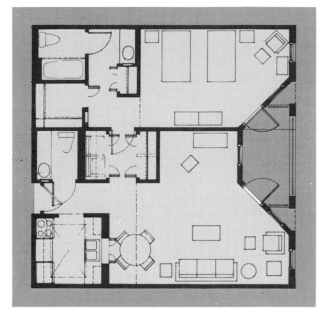

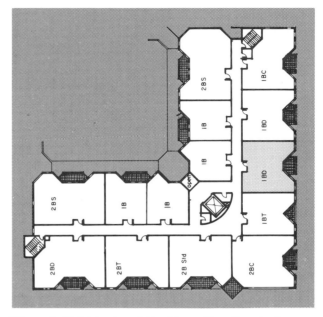

Figure 2. One-bedroom unit (Architect: Engelbrecht & Griffin Architects)

Figure 3. Neighborhood (Architect: Engelbrecht & Griffin Architects)

way to connect each unit to a larger supporting network and to provide a meaningful but understated cue for the residents' orientation.

Finally, and contrary to what younger minds might assume, we have learned that prospective residents respond well to unit designs that are somewhat unorthodox. A bay window or quiet alcove appeals. Architects should not slavishly conform to some prototypical "vision"; the resident may delight in the circumstantial.

COMMONS

Earlier, we compared the retirement community to a village. Following that analogy, its center of community activity should be a town square with principal common spaces. Our experience indicates that earlier rather spartan central facilities are giving way to increasingly elaborate programs (see Fig. 4). Many residents today are more active, so their demand for activities and services has expanded. A common central facility today may include private dining rooms, health spas, indoor swimming pools, shops, and a bank. Expanded service elements, as well as outdoor recreation areas, challenge the designer.

Planning the commons properly begins with the master plan. The commons need not be a single building. Conceptually, it can thread its way throughout the entire community. Viewed as connective, the individual elements of the commons program, such as lounges, meeting spaces, and game room, can bind the larger architecture, providing a rich continuity and orientation not found in more simplistic planning ideas. The aerial photo of Pomperaug Woods (Fig. 5) demonstrates a retirement community with a plan that centers around an outdoor common.

An enclosed arcade links various central elements and residential neighborhoods. There is no separate, isolated definitive commons; rather there is a linkage of common experiences, the village ambiance.

Even where a substantial share of commons elements are centrally located, there is no need for a centralized building. Rather, the commons offers residents a series of experiences designed to signify their perception of the larger environment. North Hill, in Needham, Massachusetts (Fig. 6), provides significant common spaces on both its first and top floors. There, members of the community are offered compellingly different perspectives of the surrounding landscape as a part of their daily activities.

Frequently, too little thought and space are

Figure 4. North Hill, Needham, Massachusetts. (Architect: Engelbrecht & Griffin Architects/Photo: Farshid Assassi)

Figure 5. Pomperaug Woods, Southbury, Connecticut. (Architect: Engelbrecht & Griffin Architects/Photo: Carl Ver Steeg)

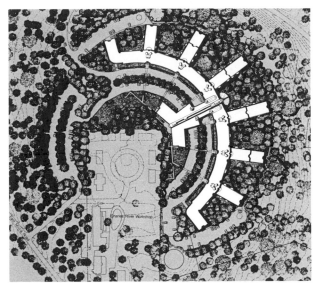

Figure 6. North Hill, Needham, Massachusetts. (Architect: Engelbrecht & Griffin Architects)

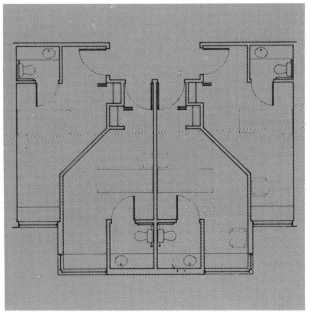

Figure 7. Nested single rooms. (Architect: Engelbrecht & Griffin Architects)

given to the beleaguered staff of a retirement community and their attendance to residents' needs. Any commons component is less than properly designed until the staff is appropriately served. Many older, established projects now require expansion of service facilities, especially to attract and retain competent staff.

HEALTHCARE

No part of the complex program for the modern lifecare-based retirement community has undergone more change than the healthcare facility. Its current form and function differ greatly from the earlier efficient skilled-nursing facility. Generally containing 30 to 60 beds in somewhat austere, double-occupancy rooms, the early nursing wings responded to limited intentions. In contrast, recent facilities reflect approaches to healthcare as an active agent for the wellness of the entire resident population. Assistance-in-living programs and small clinics are fresh responses to daily healthcare needs. Comprehensive positive care emphasizes rehabilitative services and special provisions for those who are terminally ill. Enlarged or additional spaces are needed for therapy and rec-

reation, and, in what must now be regarded as an irreversible trend, there is a need to accommodate at least one half of nursing residents within private rooms. All of this has led to expanded costs—costs that our office has attempted to counter with planning efficiencies such as "nested" single rooms (Fig. 7).

There has also been a corresponding growth in the complexity of the regulatory environment affecting skilled-nursing care. Not only do these important regulations impact construction possibilities, they also give their licensing administrators immense control over layout, form, and even master plan.

The resulting issues can harm the formal integration of the healthcare facility within the architecture of the community. Rejecting conventional visual dissociation of the healthcare center from the rest of the retirement community on functional grounds, we urge its reasonable integration within the larger composition; we stress the importance of visual continuity among the three major elements of the master plan. Where we succeed with that approach—the visual integration of the healthcare components—their presence has won enthusiasm over time.

MASTER PLAN AND SITE

The proper combination of the three basic components interlock to form a master plan for a specific site. Figure 8 illustrates a plan for a 300-dwelling unit retirement community, with development possible in two stages. Its objective was to produce a prototypical community for any number of localities. First, the concept demonstrates some of the essential functional and formal relationships of the three programmatic components, and secondly, it provides a critique of a planning process that seeks to minimize the variabilities of specific site circumstances.

The prototype demonstrates one way to interrelate dwelling units, commons, and healthcare in an efficient, expandable pattern.

A primary design determinant was that no structure would exceed three stories in height. Still, distances between each residence and the central commons are acceptable. Healthcare, commons, and service areas are efficiently related, and major public and private entrances are clearly differentiated to show clear connections to outdoor walks, roadways, and parking. As a rational model for plan development, the prototype has much to recommend it and many of its lessons continue to prove useful.

Ironically, however, experience with the design and construction of this prototypical plan prompted an enlarged understanding of the retirement community problem, a conception that has elevated the idea of context as significant.

Context should be defined as the sum of the physical, formal, and cultural realities of a particular site. Obviously, some factors present only design constraints, but many provide inspiration for the master plan and its architecture. Figure 9 projects the original master plan for Pomperaug Woods, a retirement community situated in a small New England town. Elements of the prototypical plan are easy to identify. There the lessons of the prototypical study end, and the instruction of context beings. Sloping southwest, the site is associated with an historic district, a large public park, and major shopping areas, all surrounded by heavily forested hills.

Appropriately neoclassical, the master plan centers around a large outdoor room, a New

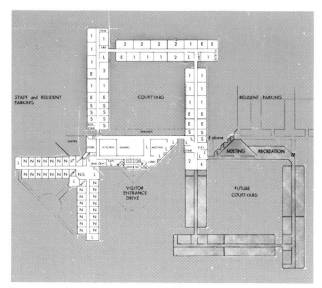

Figure 8. Plan for an expandable retirement community. (Architect: Engelbrecht & Griffin Architects)

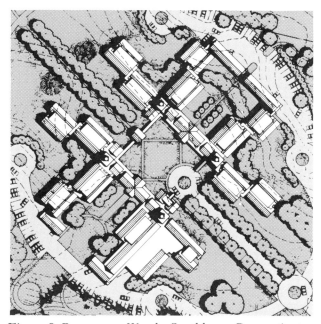

Figure 9. Pomperaug Woods, Southbury, Connecticut. (Architect: Engelbrecht & Griffin Architects)

England town common, framed by an arcade that laces dwelling units, commons, and healthcare together. Not only does the plan reflect the site's slope, it protects existing natural resources and connects the pedestrian to the park and shopping area. Figure 10 shows the architectural character, conformed to the scale, detail, and materials to the neighboring eighteenth-century houses in the historic district. Such a sensitivity to contextual concerns, in our view, must always modify a prototype, even one, as here, that is a "state of the art" plan.

Nowhere more than for retirement communities can inspired architecture be so beneficial. New communities for retired citizens are dedicated to life and deserve unique, poetic expression. They merit an architecture that is not only capable of serving and supporting, but also enriching and renewing. They demand more than tired, institutional forms. Architecture should celebrate their vitality, and that challenge remains compelling. ■

Figure 10. Pomperaug Woods, Southbury, Connecticut. (Architect: Engelbrecht & Griffin Architects/Photo: Carl Ver Steeg)

Part V

Architectural Planning

Moving from spatial and site planning toward
smaller scaled, detailed architectural planning,
Part V explores character and organization of the
public and private spaces.

39/Planning Retirement Communities

Mark Engelbrecht

Much has changed since Engelbrecht & Griffin Architects first encountered the retirement community as a design opportunity 25 years ago. Offering a range of comprehensive environments and services matched to their residents' lifelong needs, these facilities remain as alluring to seniors as ever before. The delivery vehicle varies by program (lifecare, rental, etc.,) or sponsor (profit, not-for-profit), but full-service retirement communities meet a growing need.

The complexity and size of the full-service retirement community requires integration of housing, common spaces, and healthcare components—whose increasing complexity entails significantly high delivery costs.

Responses to rising costs have been varied, but both private and public development groups have only four options.

1. Pursuit of an increasingly affluent market able to absorb the higher costs.
2. Editing the basic design program to decrease construction costs and ongoing management expenses.
3. Lowering construction costs through quality adjustments in material assemblies and configurations.
4. Development of new financial options for development and resident occupancies.

Of the preceding propositions, which are often contradictory, only the second and third fall within our purview here and deserve comment.

To build for less, build less. Unfortunately, many development groups propose to reduce the amount to be built by eliminating entire programmatic components of retirement communities, particularly healthcare. This has proved to be unwise. Without a healthcare program, be it the somewhat ambiguous "assisted living" or a licensed nursing unit, a re-

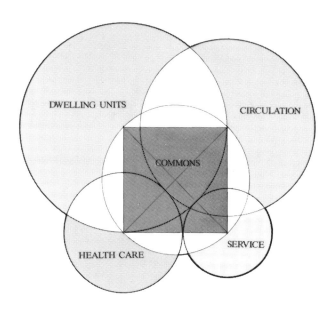

Figure 1. Allocation diagram. (Architect: Engelbrecht & Griffin Architects)

tirement community cannot offer long-term healthcare and is forced to compete with simple rentals or condominiums.

There is a better approach. The full-service retirement communities we have designed demonstrate that the proportionate areas for the programmatic elements—dwelling units, commons, healthcare, service, and circulation —have not varied much over time, even though total project areas have grown considerably. The diagram in Figure 1 demonstrates the relevant ratios and those elements that may yield area savings. Unhappily, residential areas cannot be reduced, and we would certainly counsel against wholesale cuts in services. Since the healthcare program is largely mandated by applicable state codes, that leaves circulation and commons as primary candidates for area reductions.

Combined, circulation and commons account for approximately 25 percent of gross area. The two functions should be viewed as a conceptual unity. Whenever possible, circulation should amplify common elements. As an example, in Figures 2 and 3 a retirement community plan incorporates horizontal travel routes as an integral part of the central commons cluster. Circulation spaces are visually and functionally enlarged, and corresponding real-area reductions are achieved. Another, more recent example is shown in Figure 4, which illustrates a technique for combining circulation with the common areas: atrium spaces as informal places for gatherings and directed activities. Common areas are reduced, and, since informal, unprogrammed spaces are prized, added architectural richness is generated.

Conversely, a commons/connector continuity yields interesting options for its location within the entire retirement community. The

Figure 2. Friendship Village, Columbus, Ohio, (Architect: Engelbrecht & Griffin Architects/Photo: Farshid Assassi)

Figure 3. Friendship Village, Columbus, Ohio. (Architect: Engelbrecht & Griffin Architects/Photo: Farshid Assassi)

Architectural Planning / **119**

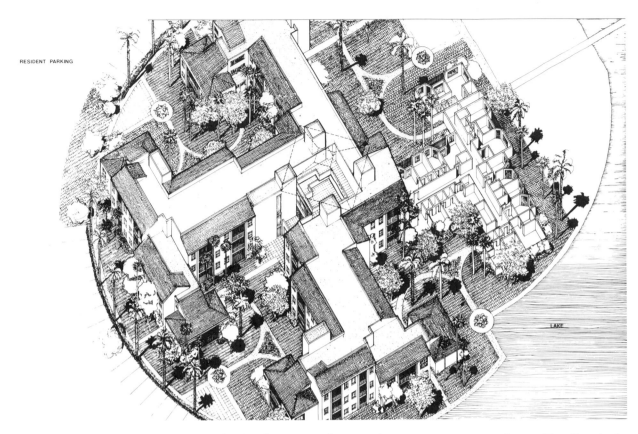

RESIDENT PARKING

LAKE

Figure 4. Metro/Sarasota, Sarasota, Florida. Combining circulation with common spaces. (Architect: Engelbrecht & Griffin Architects)

significant common spaces are located along a retirement community's natural intersections, on the vertical and lateral routes of communication.

Figures 5 and 6 show major common spaces centrally positioned within both horizontal and vertical circulation systems. Taking maximum advantage of a spectacular site, this design also optimizes spatial efficiency and yields a frugal project on net-gross accounting. Similarly, another retirement community (not shown) organizes essential common rooms along the vertical and lateral nexus of the plan. It yields a spatial "stack" that is both efficient and dramatic. Finally, to return to a project already mentioned, but freshly presented in Figure 7, we show a commons array aligned along the natural circulation patterns of a community. Had this project been arranged with two typical detached "club house" commons, significant additional lateral circulation areas would have been inevitable.

The examples of connector and commons continuity, which leads to both real-area sav-

ings and added architectural richness, are tokens of a larger attitude: the realization, both by developers and architects, that continuing care retirement communities, as full-service retirement communities, must be highly integrated environments where efficiency and quality are directly proportional to this continuity. More than programmatic analysis is required to gain integration. Designers must search for varied configurations, spatial sequences, and rational organization.

CONFIGURATIONS

Earlier, we mentioned construction quality and design configuration as two likely directions for realizing savings. Of course, some minimal savings can be gained in materials and finishes because the residents use buildings gently. But spatial arrangements yield greater economies. The more densely packed a configuration is, and the more modularized its design, the greater its efficiency, and the lower its construction cost will be. While many mod-

Above: Caretel®, Peachwood Inn/Borden Court, Rochester Hills, Michigan. Corridor. (Architect: Hobbs & Black, Associates Inc./Photo: Beth Singer Photographer, Inc.)

Left: The Miriam Hospital, Providence, Rhode Island. Signage. (Designer: Malcolm Grear Associates)

Left: Medical University of South Carolina, Children's Hospital, Charleston, South Carolina. Waiting area. (Architect: NBBJRosenfield, Columbus, Ohio Studio and Charleston SC Studios/Photo: Michael Houghton/ STUDIOHIO)

Right: James Steam Mill, Newburyport. (Architect: CBT/Childs Bertman Tseckares & Casendino Inc./ Photo: Nick Wheeler/Wheeler Photographies.)

Below: Robert Wood Johnson University Hospital, New Brunswick, New Jersey. Atrium. (Architect: NBBJRosenfield, New York Studio/Joint Venture: The Gruzen Partnership/Photo: Stephen Barker)

Caribbean Palm Village Resort, Aruba, Netherlands Antilles. Exterior view. (Landscape Architect: Leo Alvarez/Photo: Patricia Fisher)

The Gables at Old Farm Forest, Farmington, Connecticut. Atrium. (Architect: CBT/Childs Bertman Tseckares & Casendino Inc./Photo: Hutchins Photography, Inc.)

Chateau Lake San Marcos, San Marcos, California. Colonnade. (Architect: John Boles/Interior Designer: Jain Malkin, Inc./Photo: Kim Brun)

Chateau Lake San Marcos, San Marcos, California. Main dining room. (Architect: John Boles/Interior Designer: Jain Malkin, Inc./Photo: Kim Brun)

Above: Columbia-Presbyterian Medical Center, Milstein Hospital Building, New York, New York. Milstein Pavilion. (Architect: Skidmore Owings & Merrill/New York/Photo: Robert Miller.

Right: Columbia-University Presbyterian Medical Center, New York, New York. (Architect: Skidmore Owings & Merrill/New York/Photo: Robert Miller.

The Cleveland Clinic Guesthouse, Cleveland, Ohio.
Grocery section of the café and market. (Interior
Designer: Whitley & Whitley Associates/Photo: Courtesy
of the Cleveland Clinic Guesthouse)

The Cleveland Clinic, Center Hotel, Cleveland, Ohio.
Le Bistro Lobby Pub. (Interior Designer: Bathrop and
Associates/Photo: Courtesy of the Clinic Center Hotel)

Harbour's Edge Life Care Community, Delray Beach,
Florida. Dining room. (Architect: Shephard Legan
Aldrian/Interior Designer: Donald J. Stanzione
Associates/Photo: Courtesy of Life Care Services Corp.)

Above: Cleveland Clinic Guesthouse, Cleveland, Ohio. Café/restaurant. (Interior Designer: Whitley & Whitley/ Photo: Courtesy of the Cleveland Clinic Guesthouse)

Right: Flagler Hospital, St. Augustine, Florida. (Architect: Hansen Lind Meyer, Inc./Photo: Phil Eschbach)

Opposite page, top: La Posada, Green Valley, Arizona. (Architect: Engelbrecht & Griffin Architects/Photo: Farshid Assassi)

Opposite page, bottom: Abbey Delray South Life Care Community, Delray Beach, Florida. (Architect: Engelbrecht & Griffin Architects/Photo: Farshid Assassi)

Ronald McDonald House, Iowa City, Iowa. (Architect: Hansen Lind Meyer, Inc./Photo: Phil Eschbach)

Flagler Hospital, St. Augustine, Florida. (Architect: Hansen Lind Meyer, Inc./Photo: Phil Eschbach)

Park Place, Denver, Colorado. (Interior Designer: Paul Darrall/Photo: Gordon Price)

Charlotte Hungerford Hospital, Torrington, CT. Intensive care unit. (Architect: NBBJRosenfield, New York Studio/ [formerly The Rosenfield Partnership]/Photo: Hobart Williams)

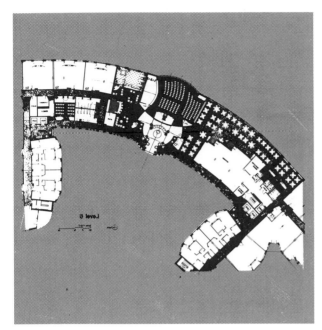

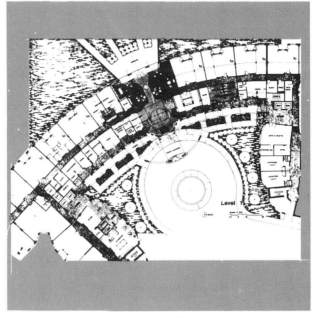

Figure 5. Plan. (Architect: Engelbrecht & Griffin Architects)

Figure 6. Plan. (Architect: Engelbrecht & Griffin Architects)

Figure 7. Pomperaug Woods, Southbury, Connecticut. Model. (Architect: Engelbrecht & Griffin Architects)

ularized, high-yield structures generate little appeal to the prospective buyer and less joy for the resident, modular design, far from being monotonous, can achieve efficient configurations and spatial compositions that benefit the larger architectural and social effort.

Figure 8 illustrates the technique we customarily use to design modular configurations that are at once efficient and appealing. This simple planning technique, a grid, forms the basic geometric field for a particular architectural configuration, and its standardization

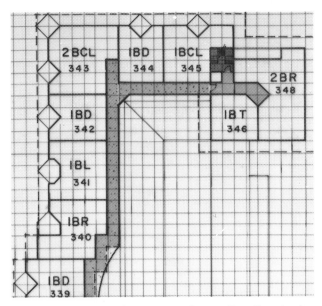

Figure 8. Modular planning: (Architect: Engelbrecht & Griffin Architects)

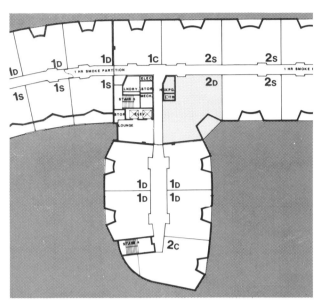

Figure 9. Plan. (Architect: Engelbrecht & Griffin Architects)

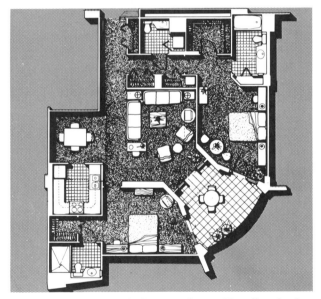

Figure 10. Residential plan. (Architect: Engelbrecht & Griffin Architects)

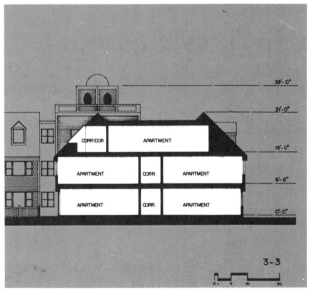

Figure 11. One- and two-bedroom apartments. (Architect: Engelbrecht & Griffin Architects)

produces real savings without sacrificing architectural richness. In fact, the geometric planning field frees the designer to deal with more significant conceptual matters, and the plans it generates are clearly understood by contractors who require consistency within construction documents, bidding, and on-site construction management.

More than plans, architectural configurations produce spatial "packages" that restore charm to residential unit design. Two examples of "space packing" techniques, illustrated

in Figures 9 and 10, show a residential dwelling unit that takes advantage of a "cornering" possibility within the larger configuration, an arrangement that enjoys a healthy net-to-gross ratio. Figure 11 shows dwelling units in a configuration that combines one- and two-bedroom apartments. This configuration yields both economic savings and a harmonious fit into historical context and zoning bylaws. Again, a densely packed configuration diminishes costs while providing a gracious residential environment.

CONCLUSION

The foregoing examples support our proposition that gaining efficiency in the design and construction of retirement communities, while essential to the success of development teams and the prospective resident, need not yield dull, institutional environments (see Figure 12). Practiced in spatial configuration, the designer can summon imagination and innovation, which will shape retirement communities that are both efficient and alluring. ∎

Figure 12. North Hill, Needham, Massachusetts. (Architect: Engelbrecht & Griffin Architects/Photo: Farshid Assassi)

40/Designing the High-Rise Continuing Care Retirement Community

Glen Tipton

In the early 1980s, as my firm, Cochran, Stephenson & Donkervoet, had just completed architectural work for Broadmead, Baltimore's first continuing care retirement community (CCRC), we started designing Edenwald. Although their programs were nearly identical, there was one crucial difference. Where Broadmead spread 240 living units and numerous courtyards and common spaces over 80 acres, on a campus plan, Edenwald's site was a mere 4.5 acres. We therefore designed Edenwald as a high-rise lifecare community.

When Martin Trueblood, then the executive director of Broadmead, learned that Edenwald would rise in town, but close to suburban Broadmead, he said that the high-rise posed very little market threat to his campus community because they have two distinct appeals, and he was right. Both continue to have waiting lists several years long.

The high-rise CCRC offers the many advantages of urban services and activities. Rural CCRCs, developed where land costs were low (or free, when land was donated to not-for-profit groups), spread low-density cottages on a campus, then provided commodious community centers to offset the lack of nearby services and activities. Today, with most sites priced on the cost per living unit, small urban sites are competitive if a high-rise can be built to an optimal floor/area ratio, and urban advantages exist.

Urban and suburban high-rise locations appeal to potential residents and developers alike. The best sites are close to shopping, churches, and medical, educational, and cultural institutions. Public transportation is an asset for residents and also eases the employment of workers in foodservice, housekeeping, laundry, and nursing assistance. Located in the midst of an office, hotel, and residential development, Edenwald stands across the street from a regional shopping center, adjoins a college campus, and is served by a municipal bus route. On a large site, a high-rise will preserve open space that creates a buffer with the surrounding neighborhoods.

MARKET RESPONSE TO THE HIGH-RISE

Many elderly now living in urban and suburban areas want the convenience and continuities a local, nearby high-rise can offer. With few entry points and typically well secured, both electronically and commonly, with 24-hour manned surveillance as well, the high-rise is generally perceived as being safe. Modern, convenient, fireproof, well constructed, finely finished, reliably maintained, and hospitably staffed, the high-rise CCRC can be a preferred way of life. In a parklike setting, it offers panoramas of sky, gardens, and skyline.

The high-rise CCRC consolidates common spaces. Since most common spaces are typically located at the tower's base, or less frequently at its top, residents need walk only a short, climate-controlled distance from a living unit, usually less than 150 feet, to an elevator, and then a second short distance to the dining room or other parts of the community center. This convenience often becomes an attractive feature of the high-rise as the prospective elderly resident ponders the concept of "aging in place." The converse of this convenience factor, based upon postoccupancy evaluations we have done of the various forms of the CCRC our firm has designed, is that the high-rise seems to attract a slightly older, frailer incoming population.

Critics of high-rise CCRCs allege that they promote less social interaction than occurs in

Edenwald, Towson, Maryland. (Architect: Cochran, Stephenson & Donkervoet, Inc./Photo: Courtesy of Cochran, Stephenson & Donkervoet, Inc.)

the campus plan, where casual meetings occur on the walks to and from the community center, and clustered cottages encourage neighborhood sociability. In actuality, comparable social generators do develop in the high-rise.

Other criticisms relate to the high-rise CCRC's costs. Structured parking is often needed. Even readily available public transportation does not overcome the sense of independence car ownership implies. Market demand for covered parking is high, and at least one space per independent living unit (ILU) is recommended. Other costs are incurred by high-rise structures to meet modern fire and building codes, but there are offsetting savings in utilities and site development, which can incur high costs in the campus plan.

DESIGN ISSUES

The high-rise CCRC represents special architectural problems: aesthetics, safety, quality of construction, and residential character, among others. The greatest challenge is to integrate in a tower all the diverse functions of a CCRC: its community center (CC), independent living units (ILU), assisted living units (ALU), and skilled-nursing facility (SNF), and to make them work as a unified complex. Since residents expect nursing care on site, the SNF

must be accessible and visible without being a constant reminder of human frailty. That poses a special challenge, because the ILU residents want the SNF, but prefer to see it or to visit it only when obliged or invited to do so. Sorting the conflicting and supporting components, giving each its vertical or horizontal path, is the key issue to be resolved.

From the several high-rise CCRCs my firm has designed, I cite two to illustrate different solutions: Edenwald, sponsored by the General German Aged People's Home, a not-for-profit group, and the Jefferson, a 325-unit, twin-tower CCRC, with twenty stories, designed for the Marriott Corporation. They represent two ways to incorporate the ALU and SNF into the high-rise ILU.

At Edenwald, the ALU and SNF are in a special unit, separate from the ILU/CC tower; they are linked by a food service component

Edenwald, Towson, Maryland. (Architect: Cochran, Stephenson & Donkervoet, Inc./Interior Designer: Arthur Shuster, Inc./Photo: Courtesy of Arthur Shuster, Inc.)

that serves ALU dining, a coffee shop, and the main dining room. All access to the SNF from the CC is at ground level, where an elevator rises to the SNF only. Three other elevators carry residents to the ILU Tower. A small amount of structured parking lies under the building, with the rest of the site used for open parking.

For the Marriott Jefferson, we proposed a vertical integration. At the Jefferson, the site is much tighter—only 1.5 acres—and the program is bigger. It was essential therefore to stack everything and separate access by dedicated elevators. Two towers containing the ILU apartments meet in common spaces at the bottom two levels, with the ALU and the SNF bridging between the towers. Underground parking occupies three lower levels. The ground level is for the CC access, service, and certain public areas. The second floor is the primary CC. The SNF is located on the third floor with the ALUs on the fourth. Floors 5 through 20 constitute the ILU tower. Elevators rise from parking through common areas

to ILU floors, while shorter elevators serve the ALU and SNF.

Access to the SNF and ALU is gained through dedicated elevators that connect the CC floors to the third and fourth floors. The elevators to the ILU tower connect all floors from the lowest garage level to the topmost ILU floor, but do not stop at the SNF and ALU floors. Dedicated service elevators serving floors 1 through 4 provide service to the dining rooms, the CC, SNF, and ALU floors.

High-rise CCRCs challenge designers to provide attractive spaces for social and cultural activities and to create accessible outdoor spaces. A neighboring college campus helps Edenwald, but the Jefferson fronts on a public urban space, the Ellipse, which, although a fine vista, is not expected to be used by the residents often. An elevated plaza at the Jefferson's CC level, with smaller spaces above for the SNF, and above that, a still smaller space for the ALU, all facing south, afford privacy, safety, sun, and refreshing views.

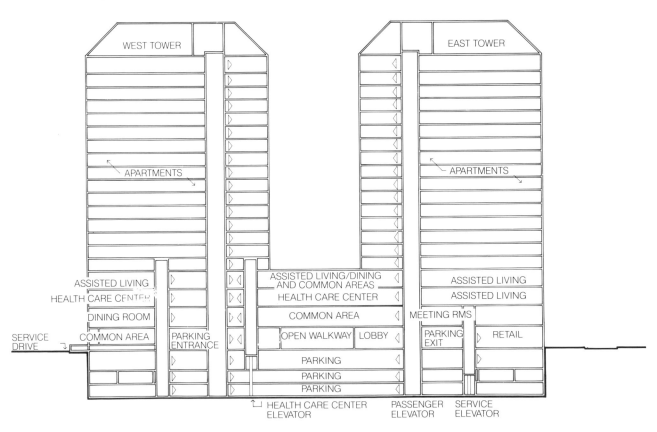

Marriott's Jefferson, Arlington, Virginia. (Architect: Cochran, Stephenson & Donkervoet, Inc./Photo: Courtesy of Cochran, Stephenson & Donkervoet, Inc.)

COST CONTROL

In high-rise design, cost control becomes crucial. To avoid costly trusses, transfer beams, and horizontal extensions of mechanical ducts and electrical circuits, there must be careful vertical coordination of structural grid and building services. That difficult task is further encumbered by the variety of functional modules that must fit the structural frame. ILUs must stack over ALUs, over SN bedrooms, over large CC spaces, over parking spaces (a formidable task, indeed), and columns should be continuous while floors should be as shallow as possible, to fit the desired number of floors within the authorized zoning envelope.

Determining where the large common spaces should be located vertically in the stack, whether below, at the top, or somewhere midway, is only partly a matter of gaining efficient vertical circulation; their location affects structure. Still, with skill and thought, the high-rise CCRC can be kept reasonably competitive with its rural campus-style alternative, which has extensive site development costs that the high-rise may not have.

In the end, the question is never merely one of costs but of lifestyles, and the urban, high-rise CCRC definitely has won adherents. ■

St. Thomas Choir School, New York. (Architect: Buttrick, White & Burtis)

41/Mall Concept: Ambulatory Care

Earl S. Swensson

OWNER'S REQUIREMENTS

The Hickory Hollow Medical Center in Nashville, Tennessee, serves as a primary-care center for members of PruCare, a health maintenance organization, and a subsidiary of the Prudential Insurance Company of America. The facility provides physician services in family practice, pediatrics, and obstetrics–gynecology. It also has basic laboratory and X-ray facilities, as well as an outpatient surgery suite and space for a pharmacy.

The client wanted to avoid overcrowded waiting areas and unnecessary patient/doctor cross traffic. Pediatrics was to be a separate area.

DESIGN SOLUTION

Our "mall" concept meets the requirements. Two major "spines" run the length of the building. The front spine, or concourse, begins at the receptionist's desk and ends at the children's waiting area. Along the way are four treatment units, each of which has its own waiting area, examination rooms, doctor's offices, and nurses' station.

At the rear, a narrow, second corridor runs the length of the building. This corridor is reserved for doctor/nurse traffic, allowing both to enter and leave their work areas without patient contact.

Other special features include color coding for ease in patient movement into waiting areas and the use of skylights along the major corridors and in the individual waiting areas. In keeping with energy conservation, the brick back-wall serves as a thermal mass, and a clerestory is designed for maximum heat absorption in the winter. ∎

STAFF CIRCULATION
PATIENT CIRCULATION

Pru-Care/Hickory Hollow Medical Center, Nashville, Tennessee. Floor plan. (Architect: Earl Swensson Associates, Inc.)

42/Circulation—The Foundation of Health Facility Design

Philip A. Monteleoni

More than most other design professionals, health facility planners must strive to design humane and caring environments, since their projects deal with so many people at moments of great physiological stress and least resistance. The design of humane, welcoming, and caring healthcare environments starts with something mundane yet fundamental: circulation.

For a built environment to be positive and not stressful, it must provide a reassuring sense orientation and be free from conflicting presences. Good health-environment planners organize a facility's circulation systems, such as corridors, elevators, tunnels, and bridges, so as to dispel confusion, to minimize inappropriate encounters, and to promote security.

Good circulation planning keeps incompatible types of traffic separate, from their sources of origin until their intended destination. Health facility circulation includes at least four basic categories; that is, the movement of (1) public, (2) staff, (3) inpatients, and (4) materials. Ideally, each category travels best along its own dedicated routing and should be protected from unintentional encounters with the other types. For major, interdepartmental circulation, however, categories one and two are often grouped.

The first two categories, public and staff, can be visualized as vertical people, mostly in street clothes, who constitute the largest and fastest moving traffic in the hospital. The third category consists of people transported within the hospital on stretchers or wheelchairs, dressed in often inadequate hospital garb, functionally helpless for that period of time. The fourth category includes carts, boxes, bins, and objects of all sorts, and is often further subdivided into distinct clean and soiled circulation paths.

The importance of keeping these elements separate can best be illustrated by visualizing an elevator encounter. In the confined space of an elevator, the close proximity of a vertical, street-clothed person next to a stretcher carrying a patient in pajamas covered by a flimsy sheet is at the very least uncomfortable for both parties. The close confinement of either of these people with a cart bearing dinner trays or taking out garbage is more than uncomfortable, it is unsanitary. Yet many of today's hospitals are still designed with only two elevator cores, one public and one service, thus unfortunately combining the patient and the trash.

Anxiety about an impending medical procedure decreases significantly when the subject knows what to expect. Analogously, anxiety about being in or moving through a large unfamiliar building can be reduced by providing people with a clear sense of spatial orientation. As long as people know where they are, they will feel less stress.

Orientation is achieved by providing strong visual cues: a pool of light at the end of a corridor, a path unified by color, or the most basic cue of all, a view of the outside. Connecting people to the outside environment as much as possible provides the additional benefit of psychological reassurance. Quite often the pain of bad news or uncertainty about the condition of oneself or a loved one can be mitigated by seeing the sky and the world outside and feeling connected to the cyclical forces of nature.

The planning and design of two recent tertiary care hospital pavilions in New York City by Skidmore Owings & Merrill share the common theme of attention to circulation. Columbia Presbyterian Medical Center's new nine-story 745-bed Milstein Hospital Building, and St. Luke's–Roosevelt new 430-bed addition at the Roosevelt site derive much of their

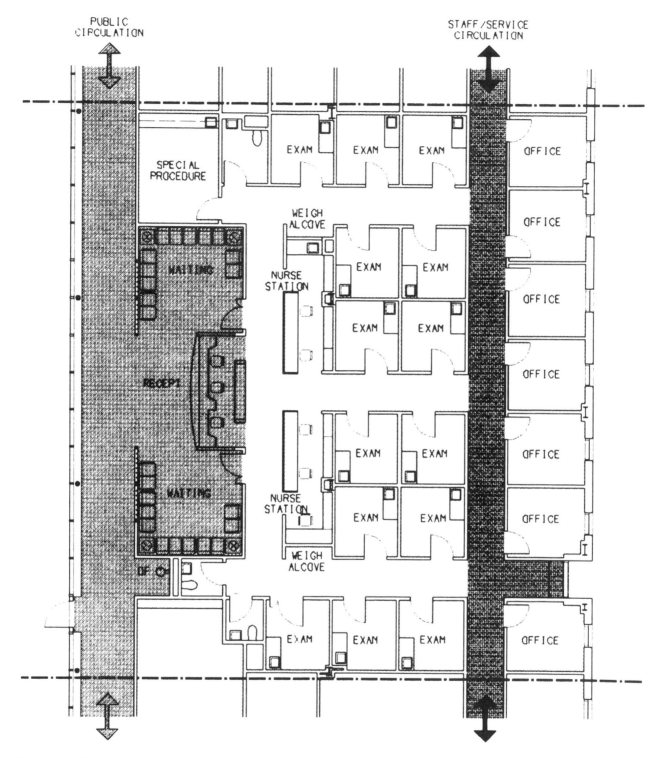

PUBLIC
CIRCULATION

STAFF/SERVICE
CIRCULATION

SPECIAL
PROCEDURE

EXAM EXAM EXAM OFFICE

WEIGH
ALCOVE

WAITING OFFICE

NURSE
STATION EXAM EXAM OFFICE

RECEPT EXAM EXAM OFFICE

WAITING OFFICE

NURSE
STATION EXAM EXAM OFFICE

OF C WEIGH
ALCOVE

EXAM EXAM EXAM OFFICE

Circulation diagram of ambulatory care module. (Architect: Skidmore Owings & Merrill/New York)

external form from the internal logic of the circulation.

The buildings are nine and thirteen stories high, respectively, and both are "anchored" by their central elevator cores. In both buildings there are three major banks of elevators, the public/staff, the patient, and their service. Each of these banks has its own dedicated lobby on each floor. In this way, each of the three major traffic types has its own set of paths through the buildings.

At the center in both projects is the public

elevator core and its floor lobbies, from which all public circulation on the floor originates. In addition to the six public elevators, this lobby also serves a continuous escalator in the Milstein building, which connects all nine floors.

When the public arrives upon the patient-floor, they are at the geometric center of the buildings, with corridors offering direct lines of sight to the nurses' stations opening off either side of the public lobby. For the safety of patients, these visitor corridors bring the public straight to the nurses' station without passing patient rooms. The nurses' station thus functions as gatekeeper for its patient-care unit and no visitor can slip unnoticed into a patient room. In addition, public corridors leading to the patient-care units are free of all other types of hospital circulation: no patients on stretchers, no carts, or equipment clutter the hallways.

Stretcher patients are brought to and from the floor via their own lobby, which connects to the patient-care unit through a separate corridor. Service traffic, arriving by its own dedicated elevator core, also connects to this "back of house" corridor.

Only in the corridors serving the patient bedrooms do the various threads of traffic finally come together: the public, the staff, the patient, and the service. To highlight the sense that the patient room corridor is the termina-tion of the visitors' journey, there are full-width windows at each end of these corridors in both projects, which connect patients, public and staff to the outside world. In addition, at the Columbia Presbyterian project, lounges that are open both to the corridor and to the outside bring natural light directly to the centrally located nurses' station.

SUMMARY

The strength of planning lies in organizing the movement of all elements in the hospital, both vertically and horizontally. The flow of visitors minimizes their perception of being in a hospital and channels them into safe, well-observed paths that inevitably terminate at the nurses' station. The flow of stretcher patients is kept separate for reasons of patient dignity, and the movement of materials has its own vertical and horizontal paths for the greatest efficiency.

The seemingly prosaic issues—people and material movement, access to circumscribed zones, and human reassurance through exterior views—are the fundamental determinants of the health facility environment. Only after these basic elements are woven into the initial planning will design development of spatial and surface enhancement have meaning and effect. ■

43 / A Social Prototype

Spero Daltas

In Saudi Arabia it is common for an entire family, often as many as thirty, to visit a patient at the same time. As a result, we separate visitor circulation completely from the medical staff circulation. The hospital in King Khalid City is on two levels: the upper for arriving visitors, and the lower for patients and medical staff. From the entrance lobby visitors proceed through skylit, landscaped courts to visit or stay with patients.

Opposite each room, a network of medical corridors allows the health functions to proceed unencumbered, unobstructed, and uncontaminated by visitors.

The entire hospital is set into the ground one-half level to allow easy access to both levels and to provide an earth cover that reduces the intense heat and wind. The efficient configuration eases servicing and maintenance and can readily be expanded. Satisfying the cultural need for separation of men and women, officers and enlisted men, and the functional need for flexibility, this medical facility is a milestone in healthcare planning. ■

Proposed hospital, King Khalid City, Saudi Arabia. (Architect: Brown, Daltas Associates)

44/The Menninger Foundation

James R. DeStefano

The new campus for Menninger Clinic, Topeka, Kansas, is a cheerful, bright, and stable residential environment that has proved to be a therapeutically beneficial atmosphere. Designed by James R. DeStefano in 1980 while he was a partner in Skidmore Owings & Merrill/Chicago, and built in 1982, the campus is a unique combination of medical, residential, and recreational facilities. It is distinctly more than a collection of buildings.

It is a total environment, created to support the highly respected psychiatric treatment programs that are the basis of the Menninger Foundation.

Set in a valley among the softly rolling Kansas hills outside Topeka, the campus has achieved a special residential flavor through its planning. One-, two-, and three-story buildings are arranged to relate to the requirements of a walking community (cars are kept on the perimeter) with needs for residential, office and treatment space, exercise facilities, and an active conference center.

The residential sector has won the admiration of patients, staff, and professional peers. The total therapeutic environment was created for the human scale.

The eighteen new buildings are contemporary in style, primarily two stories high and constructed inside and out of natural materials, including brick, wood, and fabric. Painted white brick, the exteriors nestle among the trees—less than 5 percent of the mature evergreen and shade trees were removed for construction, and those remaining interrelate with the seven existing buildings. Covered walkways serve as front porches to the living units, while partially enclosed courtyards serve as backyards.

The average patient stays at the Menninger Foundation Clinic for one year. It was obvious to the architects that a homelike environment was mandatory for this length of time, both for treating the patient and for easing his or her reentry into his or her own community. Yet the hospital is large, serving 166 resident patients.

The residential units provide sufficient space

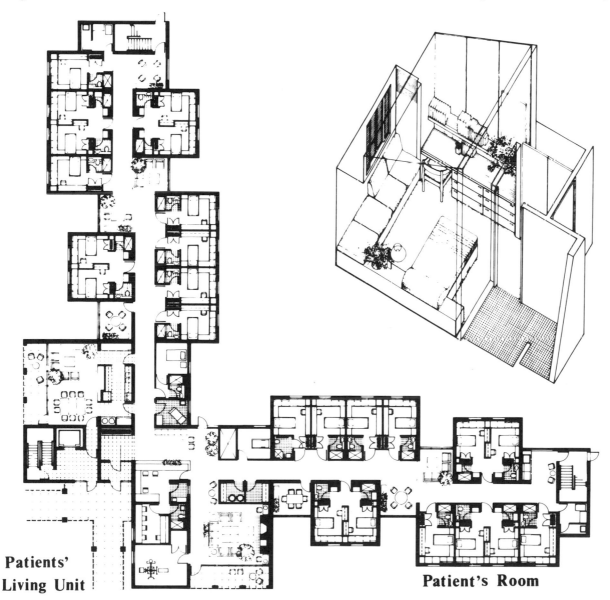

Patients' Living Unit

Patient's Room

The Menninger Foundation, Topeka, Kansas. Schematic. (Architect: Skidmore Owings & Merrill/Principal Designer: James R. DeStefano)

The Menninger Foundation, Topeka, Kansas. (Architect: Skidmore Owings & Merrill/Principal Designer: James R. DeStefano/Photo: Hedrich-Blessing, courtesy of James R. DeStefano)

The Menninger Foundation, Topeka, Kansas. (Architect: Skidmore Owings & Merrill/Principal Designer: James R. DeStefano/Photo: Hedrich-Blessing, courtesy of James R. DeStefano)

for all patients, while creating a more intimate atmosphere than found in most psychiatric hospitals. To avoid long, tedious hallways, but maintain efficient use of nurses' stations, the halls are interrupted by small alcove seating for casual patient conversations. The whole design is kept simple, but room arrangements are stepped to create zigzags. Central lounges feature fire places and several seating groupings to allow for larger informal gatherings.

The eight living units encourage interaction between small groups of patients while they benefit from the large hospital community. Furniture in all rooms is built-in. Each patient has a bed, chest, large seating area, and desk and chair. White walls and soft camel-color carpets are accented by fabric wall hangings and rusty-red bedspreads with three stripes of color: purple, green, and orange. One of the stripe colors is used as an accent on the bulletin board and seat cushions of the natural wood chair.

Additionally, privacy was provided in the double-room bathrooms by separating the shower unit from the toilet and hand basin. Patients can control the temperature of their heating and air-conditioning within a 10-degree range.

Each patient unit has a kitchen for informal food preparation. Exercise rooms are located within the residential units for patients who are not able to go to the gymnasium. Active and passive exercise is encouraged for their therapeutic benefits.

The primary goal of creating an intimate

The Menninger Foundation, Topeka, Kansas. (Architect: Skidmore Owings & Merrill/Principal Designer: James R. DeStefano/Photo: Hedrich-Blessing, courtesy of James R. DeStefano)

community was achieved with the low cluster of living units, thoughtful building design, including clerestories to reduce scale and increase patients' awareness of the out-of-doors, and extensive landscaping of the 332-acre site. This goal was further achieved through the humanizing design of interior spaces that acknowledge the importance of personal interchange within a secure community. ∎

45 / Generous Private Spaces

Bradford Perkins

In long term-care, we must redefine the models that generate today's facility designs, which are derived from healthcare and custodial models where the nurses' station and clinical support are the key determinants. Instead, we must model long-term care facilities on service-oriented residential environments

and hotels. For the Joseph L. Morse Geriatric Center in West Palm Beach we sought the character of a Florida resort, and for the Montefiore Home in Beachwood, Ohio, we designed in midwestern residential vocabulary to lessen its institutional nature.

Privacy, maximum independence, and dig-

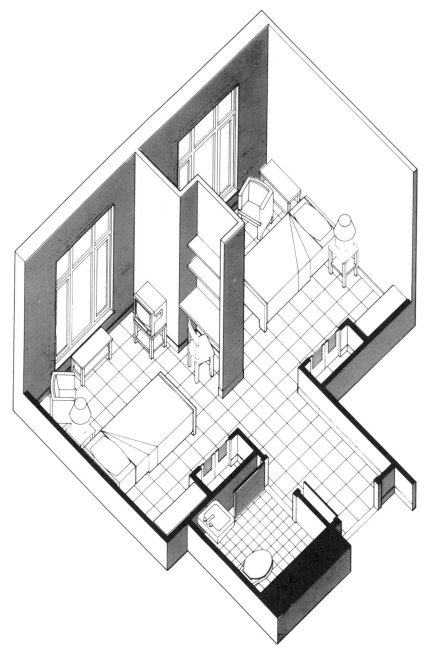

Joseph L. Morse Geriatric Center, West Palm Beach, Florida. View of semiprivate rooms. (Architect: Perkins, Geddis & Eastman Architects)

nity for each individual should replace the primary emphasis on custody and enforced socialization currently in many long-term and congregate settings. While it is important to counter loneliness, inactivity, and other common problems of the elderly, there must be an opportunity for the individual to have private space even in the traditional semiprivate room. That is why we use a special plan for this type of shared room, illustrated by the Joseph L. Morse semiprivate room.

We need to continue to rethink the typical rooms and residential units we design for our elderly. We need to experiment with room types based on more residential and hospitality industry traditions. The all-suite hotel is one example that holds promise.

We must take a critical approach to existing and proposed codes and standards. They have become a straightjacket, enforcing many of the wrong priorities. In many states the permitted area where an older person will live out his or her life is only 20 square feet larger than that mandated for a maximum-security prisoner. At 100 square feet, it is less than the overnight space in a hotel for a typical business traveler.

Other key elements of senior housing must also be rethought. Devoting 8 feet for the width of corridors is an inordinate waste of space in facilities where space is at a premium. Traditional corridors design and code requirements should be challenged and the space gained should be made part of the useful living space.

The design of common areas—the concept of a main street or community center—should also look beyond institutional traditions. These areas should become lively, attractive destinations where residents can interact and families come together. This has been an objective in each of the Main Streets we have developed in our projects, including the May Visitors Center at Miami Jewish Home and Hospital for the Aged, as well as Morse and Montefiore.

In such settings, the relationship to the outside—scent gardens, water features, and shaded settings in some climates, and winter gardens in the north—are important as well. ∎

46/Designing for Special Needs of the Elderly

Susan G. Drew

Good design for seniors takes the best in conventional housing and subtly tailors it to their special needs. Buildings can have a residential atmosphere and yet accommodate aging residents who are or will be experiencing diminishing physical dexterity. The design details are the most influential: lighting, floors, building and site organization, variety and architectural richness.

ADAPTING TO VISION CHANGES

Aging eyesight affects our ability to perceive depth, discriminate details, and distinguish colors. Decreased peripheral vision and lessened ability to discern color differences can make steps disappear. To move surely, older residents need high general illumination levels and a lighting design that avoids distractions.

Prevention of glare is key. Glare caused by windows at the end of a hallway, a strong light source, or light spilling across a corridor from an open doorway can confuse an elderly person and obscure definition of the space. By considering texture, window location, and diffused light, and by carpeting hallways, we can reduce glare dramatically.

Since the aging eye adjusts to light slowly, sudden junctures of light and dark should be avoided. Moving from a dim corridor into a bright room, or from the outside into a dark lobby, can cause momentary blindness that obscures the edge of a rug or a step. Give the eye time to adjust; a softly lighted vestibule between the corridor and a bright room, or "porch lights" that raise the lighting level act as a transition zone. Changes in floor level should be postponed until eyes have had a chance to adjust.

LAYOUT AND ORIENTATION

Building layout can be confusing if signage alone signals specific floors and rooms. Residents with vision problems, perhaps also with decline in some other senses or memory loss, need as many location indicators as possible.

Sameness and repetition are the chief sources of disorientation. Similar layouts and a regular pattern of doors give elderly residents

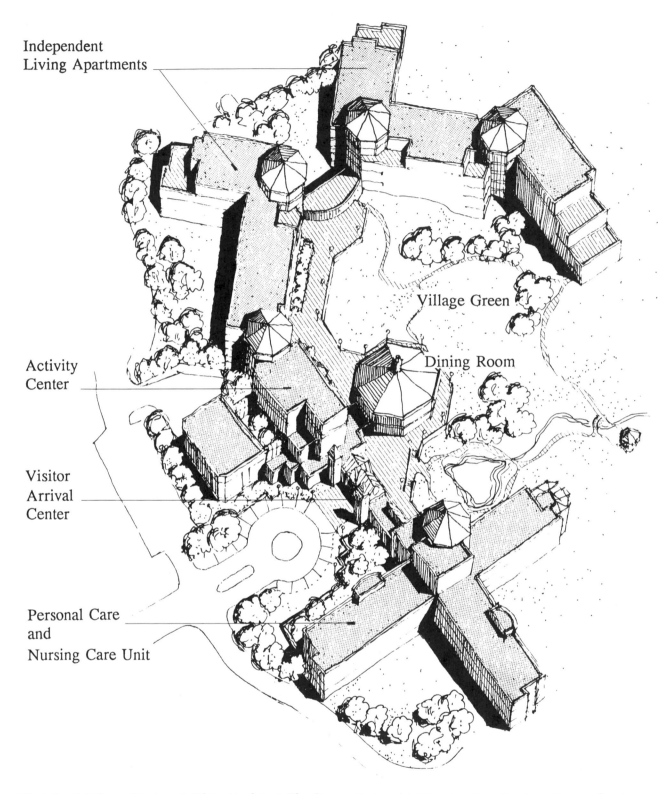

Independent
Living Apartments

Village Green

Activity
Center

Dining Room

Visitor
Arrival
Center

Personal Care
and
Nursing Care Unit

West Creek Village, Cincinnati, Ohio. (Architect: The Gruzen Partnership/Drawing: Ivan Ilyashov, Gruzen Samton Steinglass Architects)

Maple Knoll Village, Springdale, Ohio. (Architect: The Gruzen Partnership/Photo: Bo Parker)

no cues to distinguish one room from another. Creating variety in lobbies, corridors, and entries helps to identify the spaces. One wing of a building might appear different from another. Distinguishing features help: a special space on each floor near the elevator; distinctive furniture; clear signage and color coding; personalization with photographs or pictures.

Some organization helps orientation: an easily identified main entrance, a distinct vertical core, and clustered activity spaces. Windows with outdoor views give a clue to location. Internal windows, from a corridor into a common space, allow residents to identify the space without disturbing its occupants.

Multiple indicators of location work best. For example, in elevators, visual indicators can be reinforced with audible tones; clear signage can be augmented by sculpture, paintings, or architectural features; and both the lighting and the handrail shape can alert the pedestrians to steps. Music or sounds from the activity room or fragrances of baking from the dining rooms offer additional signals.

ENCOURAGING MOBILITY

Designers can promote an image of activity even to those who have diminishing strength and endurance, narrowing range of motion, decreasing muscular control, and reduced reaction time. Opportunities for exercise can be built in. Housing for the elderly should go beyond barrier-free to actually encourage mobility. The key is to create lively destination places and provide supportive access to them. The incorporation of common spaces—hobby and game rooms, coffee shops, gardens, lounges—provides the opportunity to focus on active social places. By grouping them together, the designer can create a special place that will attract residents. A location near heavily used places, such as dining areas, mailboxes, or entrances, and a configuration that allows glimpses of the activities, will encourage drop-ins without forcing participation.

Making these activity centers easily accessible will also ensure their use: seats in elevator lobbies and at intervals along hallways or walkways; restrooms periodically placed; areas of interest along the way. Elevators and self-closing doors should be timed for the elderly's reaction time. The distance to activity centers should suit the residents: a retirement complex might have a centralized clubhouse, while a nursing home would have a more local center.

ELIMINATING BARRIERS

For those with limited mobility, the environment can be filled with hidden barriers. Subtle problems with floors, sidewalks, doors, stairs, and even ramps, which escape the designer's notice, can trip up an elderly person who has a slow, shuffling, tentative gait. Doors can be an obstacle. Hinging systems should require less strength to open—sometimes automatic doors or two-leaf doors are appropriate. Siting, building height, and massing can create wind traps that put pressure on outward swinging doors unless they are shielded by overhangs and checkwalls.

Barrier-free standards focus on wheelchairs, but architects also should recognize that the elderly often use walkers, have diminished strength, control, and reach, and may grab household fixtures for support.

With aging comes loss of dexterity and strength, often compounded by arthritis. Manipulation of switches, knobs, buttons, and controls becomes more difficult, especially if they require precise finger movements. Devices that respond to the palm or an arm, such as lever-type door handles and push-button light switches, are preferred, and they should be located to allow the chairbound and ambulatory resident to operate them without bending or stretching.

RETAINING CHOICES

In retirement housing, seniors look to their local environment for personal experience, activities, and sense of community. Buildings and grounds need to provide richer detail and more spatial variety than conventional housing complexes. Places to pursue special interests, alternative pathways, personalized units —all serve to increase a person's sense of control and feeling of home.

The need for variety isn't limited to apartment or cottage dwellers. More severely disabled residents who may spend a great part of the day in a chair or bed still should retain as much command over their surroundings as possible. The capacity to personalize their rooms is important. The placement and choice of window can respond to a range of needs: mullions positioned to preserve the view of a seated or reclining resident; shallow exterior windowsills to allow a seated person to look down to the street; and openings designed for operation with minimum strength from a chair. Ideally, in nursing homes the majority of environmental controls should be within reach of the bed.

Thoughtful design and landscaping of housing for the elderly can go far to satisfy older residents, but good management must supply the services and amenities and set a tone of respect, support, and active community. Today, architects, operators, and developers are working together to recognize the special needs of senior housing: to improve the living environment of the elderly; to prolong their independence; and to afford them a greater degree of control in their daily lives. ∎

47/Intimacy, Nooks, and Cues

Lynn Tamarkin Syms

My initial insight is that the nursing home frequently comprises the whole universe for many residents. Often that universe is confined to the floor where the resident lives. That world should be as diverse as possible—not only to increase stimulation and response to surroundings, but to create more interesting places for working staff.

My solution is to break space visually into small areas. Furniture groupings are made for groups not to exceed six people; lamps stand on tables to lessen the need for ceiling lights, and furniture is scaled consistent to the smaller stature of the average older person. Fabrics have varying textures, and hues are pleasing to the eye and hand. Reception desks should be compatible, with a low section where the wheelchair person can establish comfortable eye contact.

NOOKS

On residents' floors, most plans begin with a central core, usually the nurses' station. Such plans encourage long, straight corridors unrelieved by any architectural significance. A "spoke" or "hub" configuration relieves that confinement. Where possible, I will use the smallest scrap of unused space, even an indentation in a wall, to create a stopping point as a resting place. It should accommodate a chair or wheelchair. With an attractive wall lamp, a picture, and wallcoverings, you have a place to pause in a long corridor.

MEMORY CUES

Residents often fail to identify their wing or even their rooms. Color alone does not give sufficient identification. Different colors are

Duncaster, Bloomfield, Connecticut. (Photo: Dianne Davis)

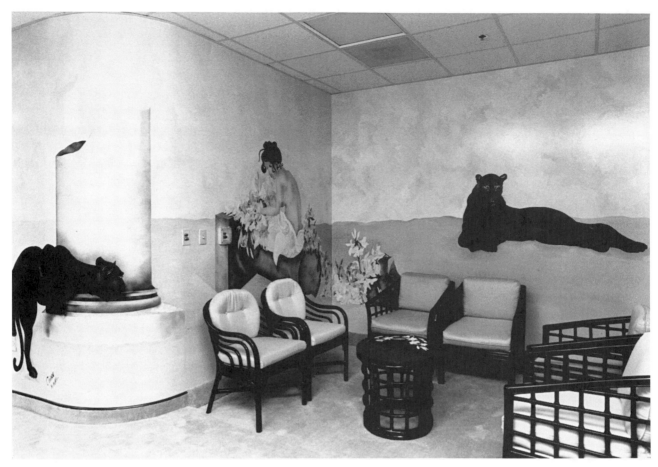

The Miami Heart Institute, Radiology Department, Miami, Florida. (Artist: Oriente Davila/Photo: Courtesy of the Miami Heart Institute)

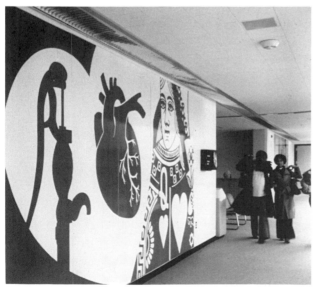

Outpatient Department, Boston City Hospital, Boston, Massachusetts. (Graphic Designer: Malcolm Grear Associates/Photo: Malcolm Grear Associates)

helpful, but art—a painting, a statue, a construction, a hanging quilt or tapestry—is a stronger cue. Outside residents' rooms, I have found that simple geometric shapes—different from one another, but not so diverse as to create visual chaos—may make a personal "tackboard" of color and texture for a memory cue. Another device is an old-fashioned picture frame fastened to the wall by hinges; inside, one sees personal snapshots, small mementos, a name, and room number.

At the opposite side, memory is linked to learning. In one large hospital area, where children assemble for multiple transfusions that last four to six hours at least once a week, focus and gaiety are wanted. On its white walls, painted scenes will challenge a young mind: individual scenes tell a story, or teach numbers and letters. ■

48/Fifty Points of Responsive Design

Architectural Design Considerations

"The average age of a retirement housing resident in this country is 81. Let's remember who we're designing for."

1
Recessed entry. Provides unit identity. breaks long corridor image.
2
Convenience shelf in corridor at entry. Place to set package when getting out key. Useful for resident displays.
3
Circulation spaces 3'–4" minimum wide. Allows easy movement of wheelchairs/walkers.
4
36" entry door with viewer, number, and name holder. Wide door for furniture movement, good security; no door chain allows emergency entry.

5
Door hardware to minimize accidental lock-out. Use of concave key cylinder allows insertion of key by unsteady resident.
6
Lever handle hardware at all doors. Easily operated by persons with limited dexterity.
7
Raised panel doors with matching bifold doors at closets. Use handles; no knobs or mirror units. More residential character, easier to operate.
8
Insulated-glass at window. Extended window sill for display. Hardware easily operated. Combination door/window unit if access to outside required.

9
Low pile carpet with thin pad. Deep pile causes tripping.
10
Large storage area for multiple uses.
11
Adjustable shelves for flexible storage arrangement.
12
Full length mirror on door for checking full height appearance.
13
Self-cleaning range/oven with front controls. Timer device to prevent accidental use past 1 hour. Front controls limit accidents caused by reaching over hot surfaces.

14
Frost free refrigerator with automatic ice maker. Manual ice trays difficult for older adults.
15
Cabinet above refrigerator moved forward for accessibility/useability.
16
Top of wall cabinets not above 7'–0". Higher cabinets inaccessible.
17
Kitchen base cabinets with roll-out shelves. Limits bending to reach contents.
18
Counter surface of a light color. Contrast easier for persons with reduced eyesight.
19
Allow for microwave and dishwasher options in kitchen. Consistent with appliances residents may desire.

20
Pass-thru shelf with shutters between kitchen and dining. Provides view from kitchen, allows close off from dining.
21
Cushion sheet vinyl in kitchen and bath. Softer and warmer to walk on. Important to people with reduced circulation.
22
Wood finish cabinets at kitchen and bath. Residential character more acceptable to resident.
23
Bathroom door, minimum of 2'–8", swings outward for access in emergencies. Makes circulation in bathroom easier.

24
Recessed medicine cabinet on side wall full frameless mirror over vanity makes room seem larger. Avoiding recessed cabinets in common walls improves sound control between units.
25
Towel racks with grab bar stability. Prevents accidents caused by grabbing towel bars not able to support such weight.
26
Five adjustable shelves at linen closet. Provides flexible storage of towels/linens.

Mechanical/Plumbing/ Electrical Considerations

"Understanding the real issues ... a prerequisite to making good ideas into good buildings."

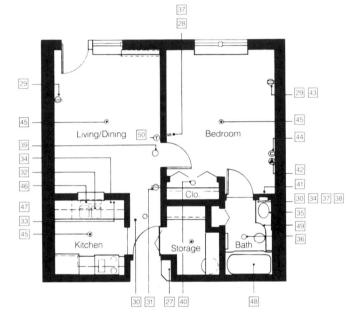

27
Accent light above or side of entry door. Identifies unit. Minimizes overhead lighting. Improves corridor image.

28
Electrical receptacle wired to switch at entry and at bedroom door. Allows turning on table lamps before entering room.

29
Mount electric outlets 16" above floor. Limits bending.

30
Place TV/cable outlet on each wall in living room to permit flexible furniture arrangement.

31
Convenience receptacle in hall. Allows lamp on small table.

32
Task lighting above counters in kitchen reduces shadows caused by ceiling fixture. At dining area ceiling, use light track wired to dimmer switch for flexible table location.

33
Garbage disposal switch remote from unit. Prevents accidental use when hands are near unit.

34
Special receptacle at bath and kitchen sink prevents accidental shock.

35
Wall mounted incandescent light over bathroom mirror for good illumination. Provides better light than medicine cabinet light and fewer shadows than overhead fixture. Better for putting on makeup.

36
Ceiling heat lamp wired with timer switch. Supplemental heat for persons with less tolerance to cold after bathing.

37
Illuminated switches at bedroom and bathroom lights. Ease of identification at night.

38
Bath exhaust fan switch separate from light switch. Avoid fan sound except when needed.

39
Ceiling mounted smoke detector (wired, not battery) outside of bedroom door. Best location for detection and limits false alarms. Second unit could be in bedroom for added safety.

40
Overhead light for increased visibility in bedroom closet. Improves visibility of wardrobe for persons with decreased eyesight and color perception. Rod @ 60" for long dress.

41
Nightlight/receptacle. Improves night time visibility.

42
Telephone outlet on bath side of bedroom. Avoids walking around bed to reach telephone.

43
No switched outlet at bedside because of use of clock radios. Switched outlet more useful for table lamp on opposite wall.

44
Emergency call switch at 24" above floor in bath, 48" in bedroom. Switch can be operated from bed or bathtub where most emergency calls originate.

45
Semi-recessed sprinkler heads. Improves aesthetics of residence.

46
Individual water heater if needed. "Low-boy" type to maximize storage availability.

47
Double bowl sink with single lever faucet set and sprayer. Single lever allows easier control of water temperature for resident with reduced dexterity.

48
Fiberglass tub and shower unit with slip resistant finish, integral grab bars. Fold-down seat in tub. Integral seat in shower. Sliding doors in lieu of curtain for safety. Lever type shower control with pressure balance anti-scald system @ 4'-0" above floor. Detachable spray wand. All items intended to facilitate easy and safe bathing.

49
Wood vanity with top @ 2'-8" and extension over toilet tank. Lavatory with single lever faucet set, storage rack on cabinet door. Provides increased counter space, storage accessibility and ease of lavatory use.

50
Thermostat with large numerals at 48" above floor. Mount next to door frame to keep wall clear for artwork.

49 / Some Practical Observations

Stephen R. Roizen

Retirement housing cannot be built with an expectation of redecorating every two or three years. Since the population is relatively long-term and stable, decor must not be too flamboyant or high-fashioned, and it must be serviceable. Classic regional design is safe and generally appreciated by the senior population. Washable, easy-care environmental surfaces are a must.

Hospitality in a retirement community takes on a new time dimension. Residents have a great deal of time. Unlike a hotel lobby, where transient guests sit only long enough to wait for a limousine or a guest's arrival, residents may sit for hours awaiting mail, talking, seeing the flow of people, playing a card game, or working in the craft room. Comfort and function become important.

Seats must be designed to comfortably fit a 5-foot-tall, aging woman for long periods of time. They must be easy to glide when at a table, with washable seat upholstery (we may occasionally have stress incontinence) and arms that ease getting up and sitting down. If this sounds like a vinyl geriatric chair from a nursing home catalogue, avoid it, and avoid sofas with big overstuffed pillows. Attractive seating exists.

Chairs should be straight-backed, for the most part. They should have just enough cushioning to reduce the hardness of a wooden seat. They should not have plush, overstuffed seat or back cushions, which tend to sink the user into the chair, causing poor posture, resulting in back pain, and making rising difficult without assistance. Sofas, as a rule, do not work well for the elderly. Again, cushions sink in, and a sofa's arms are not available to support the elderly person in seating and exiting from the seat.

To promote socialization, especially among residents spending extended time in one area, both acoustics and lighting need special consideration. Background noise offends the aging ear and especially offends residents who use hearing aides. Sound that is "normal" background, or "white noise" to a younger person, gets magnified and distorted by a hearing aid, making certain areas unbearable. While aesthetically pleasing, a decorative water fountain can disturb an older adult. Background noise bothers, and added to that stress is running water's tendency to urge relief of the bladder. A person with normal stress incontinence can find a fountain a major obstacle to enjoying an otherwise delightful area.

Lighting can cause difficulties for the aging eye. The aged eye dims vision and fades colors' brightness. Pastels and soft colors should be chosen with care and used in areas where there is adequate bright (but not glaring) light. When exposed without proper reflectors and shades, fluorescent lighting can be harsh and irritating. Pools of light can distort height and depth, causing stumbling or tripping.

Mealtime is an especially important time for the elderly in a retirement community. Anticipated all day, it is an opportunity to get nicely dressed and to see other residents, to gossip, and to enjoy good food. If the ambiance is not conducive to socialization, if it offends because of noise or lighting, then the most delicious cuisine will not make mealtime a pleasant experience.

A series of small dining rooms works well. Different locations, shapes, and sizes promote a feeling of warmth and intimacy, reduce noise and give flexibility for serving small groups of people. In a retirement community where the resident has a choice of either lunch or dinner, generally, the majority come to the evening meal. In a large dining room with only a few residents for the noontime meal, the space seems cavernous and the atmosphere can become tense and uncomfortable. Moving the seating into a smaller dining room, where nearly all the tables are utilized, may make the noontime meal a more pleasant experience for the residents.

While apartments must be comfortable, spacious, and provide larger kitchens than any retiree will ever use, the apartment is almost secondary to the existence of the community. This may be a bit of an exaggeration, but the community space is tremendously important as an extension to the apartment. ∎

50/Regional Expression

Albert Bush-Brown

Some of the most hospitable recent health-care architecture is designed to express regional character and to blend with neighboring historic buildings.

Picking themes from St. Augustine's Romanesque Spanish style, Florida's Flagler Medical Center introduces tiled roofs, elongated vertical proportions, and a hanging oriel. The wooden domestic architecture of New Jersey's Cape May is reflected in the Victoria Manor Retirement Facility. Near Roseburg, Oregon, a congregate care center, Linus Oakes, recalls regional barns, houses, and ranches. A house in Gladwyne, Pennsylvania, designed about 1910 by the Philadelphia architect, Frank Furness, was converted to a guest center, and its garden and treed alley are prefaces for the new senior residential wings. The

Linus Oaks, Roseburg, Oregon. (Architect: Sonderstrom Architects/Photo: Courtesy of Sonderstrom Architects)

St. Catherine's Village, Madison, Mississippi. (Architect: Cooke, Douglass and Farr Architects/Photo: John O'Hagan)

Sarasota Memorial Psychiatric Center, Sarasota, Florida. (Architect: Hansen Lind Meyer, Inc./Photo: Phil Eschbach)

interior and exterior of Ambulatory Services II at Boston's Brighams & Women's Hospital recall the rhythmical bay windows of Boston's Back Bay.

Such stylistic expression and reflection of the old in the new can capture domestic scale and offer a special appeal to the prospective, usually local, applicant for residence. Stylistic expression also offers interesting architectural detail and encourages lively massing and silhouette. By harmonizing the new institution with its context, reflecting the scale, rhythms, and stylistic themes of neighboring streets, an institution can foster a sympathetic relationship to the community.

Properly presented, regional expression may offer a marketing theme. A California retirement village with a Mediterranean theme names its pavilions after various Greek islands. The architectural firm that nimbly captured the Southwestern village character at La Posada, along the Santa Cruz Valley south of Tucson, Arizona, also designed a retirement community for Taunton, Massachusetts, where they succeeded in gaining the sense of a New England village. Chimneys and gables are interspersed along a row of stepped façades arranged to form a landscaped commons, with a clock tower marking the commons building. That firm also gave a distinctively Floridian, yet modern character to Abbey Delray South at Delray Beach, Florida, completed in 1982. ■

Part VI

Hospitable Models

More than a dozen examples of hospitable design and services are illustrated in this section. What can be learned from Miami's Baptist Hospital? From Caretel? From the Corrinne Dolan Alzheimer Center? How to organize an adult day-care center? Hospice? ICU and nurses station?

51/Hotel Services for Healthcare

Robert B. Rees

Today it is not enough to provide quality medical care; the public also expects quiet, comfort, and amenities. Hospitals have an average cost per day of $500, whereas hotels charge approximately $125. How can we surround excellent medical care with service and settings comparable with the best hotels?

At Baptist Hospital of Miami, our basic goal has always been to provide clinical care in a hospitable environment. When, in 1958, Mr. Arthur Vining Davis provided a million dollars and land to build Baptist Hospital, his gift carried a stipulation: The Hospital should resemble, believe it not, the Boca Raton Country Club. For four decades we've tried to do that. Davis was visionary. He believed sick people need not only a quality facility, but that they need to be cared for in a friendly, comfortable, and nonclinical environment.

We created a physical facility that resembles a premier hotel, and we've received a national award for our landscaping and been featured in *Architectural Digest*, *Newsweek*, and other journals. The entire facility has a tile roof, stucco walls, and driveways lined with palm trees. Even our Emergency Department, built in 1984, was designed for patients' satisfaction, privacy, and comfort. When patients enter, they don't go first to a register requesting billing information or to a treatment room; they enter a lobby with a large skylight and are seen by a volunteer and a triage nurse. Patients are treated in private rooms, and those who must wait for X-rays and tests have television sets and may order luncheon.

Since 1979, we've embarked on an $84 million renovation and building program, always keeping in mind Baptist's need to look and act like a fine hotel. A recent addition, Lake Pavilion, is a $22 million rehabilitation and obstetrics center. It introduces our best amenities program. The obstetric patient is usually healthy and enjoys hotel services. Eight labor

Baptist Hospital of Miami, Miami, Florida. Birth Center "hotel suite." (Architect: The Ritchie Oganization/ Interior Designer: Lisa Alvarez/Photo: Medical Services, courtesy of Robert Rees)

and delivery rooms, with recovery room, are in the "LDR/hotel," where examination lights and other apparatuses are concealed to preserve the domestic atmosphere. In each of 48 private rooms, an armoire encloses a remote control color TV, a stereo, a VCR, and a refrigerator stocked with sodas and sparkling water. Each window is also a door opening to a private balcony. Wall sconces and the furniture were custom made, including a sleep chair for the father, if he'd like to stay overnight.

We offer candlelight dining every evening on two large patios located in the same building. A gourmet menu offers lobster, steak, or whatever the patient selects, and dinner is served on fine china in a private setting. Our chef, Jose, prepares the gourmet meals, and our hostesses serve them in our VIP rooms. Room service is also available, ten hours a day; the patient needs only to call our hostess and the order will arrive within twenty minutes.

We developed our first VIP room in 1985. We took a normal four-bed patient room and changed it into our first VIP setting, an individual bedroom, with a living room and a folding bed, a remote-control TV, and a separate dining area with a refrigerator and sink. We are now building 36 similar rooms at Baptist. The bedroom portion of our new VIP suite has wood molding along the ceiling, full-length mirrors, marbled counters, portable phones, maid service, and prime-time movie channels; continental breakfast arrives with *The Wall Street Journal*. A computer terminal is provided in each room for the executive who would like to work during recovery. A patient guidebook introduces services, a hotel idea we decided to develop for Baptist. It provides names and numbers to call for room service, gourmet meals, TV services, or whatever you'd like to have in the hospital, such as dry-cleaning service. We offer gift certificates that visitors can buy for patients to use in our dining rooms and gift shop.

What more will make our patients feel like hotel guests? We may invest $200 million in the hospital, but if we don't teach our employees good guest relations, we've achieved nothing. Several years ago, we started giving our 2700 employees a six-hour guest-relations training program, again an idea we got from the hotel industry. Our employees are urged to respect our patients' privacy; it's simply a matter of being respectful, caring, and responsive.

At Baptist, the lodging complex is a 31-unit apartment building for our outpatients or our inpatients' families and visitors. A volunteer service shuttles patients back and forth between the lodging and our main campus.

What will we do in the future? We believe that successful hospitals will provide quality care in a hotel setting. We'll recruit people and ideas from the hotel, motel, and restaurant industries.

Baptist Hospital of Miami, Miami, Florida. Typical semiprivate room. (Photo: Medical Services, courtesy of Robert Rees)

Baptist Hospital of Miami, Miami, Florida. Gourmet meals. (Architect: The Ritchie Organization/Interior Designer: Lisa Alvarez/Photo: Medical Services, courtesy of Robert Rees)

And we will market our services and facilities. Baptist has recorded its first commercial, a 30-second TV spot airing in the Miami area: "When you're away from home. Luxurious accommodations with all the amenities that you want and expect. Lush, tropical walkways, beautiful surroundings, intimate gourmet dining at sunset, and of course, time with the family. The New Family Birthplace at Baptist Hospital. Five-star treatment without a five-star price. For reservations, be sure your obstetrician is on the Baptist Hospital staff. Call The Baptist Hospital Physician Referral Service 596-6557."

We believe the successful hospital will provide hotel services in a hospitable setting. At Baptist of Miami, we will continue to seek ideas and people to improve the hotel comforts for our guests undergoing medical treatment. ■

52 / Welcome and Guest Services

Dianne Davis

A patient within a healthcare community needs various kinds of communication to sustain both a sense of individuality and a feeling of membership.

GUEST SERVICE DIRECTORY

The "welcome" pamphlet or brochure is an important introduction. To be sincere and informative, the booklet may take the form of a guest services directory, familiar in some hotels. Miami Baptist Hospital in Miami, Florida, distributes *Patient Guide*. The Healthcare Medical Center of Tustin, California, gathers information within a well-designed jacket, with an index to a cascade of pages devoted to guest services. It includes a financial program

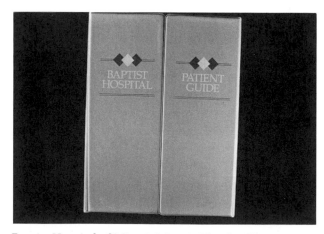

Baptist Hospital of Miami, Miami, Florida. The cover of the patient guide.

named *Healthline*: information about interpreters, the women's auxiliary services, gift shop, mail, flowers, and the laundry and valet; dining room hours for meals; food and nutrition; meditation and prayer room; patient representative; social services; and "hot line," all printed in large type.

How guests may use telephones, television, and radio, and how they may obtain newspapers and other literature are described on one page that also describes a book cart that is a free service brought to the patient's room by dialing one of two extension numbers.

Transportation, parking, safe storage of valuables, lost and found, and air-conditioning —a mixed array—are described on one page, followed by financial information, billing, and notary service. The welcome pamphlet ends with requests for an evaluation of the patient's experience (form provided) and some comments about employee recognition and visitor information.

A separate folder, a good marketing tool, explains Room Service (at no extra charge) and the menu. Like its companion directory to secretarial services and hotel accommodations for family members, the entire booklet reinforces the goal of a medical center: ". . . caring for your comfort is just as important as caring for your health. . . . An environment similar to a fine hotel while you receive high quality medical treatment," sums up the objectives of the Tustin Healthcare facility.

Columbia Presbyterian Hospital in New York City publishes its *Bedside Guide* in separate editions of Spanish and English. Among several informative paragraphs are sections devoted to a future expansion and opportunities for making donations. The statement of a patient's bill of rights consists of nineteen carefully worded points. They include the rights to privacy and confidentiality of records, the right to designate an assigned private accommodation a nonsmoking area, and the right to ex-

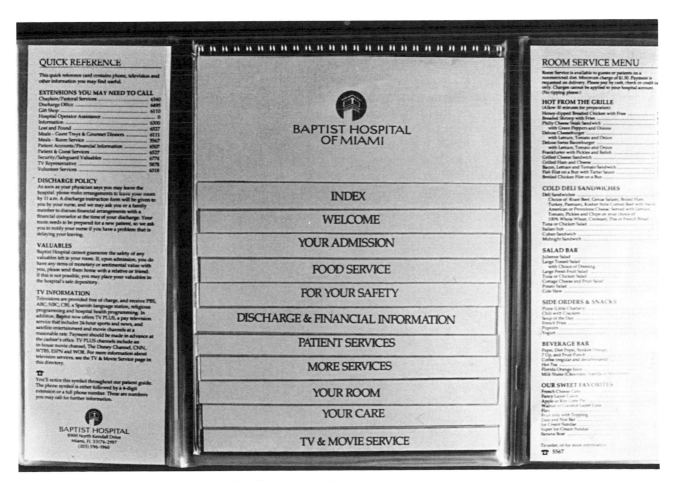

Baptist Hospital of Miami, Miami, Florida. The patient guide open.

press complaints and receive written responses.

The welcome booklet for Rhode Island Hospital in Providence introduces both the hospital and its link to the city's cultural heritage. In clear sentences and large type, the booklet states policies about admission, proscription against smoking, use of television and telephone, a 15-point patient's bill of rights, and sections showing the availability of banking services, visiting hours, food services, clergy and chapel, interpreters, blood center, records, and, inevitably, the hospital bill. All this information is bound within a cover that bears a reproduction of Claude Monet's *Le Bassin d'Argenteuil*, a painting owned by the Rhode Island School of Design's museum, whose donors, the Metcalf family, have been generous contributors to the hospital as well.

HOSPITALITY-ORIENTED SERVICES

Often a room has been cleaned while a guest is absent. Upon returning, the guest finds a housekeeping tentcard indicating that the room was "tidied and checked while you were away and if anything is needed, contact 'Carol' at number 971."

Two innovative concepts are changing the traditional hospital welcome; Miami Heart Institute's Ambassador Service and Tustin Medical Center's Unique Resource Center are examples of modified hotel services. In Orange County, California, Tustin's Resource Center successfully blends traditional hotel concierge services, health education, and physician referrals, conveniently located in the main hospital lobby. Besides providing assistance, the center has become an asset in marketing professional services.

Service Directories, amenities and housekeeping tent cards describe support services and help smooth a patient's stay. These organized, informative communications are appreciated by patients, visitors, and staff. They save time, eliminate repetitive questions, and assist

Healthcare Medical Center of Tustin, Orange County, California. (Photo: Stevan Porter)

in image building—communicating "we care." A directory of support services is a good marketing tool. It also frees nurses, telephone operators, and support staff to address important issues. ■

53/VIP Patient Suites

Karen Meyers Ziccardi

Hollywood Presbyterian Medical Center, at Costa Mesa, California, opened its deluxe VIP suite in 1988. Designed by Karen Meyers, president of Interior Design Development, Inc., it transformed an ordinary two-bed corner room into a first-class suite that has all the amenities of an elegantly appointed hotel suite: soft, upholstered furniture, lush carpeting, limited-edition art, and panoramic views of the Hollywood Hills. The suite accommodates a generous visitors' seating area with a separate television console and a sofa that converts to a comfortable bed.

Occupants of the VIP suite may subscribe to the Golden Pass Amenity Package, which includes a deluxe fruit basket delivered upon ar-

Hollywood Presbyterian Hospital, Hollywood, California. (Interior Designer: Interior Design Development/Photo: Milroy/McAleer Architectural Photography)

rival; selections from a "Get Well Gourmet" menu featuring dishes designed by celebrity chefs, meals served on fine china with elegant linens, crystal, and silverware; private direct-dial telephone; fresh flowers; luxurious bathrobe; deluxe toiletry items; free parking for guests; daily newspaper delivery; 24-hour visiting hours; visitor screening through the information desk; and daily visits from the hospital's patient representative, a clinical dietitian, and a member of the administrative staff.

The VIP suite concept, I believe, will become a valuable patient amenity package in the future. The success of this project indicates patient desire to select a highly individualized level of hospital accommodation and service. ■

54/Nurse Station and ICU

Herbert Bienstock with Janet Hays

The intensive care area of the Charlotte Hungerford Hospital in Torrington, Connecticut, is comfortable, airy, and spacious, thus easing the tensions of family, patients, and staff as they attend serious illness.

The plan, windows and lighting, colors, and ceiling arrangement are all coordinated to give the nurses and patients the highest possible degree of support.

The decentralized work stations, which bring nurses close to patients, ease healthcare tasks and comfort patients. Large windows in each patient room provide views to the outside and bring natural daylight into the work core of the unit; a ceiling fascia over the nurses' work area permits indirect uplighting, creating a sense of extra height and more light over the work. The blue fascia and pink soffit enliven an area that is often severe or mechanical. ■

55/Easy Street: A Definition

David A. Guynes

Easy Street represents an environmental approach to creating functional, motivational spaces for patients to practice daily living skills. The central therapeutic purpose is to simulate obstacles associated with life outside the home—in short, the urban landscape. This clinically driven idea has been around for decades; however, it has always been implemented without benefit of context. Easy Street places different kinds of activities within the context of modular components, and thus creates continuity between each separate element.

Each Easy Street Environment is designed uniquely for a specific location. The spatial considerations and clinical criteria are evaluated through a site survey. Anecdotal design elements represent the indigenous community. This, in effect, provides the recognizable visual context whereby the patient begins community reentry. Local landmarks and whimsical visual cues add to the dynamics of the space.

REHABILITATION ENVIRONMENT

On one level, Easy Street is a training environment, that is, an obstacle course with both physical and cognitive challenges. On another level, it is an environmental tool the therapist can use to motivate the patient during the long and often painful process of rehabilitation. The emphasis on functional outcomes is the key objective for the therapist, and it is central for the patient to regain the confidence and skills necessary to lead a full and productive life. Easy Street is a dramatic example of how motivation can be stimulated in an innovative and creative way. ∎

Easy Street. Model. (Designer: Guynes Design, Inc./Photo: Al Payne)

56/Magnetic Resonance Imaging

Wayne Ruga

A good example of hospitable design is the Imaging Room of the Castro Valley Magnetic Imaging Center, California, which contains an anxiety-provoking piece of diagnostic radiology equipment. Intended to enhance the quality of experience, the murals offer soothing, restful views to shift the patient's attention away from the forty-five-minute procedure that requires absolute stillness. ■

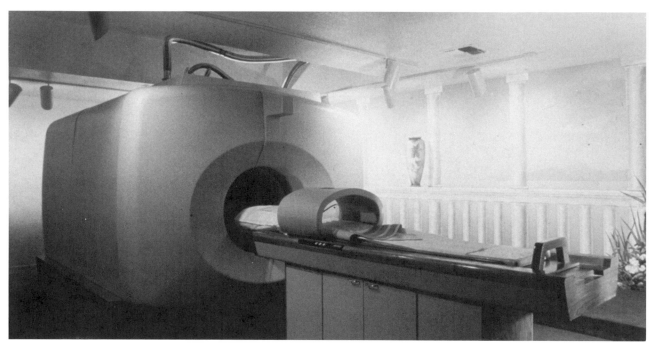

Magnetic Imaging Center, Castro Valley, California. (Designer: Jain Malkin, Inc./Photo: Colin McRae, courtesy of Wayne Ruga)

57/Corinne Dolan Alzheimer Center

Margaret P. Calkins

The Corinne Dolan Alzheimer Center was uniquely designed to provide a therapeutic environment that supports a creative program for people with Alzheimer's disease. Developed with the help of a grant from The Robert Wood Johnson Foundation, the center was designed by Stephen Nemtim of Taliesin Associated Architects. From the design and location of activity rooms to the type of bathtubs, each feature has been rigorously examined to meet the needs of people with Alzheimer's disease. Some guidelines were based on anecdotal experience, and the center is testing the effects of various building components.

The center consists of two identical units, separated by shared bathing and staff areas. Each unit's open plan enables one staff member to supervise the focal points for activity programs. A residential-style kitchen encourages residents to continue life-long domestic patterns. Standard-height counters and tables enable people to sit while working, and, though normally open for general participant access, the kitchen can be closed off to allow staff to prepare meals safely and efficiently.

Adjacent to the kitchen, the dining area is furnished with wheelchair-accessible matte-surface tables, designed to fit together in various configurations where residents can dine in familiar groups of one to six.

The hallway surrounding the kitchen and dining areas is critical. Wandering necessitates flow, without any dead-end corridors, and so-cialization is stimulated by making dining areas visible. Flexible dividers enable testing of the effects of various barriers or transparencies between the dining room and the halls.

The bedrooms arranged around the hall are furnished by residents and have Dutch doors that, while maintaining privacy, admit natural light into the central areas. The entrance to each bedroom has a display case for a resident's treasured mementos; that secure place for valuable personal items cues residents to their individual bedrooms. It also helps others to know and understand each resident better.

Located on each bedroom's exterior wall, the toilet is clearly visible from the doorway—an important cue for helping residents maintain continence.

While primary artificial light comes from low-glare uplighting, a large, curved window is the most striking architectural element in each room. Offering grace and elegance, it signals that residents are not living at home, but

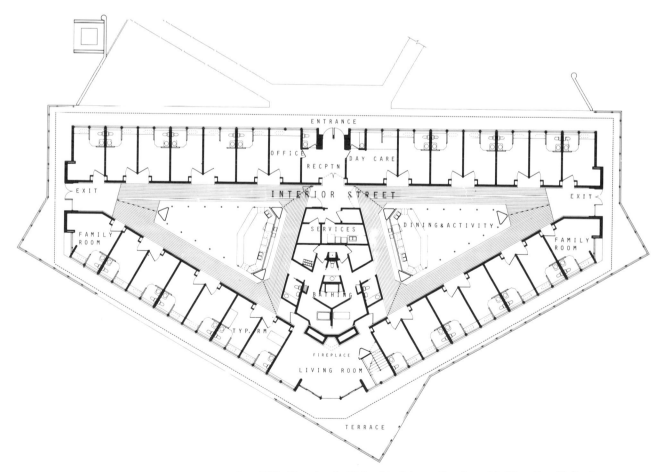

Corinne Dolan Alzheimer Center at Heather Hill, Cleveland, Ohio. (Architect: Stephen M. Nemtin, Taliesin Associates Architects, Frank Lloyd Wright Foundation)

rather in a pleasant, residential facility.

A gracious living room with a gas-log fireplace is one of four common program spaces. Within each unit, a family room is used by small groups and for family visitors. The fourth room is a craft room fitted for a variety of projects, including painting and woodworking.

Several small nooks for casual conversation and visiting are located adjacent to the exits, and the staff have a clear view of them. Each exit door is equipped with an access-control device, but is unlocked during clement weather, so residents can easily enter the park.

The two-acre, secured park is designed to provide a variety of activities and experiences. Adjacent to the walkway, the upper patio overlooking the garden has chairs and tables. There is a great variety: picnic tables, chairs near a curved garden wall, paths, woods, scenic views, and grassy areas where residents play croquet or practice putting. The gardens provide color and vibrancy year-round, and the plants are nontoxic. All paths circle to the main path so that participants explore in comfort. A variety of additional areas are planned: from a flagpole to a clothesline, from a hand pump to a small playground for children. ■

58 / Caretel®

Horace D'Angelo, Jr.

Now is the time to deinstitutionalize long-term healthcare facilities. No longer should they be merely clinically oriented institutions lacking life-enhancing amenities.

Peachwood Inn and Borden Court, the first healthcare facility built on the principles of Caretel®, combines the services of long-term care with hotel services. Based on the three components of Caretel: design, program, and management, Peachwood Inn and Borden Court provide hotel-style healthcare concerned with the physical and emotional well-being of the residents, families, and staff.

Set in the wooded, rolling landscape of Rochester Hills, Michigan, Peachwood Inn and Borden Court, with its gabled roofs, portico, and hand-carved wooden doors, presents the image of a conventional brick-and-stone country manor house, complete with chimneys and courtyards. Enclosed by the building's wings, the courtyards offer secure, beautifully landscaped and furnished areas for tranquil strolling, sitting, and the enjoyment of vistas. Intimate interior community spaces, many with fireplaces, give warm and friendly settings for visiting and other activities in spaces removed from the bedroom areas. As in

the hospitality industry, residents and guests may elect to spend their time in smaller, more private community rooms or to join others in the larger common areas.

The front lobby and reception desk resemble those of a fine hotel. Traditional furniture, fabrics, and wall coverings, combined with colors, such as peach, federal blue, teal, rose, and forest green, add to the homelike appearance. All rooms have outside walls; clerestories, skylights, and large windows admit abundant natural light. A hospitality director is charged with welcoming all new residents and their guests and sees to their comfort throughout their stay. The entire staff is trained in hotel-style hospitality skills.

Picadilly Lane, Peachwood's Main Street leading to the residential areas, is the shopping area. There, residents find Aunt Peach's Ice Cream Parlor, Etc. Gift Shop, Bogey's Movie Theater, Shearlock's Home (a hair salon), the Jenny Lind Guest Room, and the Bugatti Bar and Bistro. The Bugatti Bar and Bistro, named for the 1927 Bugatti parked outside its door, is a gourmet restaurant. The amusing shop names add levity to a variety of interesting and cheerful places to entertain residents' guests.

The lane promotes resident-to-resident friend-ships.

The shops, restaurants, and community areas give residents a chance to involve their families in their life at Peachwood or Borden Court. One of the hallmarks of Caretel is to give residents a choice of spaces and occasions for entertaining guests. An excellent example is the Bugatti Bar and Bistro. Its menu, the tuxedoed director of foodservice, and the bar/bistro's service and ambiance not only afford a pleasurable experience, but give the resident choices—"Shall I go? Who shall I invite? What shall I order?"—that stimulate independent thinking, planning, and socialization.

Another example of promoting family interest and participation is the Jenny Lind Guest Room. Decorated with Victorian antiques, the Jenny Lind Guest Room is Peachwood's hotel-style bed and breakfast for out-of-town family members.

Individually decorated bedrooms in the main facility are clustered in self-contained "neighborhoods" suggesting a community. All sleeping accommodations are on outside walls with large windows and window seats overlooking courtyards or the surrounding woods. Each room has a private bath with step-in shower. Residents are encouraged to add their own favorite furniture or memorabilia. There is a choice of ten room styles, which range from moderately priced accommodations to luxurious suites. Wing walls in the multiple-person rooms add to each resident's privacy. Brass nameplates at the doors reinforce identity, the idea of ownership, and individuality. All hallways are short and end in flared areas that contain seating. These spaces provide yet another place for privacy or quiet conversation. The nursing stations, located centrally in each wing, resemble hotel concierge desks, reinforcing a nonmedical atmosphere.

As in fine hotels there are multiple dining rooms. Small, light, and airy, neighborhood dining rooms offer intimate seating areas. Table service prevails, and several dining rooms are available for private parties. One includes a kitchen where a resident may cook or bake for guests. These smaller dining rooms and the Bugatti Bar and Bistro allow the resident to entertain guests as they would in their

Peachwood Inn/Borden Court, Rochester Hills, Michigan. Picadilly Lane. (Architect: Hobbs & Black Associates, Inc./Photo: Beth Singer Photographer, Inc.)

homes. Encouraging the resident's self-esteem, independence, and vitality, the variety also gives them choices, a privilege that many lose in long-term-care facilities.

The family is essential to the success of the Caretel concept. If families find the surroundings comfortable and attractive, they are apt to visit more often and for longer periods of time. Combining the best of the hospitality industry with fine medical services is what has made Peachwood Inn and Borden Court a flagship of future healthcare facilities. ∎

59/Medical Center Inns and Hotels

Bruce I. Fisher and Ronald P. Steger

The "medical hotel" (also called a "recovery hotel") enables patients to recuperate under physicians' supervision in a nonhospital environment. Designed for patients who would otherwise be hospitalized, the medical hotel helps the transition from hospital to home.

The medical hotel responds to a vital need. It sharply reduces medical costs, opens critically scarce hospital beds, and relieves shortages. Additionally, since many surgical procedures that were done in hospitals can now be performed in an outpatient surgical center, the patient may need to be transferred to short-term care—the medical hotel.

A key component of the medical hotel is a "care partner." A prospective guest is encouraged to have a family member or friend live in and assist in caring for the guest's nonmedical needs. While not all guests will require such assistance, a care partner is encouraged to participate in order to involve family or friend and to educate them about the guest's illness and recovery process. This process alleviates apprehension that family members may otherwise feel when the patient returns home.

The medical hotel differs from a traditional hotel in that it provides unique services to guests with healthcare needs, including:

• Regular visits by their physician.
• Ancillary healthcare services ordered by their

New Haven Medical Hotel, New Haven, Connecticut. (Architect: Robert Wendler & Paul Pizzo, Architects)

attending physician, that is, nursing, physical therapy, laboratory, radiology, and other services as required.

- Lectures and discussions that address specific diagnoses, and a library of medically oriented videotapes available in a special health education center, which will be accessible to all guests and their families during their stay.
- A concierge/emergency medical technician stationed on each floor to attend to the guests' needs.
- Rooms built to accommodate the special needs of guests, including handicapped accessibility and emergency call devices.
- Two heated swimming pools, one of Olympic size, the other a hydrotherapy pool constructed with lifts and ramps.

Two types of patient are candidates for the medical hotel program:

- Medical or surgical hospital patients who no longer have acute-care needs, but are not yet medically ready to be discharged. These patients can complete the last few days of their recovery at the medical hotel where the nonhospital environment encourages the transition to independence and self-care. It is important to stress that the combined length of stay in the hospital and the medical hotel will not exceed the current average length of stay in the hospital.
- Patients who previously would have had surgery in a hospital setting now will be able to be admitted directly to the hotel after surgery in an outpatient facility, thereby completely avoiding an inpatient hospital stay.

The medical hotel is an innovative concept that will gain rapid acceptance.

A recent and growing development is the "hospital hospitality house," primarily for patients' families but also serving outpatients. The National Association of Hospital Hospitality Houses, Inc. has its headquarters in Muncie, Indiana. ■

60 / Lodging Facilities at the Cleveland Clinic Foundation

Joseph Franko

The campus of the world-renowned Cleveland Clinic Foundation (CCF) includes two hotels, comprising nearly 550 guestrooms, which are owned and operated by subsidiaries of CCF.

Occupying parts of a 48-block site, just east of downtown Cleveland, the hotels, about two blocks apart, are separated by the spacious, landscaped mall that is the center of the CCF campus.

The Clinic Center Hotel was built by a private hotel company in the early 1970s. Purchased by the Clinic in the early 1980s, it serves the Clinic's patients and professional staff. Offering 348 rooms, the hotel is a deluxe facility with first-class services that compete with other downtown hotels for the general public. Among its distinctive features is a penthouse floor of lavishly decorated suites with complete butler service. World famous celebrities, royalty, heads of state, and leading business, entertainment, and political figures have occupied the penthouse floor. The hotel also has a Regency floor with executive-class suites and valet service.

The hotel offers other services: room service, concierge, gift shop, shoe shine stand, a travel agency, express check-in and checkout, a national toll-free reservation system, valet parking, and three restaurants: a pub-style facility, a family-style coffee house, and the glamorous Classics, regarded as one of Cleveland's finest restaurants. Connection to the main clinic buildings and a parking garage is through an enclosed, climate-controlled skywalk.

Nearby, the Cleveland Clinic Guesthouse, opened in November 1988, has 200 units providing inexpensive lodging to patients and their families, with emphasis on long-term stays. While the Guesthouse offers no bell or room service, rooms are larger and more comfortably furnished than those in a commercial motel. One half include full kitchenettes, and twenty-four are two-room apartments. All floors include a lounge and game area, as well as laundry facilities. Adjacent to the Guesthouse, Cleveland Clinic's Cafe and Market offers seated or carryout dining, as well as "deli" items, baked goods, produce, meat, dairy, and canned goods, for the general public as well as those who are staying in the Guesthouse. ■

Cleveland Clinic Hotel, Cleveland, Ohio. (Architect: Whitley & Whitley/Photo: Courtesy of Cleveland Clinic Hotel)

61 / The Hospice

Mark Engelbrecht

The Hospice for Boca Raton, a small institution for the terminally ill, evolved out of three primary design objectives. First, the architects wanted the Hospice to express the concept of a "caring" community focused upon the well-being of its residents. To this end, a highly articulated family of forms was used to define the architecture.

Second, the design team wanted to explore the important relationship between the natural order and psychology of the hospice experi-

ence. An architecture carefully related to interior gardens and the wilder, natural surrounding landscape responded to this objective.

Finally, the forms and materials of the Hospice in Boca Raton reflect the indigenous domestic architecture of this historic community. This usage provides a continuity of environmental language that intends to link the Hospice to residential associations.

In addition to caring for patients who are

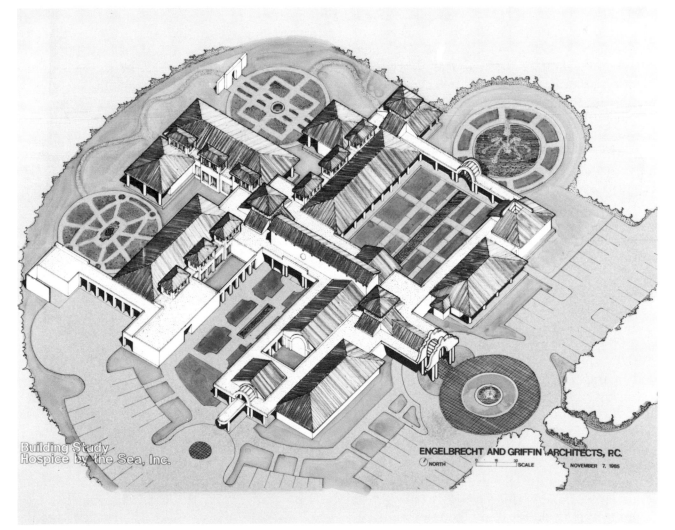

Hospice by the Sea, Boca Raton, Florida. (Architect: Engelbrecht & Griffin Architects)

expected to live no longer than six months, The Hospice by the Sea at Boca Raton offers ambulatory adult day care, home-care services, a children's day-care center, and an outdoor playground for employees' children. There are also family rooms with kitchenettes, an educational wing with a library and classrooms, a chapel for funeral and memorial services, and a room for bereavement counseling. Designed to be a cohesive group of connected buildings, the Hospice integrates diverse activities and offers views into varied gardens; several gardens are visible from terraces adjacent to patients' rooms. ■

62/Adult Day-Care Centers

Dianne Davis

For many families with elderly parents or relatives living with them, especially where both spouses work, the adult day-care center provides a reliable daytime agency. The centers offer professional supervision in a congenial setting with beneficial, recreational activities and at a cost less than alternatives, such as putting a parent in a nursing home or having private nurses in the family residence. A rapidly developing service, the adult day-care center meets the physical, emotional, and financial needs of America's fastest growing group, the dependent 80-year-old.

They offer care, friendship, amusement, and sociability to the frail or disabled who live at home and do not have or require 24-hour institutional care. Remaining independent, they form new friendships and renew activities, and their families feel secure about a friendly social center that cares and is medically competent. In addition, the adult day-care center promotes dignity, community ties, and sense of membership. Served by door-to-door shuttle vans, they are located in shopping centers, schools, hotels, and healthcare facilities.

To assure quality care and meaningful activity, a large, flexible open space is essential. It should support eight essential components: reception; staff/conference office and lounge;

nurses' observation/treatment room; multipurpose activity and quiet areas; kitchen; bathrooms; and storage. Their design should emphasize six features: freestanding, movable partition walls in the multipurpose space; a personal care (beauty salon) area; a dual-height island or counter near the kitchen; a carpeted "living room" and quiet area; an indoor "porch"; and, where possible, an enclosed garden; a walk-in shower; and, critically important, a twin laundry unit.

Some special items greatly enhance emotional satisfaction. Attractive plant containers, bird cages, gerbil boxes, and fish tanks stimulate interest and conversation. Sprouting a seed to flower is an engaging event; bulletin boards can display clients' art and activity photographs. The sense of expectation and belonging is increased by personalized mugs, scarves, and craft aprons. Noise caused by a TV's volume can be controlled with TV and radio headsets that give the hearing-impaired individual sound adjustment.

While *Planning and Managing Adult Day Care*, by Linda Cook Webb, provides detailed information, and the National Institute on Adult Daycare in Washington, D.C., offers a support network, the essential objectives are known: flexibility, essential for conducting diverse activities simultaneously; sensory cues;

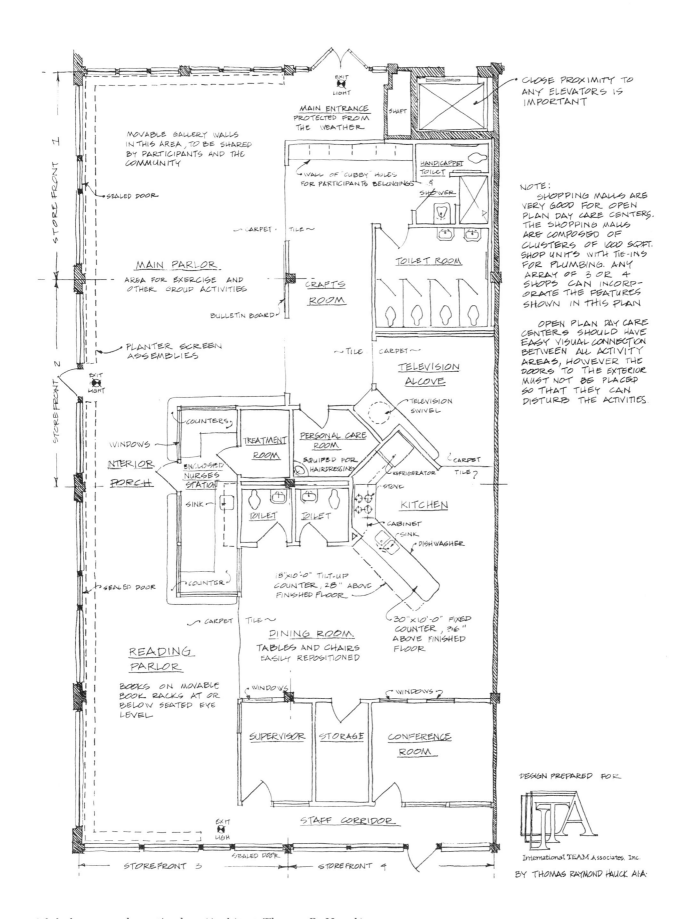

Adult day-care schematic plan. (Architect: Thomas R. Hauck)

opportunities for privacy as well as social interaction; and a warm, inviting, and stimulating homelike atmosphere. Clear signs are needed, and parking should be close to well-marked entrances.

Adult day-care centers provide a safe environment with a variety of health, social, and related support services, including leisure activities, exercise classes and, most of all, companionship. ■

Part VII

Special Design Features

Building upon the preceding essays—the shaping of space and spatial sequences to achieve privacies and memberships within active healthcare communities—Part VII offers practical, notably personal advice about horticulture, graphic design, lighting, color, acoustics, furniture and hardware.

63/Buds, Berries, and Branches: Gardens for All Seasons

Albert Bush-Brown

Many hospitals and nursing homes could be made more attractive if they attended to landscape design and horticulture. Barren parking lots, crude walkways, empty vistas, and ragged, pathetic plantings are neither hospitable nor necessary. Not much joy is inspired by battered trash cans, cement walks, and plastic greenery in a lobby. Even a small garden offers delight and a sense of caring. It does not have to be elaborate or sophisticated, and it need not be expensive to start or maintain.

It should, however, be imaginative and profound. Seasonal change should reveal manifold bounty: leaf and flower, then fruits and berries, followed by bare trunks and branches, and Spring's burst of buds and shoots. Seasonal response requires structure and variety. The pervasive institutional and suburban plantings do not respond. A clipped lawn, spreading junipers, yews, and other evergreens remain fairly constant all year. Spotting impatiens and marigolds along borders is a meager and wistful effort at coloring monotony. An evergreen border may be easy to maintain, but even the best ilex lack the changing leaf and fascinating branches of a Japanese maple or other deciduous trees. Even more rewarding is that imagery and depth which the celebrated English gardener, Gertrude Jekyll, achieved when she loaded garden beds with perennials' color, texture, and shape. "No soil should show, except in winter," she advised, and even then, I suspect, she preferred to see stalks, seed pods, and fallen leaves.

To design landscape is architectural. Trees are columns and roofs; plants and shrubs are walls and sculpture; and lawns and terraces are floors. Arranging them to form paths and nodes is spatial design, and it can be gained economically. Vistas and spaces can meander like a path through a meadow, or they can be formal rows and axes, like an orchard. In either case, they will be strengthened by hedges, walls, fences, gates, and trellises. White or split rail fences glide over the rolling pastures in Kentucky and Virginia, and New Englanders regularly restore the ancient ledge rock walls near Newport and the glacial granite walls in Cape Cod. Structures are especially important in winter. When trees are bare and stark, the sheltered terrace traps the sun. Even as a frozen pond glistens in the distance, a bench or chair will be warm and inviting, and the sunstruck wall that holds a vine will catch the shadow of an apple that has browned and puckered on its February branch.

Opening views and selecting glimpses to distant landscapes or buildings through a fence, wall, or hedge is the first act in siting a garden. A second is to locate flat places for terraces, benches, chairs, wheelchairs, and tables. A third is to invite the terrain itself to suggest the garden's shape: a stair and terraces to climb a hill; a pool, willow tree, and ferns to mark a swampy hollow; or heathers, chrysanthemums, birches, and Scotch pines to accent large rock outcroppings. Save the rocks. A jagged boulder nested in dark leaves thrives on rain and sun. Know the soils. An acidic soil brightens the oaks' and maples' reds, while a lime or sweet soil heightens the yellows of beeches and willows. Seek native and acclimated plants. The yuccas and cactuses that are dramatic in Arizona look silly in Vermont, and, however much a New Englander transplanted to Palm Springs or Palm Beach may yearn for them, the solitary elm and clumps of white birch in a New Hampshire intervale do not thrive on a desert or seashore. What grows wild near dumps and along highways may offer better clues to success with native plants and trees than any exotica proffered by the local nursery.

All gardeners have prejudices. My own run contrary to the costly gardens some hospitals and urban nursing homes try to develop. To aspire to a formal garden where clipped yews and topiary hemlocks are disposed symmetrically, with lawns, statuary, and reflecting pools, is to court high costs. It can also be very dull. I prefer wild, lush, free planting. I am little interested in lawns and have never emulated the golfer's green, but I delight in grasses, fields of them, with elegant stems, leaves, and seedheads—striped rushes, feather, barley, timothy, pampas, fescue, quaking, zebra, and orchard grasses—tall and waving, with poppies, daisies, Queen Anne's lace, brown-eyed Susans, buttercups, and red clover mixed in. Then mow paths through the meadow. Once seeded, cutting it once in July and again in October is all it takes.

While great effect comes from massing a bouquet of lupin here, striking a chord of roses there, and cascading ferns on a rocky bank beyond, purity and simplicity are not always admirable. A bramble of rambler roses, with Japanese or Siberian iris and several azaleas among them, all at the foot of a holly, offers surprises from spring well into summer. That is heresy to those gardeners who clip privet into spheres and cubes, and lay out neat rows of begonias and petunias. My wayward fancy for introducing errant beans, onions, rhubarbs, and carrots into beds of astilbe, hostas, and dahlias may offend (and bar my admission to respectable garden clubs); still, it draws admiration for its seemingly careless palette.

Many classic plant groupings are vivid. Lupins massed with foxgloves and delphiniums start the summer dramatically. Wild clematis, box, and yew are a subtler palette. Still subtler are grays and silvers struck with dusty miller, globe artichoke, and several herbs, accented by two low blue spruce birds' nests. A dark purple theme—tall beech, lower plums, and still lower barberries—best displays its seasonal maroons, pinks, and greens when keyed by golden junipers, or cypress, with a few notes of yellow euonymus and iris. The golden daffodils poets extol are hosted by woodland meadows, and Matthew's biblical apostrophe to the lily's graceful ease places them in fields, where, among grasses, indeed they can be splendid.

The springtime garden is easier than others,

Carmel Valley Manor, Carmel Valley, California. (Landscape Architect: The SWA Group/Photo: Dixi Carrillo)

but it is also transient. Welcome and brilliant, the primrose, bluebell, tulip, narcissus, hyacinth, and anemone do not last long; the golden broom flowers, sags, and is spent. Pear, crab, plum, and cherry linger, then pass quickly, and as summer arrives, the forsythia that dazzlingly harbingered spring becomes a dull foil for vibrant lupins, larkspurs, delphiniums, and foxgloves. Still later, quiet autumn hedges present long-flowering chrysanthemums and the best of roses, those that bloom in the fall. Unless there is an Alaskan daisy, the first sharp frost ends the display.

But the garden that contains more than ephemeral annuals and the stabler perennials will not finish at fall. Given trees and shrubs as its structure, a garden can be rewarding year-round. Fall and winter will display oranges, blues, reds, and yellows in the fruits of the mountain ash, viburnums, pyracantha, and cotoneasters. The apples of some crabs are cardinal red. Holly berries and mistletoe are famous. Milkweed bursts cotton, and color comes to the leaves of gooseberries, raspberries, and currants, which bear bright berries. Although the tender basil falters, other herbs, such as the mints, dill, sage, sorrel, chives, tarragon, chamomile, and marjoram, enter the winter with flourishes. Then as wind and cold persist, the garden, now dormant, is the domain of the bare branch and evergreen, the red-twigged dogwood, bamboo silhouettes, lingering viburnum berries, flaming pyracantha, and, if you are fortunate, yellow flowers on bare-stemmed winter jasmine—and so the garden rests until snowdrops and crocuses spring up at the snow's melting edge.

SPECIAL LANDSCAPES

Medford Leas

Landscape is the pervasive theme at Medford Leas Retirement Community, an early continuing care retirement community in Medford, New Jersey, 17 miles east of Philadelphia on the edge of the famous Jersey Pine Barrens. There, thanks to Lewis W. Barton, a horticulturist who was instrumental in founding Medford Leas, residents (and visitors) today enjoy the Barton Arboretum, whose woodlands ride over varied terrain, offering spreads of wildflowers in meadows, groups of native and exotic trees, a rhododendron garden, and an extensive display of daffodils. The "blossom calendar" begins with crocuses, daffodils, and forsythia in March–April; rhododendrons, Bradford pears and jade crabapples in May–June; and roses, magnolia, and mountain laurel in late June. An herb garden, roses, and day lilies are best in July, but roses continue well into autumn, and franklinia, named for Ben Franklin, blooms in August. The pyracantha fruit of September and the jade crabapples of October and November are spectacular red-orange accents against the winter's brown deciduous foliage.

Viburnum berries, pyracantha fruit, and crabapples account, in part, for the avid bird-watchers at Medford Leas. A list of birds seen by residents is checked each day on the bulletin board, and birding becomes especially active as spring and fall migrations near. Those residents who prefer to take their count closer to their own terrace hang feeders and nesting boxes within view of favorite sitting areas, where binoculars and Roger Tory Peterson's guide books are near to hand.

Medford Leas offers still more: a vegetable garden with residents' plots, a cutting garden featuring peonies, a library emphasizing horticulture, excursions to distant gardens, lectures, a bog along Rancocas Creek and a nature study center, with a greenhouse, located near the new tennis courts.

Perhaps the epitome of the landscape theme at Medford Leas is the open atrium garden, which is seen by all who pass into the dining rooms and living room. Even those residents who may not go out-of-doors in winter can enjoy the blue Atlas cedar in snow, ice on the pool, and the jewel-like berries on crab trees, dogwood, and hollies.

A national or even a regional horticultural or garden society could well form a retirement community around their members' interest in outdoor and indoor gardens. Why not build upon that natural delight which brings thousands of domestic and foreign visitors to Longwood Gardens, near Wilmington, Delaware, each week?

Medford Leas, Medford, New Jersey. (Photo: Albert Bush-Brown)

Bermuda Garden for the Blind

Although "touch gardens," "scent gardens," and "braille-labeled gardens" exist today in many botanic sites, the Garden for the Blind at the Bermuda Botanical Gardens remains an early favorite, if not the most elaborate. Here, the garden beds are raised to touching or wheelchair height, forming a walled, tranquil space. The touch of sun and wind, like the sounds of water, birds, and rustling leaves, increases the sense of scent.

The beds are planted with thyme, lavender, sage, laurel, rosemary, and other herbaceous, aromatic leaves.

For more than sixty references to Gardening for Handicapped and Elderly Persons, see the bibliography prepared as circular 1981–1 by the National Library Service for the Blind and Physically Handicapped, The Library of Congress, Washington, D.C., 20542. The list includes a section devoted to plant cultivation as rehabilitation therapy. ■

Garden for the Blind, Bermuda Botanical Gardens, Bermuda. (Photo: Albert Bush-Brown)

64/Signs Without Words

Malcolm Grear

In contrast to many mental health facilities where patients are contained by walls or fences, Oakwood, in Somerset, Kentucky, was built to be open and residential. Built in clusters of two houses, with each house serving twelve children and their counselor, the clusters encourage children to stay, without coercion.

The surrounding community approved, but no one wanted Oakwood next door. Even during construction, Oakwood was referred to as an insane asylum, and petitions demanded fences.

When nearly completed, and with children already resident, we were asked to design signage that would give visual vitality to the architectural structures that many felt imposing. We aimed to change the community's viewpoints. Visually, we wanted to say that Oakwood is a safe and desirable place. The majority of the children at Oakwood would be coming from Kentucky's mountains and farming sections. Moving would be a major adjustment. We wanted to incorporate familiar things such as native materials, bird houses, and recyclable objects. Logs from the mountains were debarked by hand axes for play structures. Discarded tractor seats were sandblasted and painted to become outside seating. Concrete culvert pipes were turned vertically and filled with dirt to become vegetable gardens.

Very little effort was required to convince sculptor Hugh Townley and cartoonist Ed Koren, both well-known artists, to join our effort. Hugh produced a large sculpture composed of three parts. Convincing the state officials that the sculpture could be the main entrance sign was no easy chore, especially since it was not listed in any catalogue of parts. Some community officials also felt that the sculpture was too abstract and no one would understand it.

Oakwood Comprehensive Training Center for Mentally Disabled Children, Somerset, Kentucky. (Sculptor: Hugh Townley and Edward Koren)

As the sculpture was being installed by workers, who were mainly from the mountains, one of them asked me, "Mr. Grear, what does it mean?" I turned the question back to him. I asked, "What does it mean to you?" He stepped back, looked up at the sculpture for a few seconds, and said, "Well, it's like a piece of music. If you put the right notes together it makes a pretty sound." I don't think that I could have done as well.

Ed Koren prepared small drawings that we enlarged and had cut from several layers of wood, and these were laminated by Hugh Townley. Then Ed painted directly on the wood. The children and their counselor gave those creatures names. To draw the nonambulatory children's eyes skyward, we designed bird houses for martins and placed them outside their windows. Martins are recognized and respected by most Kentuckians.

I also designed a sculpture and placed it on top of a pole. It turns slowly with even a slight wind. The piece was built by a local welder, who thought that he was making a fancy TV antenna.

We designed banners and flags. Their poles or supports were shaped to suggest the banner. The poles remain visually active even when the banners are missing. The children make the banners from the patterns we supplied.

Drapery patterns throughout the center are based on letter forms. Prison inmates were taught to silkscreen fabric, and they make the draperies as part of their industrial program. We also created special elements such as sculptured forms for the children's balance skills and painted patterns on paved areas to develop coordination skills.

We suggested that terrariums for the non-ambulatory section be maintained by ambulatory patients. The plants and creatures could be taken from a small swamp on the property; we drew attention to the swamp by placing brightly colored poles within it.

It was difficult to convince the people in the state bureaucracy to plant five acres of wild-flowers on a hillside, since they thought of them as weeds. We prevailed.

The entrance sculpture by Hugh Townley has since become an important symbol for the total community, almost like their bell tower. Its outlines are now used in relief on plaques that the Chamber of Commerce distributes, and the shapes, drawn in silhouette, have also been used as a symbol in the local newspaper. The sculpture signifies more than the center itself.

In a touching description, the children wrote: "The umbrella shape suggests sheltering, while the circular shapes represent three rings of hope. The cutout heart in the third form indicates love."

As designers, we can educate our public. If we had given in too easily, the sculpture would not be there. In its place, a large sign would proclaim that this is the Comprehensive Training Center for Mentally Disabled Children. It is also noteworthy to think about teaching prisoners to silkscreen. Total commitment is necessary to design creatively. The late Louise Nevelson said, "I have always wanted to show the world that art is everywhere except that it has to pass through a creative mind." ∎

Oakwood Comprehensive Training Center for Mentally Disabled Children, Somerset, Kentucky. (Designer: Malcolm Grear Associates)

65 / Lighting for Dramatic Effect

David Rockwell

There is more to light than brightness for reading and safety. Light creates space and defines objects. It also creates mood. Light can ruin a well-shaped space or make a poor space sparkle. It can transform a large hostile space into intimate areas or make a small space seem open and airy.

At Il Bianco Restaurant in New York City, lighting helps to create a dining area on an incidental terrace. Defining the space and dramatizing foliage and flowers, light creates shadows that bound the terrace from the adjacent street. To complete this haven for diners, an overhead trellis incorporates low-voltage spotlights directed at each table, suggesting filtered moonlight. What had been a cold streetside urban plaza now is warm, visually secure, and appealing. Of the four lighting components in the outdoor dining terrace, the most important is the ambient, or overall, lighting level. The glowing backlighted fabric ceiling creates the effect of filtered sunshine. Secondary light is directed at the tables to provide sufficient lighting to avoid eye fatigue and render the food in its proper colors. Two additional systems decorate the walls and cast light upwards to the trees—visual accents that draw one's eye gently through the space.

Lighting in the Cafe Roma in New York City opens the interior space toward an artificial view, in this case, abstract. A brick wall painted in pointilistic style, from light blue at the bottom to deep blue at the top, responds to a lighting system that changes the wall's colors, from cool blue to rich red/lavender. Thus, the diner's environment is modified to suit the occasion—bright and lively for breakfast, warm and soothing for dinner.

No single source or type of light alone offers depth and nuance. The new cancer unit at the Hartford (Connecticut) Hospital, completed in 1990, is an excellent orchestration of recessed quartz downlights, low-voltage adjustable clear

Baptist Hospital of Miami, Miami, Florida. Women's Diagnostic Outpatient Center. (Architect: TRO/Ritchie Organization/Interior Designer: Lisa Alvarez)

alzak reflectors, incandescent lamps, and fluorescent light. At Children's Hospital, San Francisco, and the new labor and delivery rooms for the University of California, San Francisco, the lighting designers and architects succeeded in creating hospitable space.

Light shapes space and form. An especially dramatic example is the reception area of the Women's Diagnostic Outpatient Center at Miami Baptist Hospital. Light defines spatial sequences and hierarchies, as at the Cleveland Clinic. Light marks climaxes and turning points, as at La Posada in Green Valley, Arizona.

Il Bianco Restaurant, New York, New York. (Architect: Haverson/Rockwell Architects/Photo: Paul Warchol)

Light is powerful and flexible. Its elusive qualities change with brightness, color, temperature, source (fluorescent, incandescent, low-voltage, metal-valide, etc.), and tightness or size of beam. Light's protean power is al-most endless. When used creatively, light can affect comfort and mood. It modifies our perception of space; it models and hides or dramatizes. Long after Edison, candles still grace a fine table. ■

66 / What Color Shall It Be?

Albert Bush-Brown

Apparel fashions featuring lavender or chartreuse may last a season, but hospitals have been wearing apple green for decades. Whether it ever looked fresh, clean, or antiseptic is less certain than the reaction it surely summons: Ugh! Hospital green!

Dismissing much taste and color theory is not to say that color obeys no rules. Nor does it imply that my enjoyment of autumnal browns and oranges, with just a splash of purple somewhere, is better than your taste for springtime blues and greens. In these matters, money, education, verve, status, and tradition all play a part. Since the invention of white lead paint in the 1820s, heritage and regional pride have kept New England clapboards ready to stage May's forsythia, June's azaleas, and October's maples, all brighter for a white setting.

Red-stained barns in southeast Pennsylvania, quarried rock in the Brandywine Valley houses, and redwood weathered silver by California sun confirm natural, regional origins of color. Urban style, combined perhaps with inhibition, may mute a personal taste, though today street attire shows less decorum, and the exhibitionist plumage and exposure of the mating season abounds, even in London and Boston. More than a millennium ago, royal prerogative preserved purple for the Byzantine Emperor, who was porphyrogennitos, literally, born to the purple. Until the fifteenth century, when Flemish painters defied Christian iconography by painting her robe carmine, the Virgin Mary owned lapis lazuli's blue, as she would again for centuries thereafter. Such a distinctive color signal is prized by Avis, Hertz, and the Bonwit Tellers of the retail world, but commerce does not allow any color to be owned for long. Still, we keep the festive yellow in Easter and the red in Christmas, and conservatism selects the "sincere blue" suit one of my friends reserves for funerals, weddings, bar mitzvahs, and job interviews.

Not every man with a couple of gallons of paint should be let loose to roll colors on hospital walls, even if he is Rothko or Pollock. Either painter would be better than most custodians and superintendents, and their art could greatly calm (in Rothko's case) or excite (in Pollock's) many a healthcare space that needs those effects.

Much literature about color arises from artificial premises. Consider, for example, an admonition to avoid strong reds. They excite; they are belligerent, hot, and intrusive. Red's aggression is demonstrable; see warning lights and signs marking exit or stop. Hear van Gogh speak about his *Night Cafe:* "I tried to express through red and green the terrible passions of humanity."

But is red to be avoided on Valentine's Day? Is the luncheon with red roses and linens prepared by a hostess in a red dress to be regretted? Not on your life! Is the red we are advised to shun to be pervasive, covering the ceiling, floor, and all the walls? Or is it a background for black leather, chromed furniture? Doesn't red have many beneficial, desirable uses? Doesn't their usefulness depend upon your purpose and the context? Shouldn't we amend the admonition to say, "Like every other hue, red in some contexts and for some purposes may be exactly the color we want?"

What do you mean when you say "blue?" Do you mean what I enjoy, the dashing cerulean blues and flashing iceberg blue-greens of a shimmering aurora borealis? No, those are the last blues that come to your mind. You mean "blue," really blue, the blue that can range all the way toward green, all the way to purple, all the way to midnight black, all the way to a cloudless October sky: a generic *blue.*

Like every other hue, blue has various

shades. Mixed with white, it has different values: it can be pale and light; or strong and dark, a navy blue. Composing with values alone, from a hue's lightest value to its darkest, we shape form and space: pale ceilings, darker walls, lighter pilasters, and darker alcoves. Is such composing with values what Delacroix meant when he boasted, "Give me mud, and I will paint the skin of Venus?"

At some point in its sequence of values, a hue is most intense. At that value, a blue is stronger than a green or yellow at the same value. Like the least intense, the most intense value has its use. It makes a spectacular accent on exterior architectural form. Sunlight brightens the intensely red door, green shutter, or blue wall. Florida, Arizona, and Mexico relish strong exterior color. Inside, intense color is best used sparingly, preferably as signal, accent, or landmark. Unless an atrium or tropical sun lightens it or white contrasts it, an interior with an extensive expanse of intense color will seem oppressive.

Hue, value, intensity, and their mixture, those are the mechanics of color. Their optical effects are demonstrable and useful.

Left there, we are tempted to trip on an artificial premise: judging a single hue without context. Colors exist in place. They live with other colors in places that have height, length, width, light, and shadow. Each of these factors affects a color's value and intensity. Light is critical. Strong light on a painted surface may pale a hue's value and decrease its intensity, while dim light, by darkening its value, may intensify a blue, yellow, or even a red. Although it obeys different mechanics, light through stained glass makes the point: high morning light at Amiens Cathedral embellishes its windows' reds, oranges, and yellows, which become less intense when twilight draws brilliance from deep blues and dark greens that were muted earlier in the day.

The Danish architect, Steeneiler Rasmussen, proposed a fascinating though debated thesis: southern light relishes warm colors; northern light, as in Vermeer's studio, brings out the best in cool colors. Rasmussen suggests we select colors that the source of light will enhance. Before we jump to sunny morning yellows and moonlighted evening blues, understand what he means: yellows and blues can be either "cool" or "warm," depending upon their blending with other hues. A warm yellow in northern light can appear muddy; a cool yellow will sparkle. Vermeer often showed that brilliance. His yellows throb against variously valued blues. Painting walls a warm yellow or orange to cheer up a north-lighted living room can be disastrous.

Context is everything. The periwinkle that looks so dramatic with black is a disappointment with browns. "In order to change a color," the painter Michel Eugene Chevreul observed, "it is enough to change the color of its background."

More about context: different hues in various values and therefore with various intensities can be combined in palettes to form harmonies and contrasts. Palettes are fun to compose. The literature that draws us to consider single colors in isolation, or color charts and wheels, can inhibit our instinct and dim our enthusiasm for palettes. We settle for accents on off-whites, whatever off-white may mean to some local painter. Nothing is inherently wrong with the pervasive greens and beiges that cover nursing home and hospital walls. When not relieved or accented by other hues or different values, they are dreary and bore us. They lack the harmonies and contrasts a palette of hues and values provide.

Since the Impressionists, green with blue has been popular. Less fashionable today is the Pompeian palette of deep red and yellow ochres with lampblack. Instead, Art Deco mauves and pastels are currently in vogue. All such palettes are especially successful when the hues are separated by a line of black or gold or white. Whites help hues read true, with depth. Then that richness which artists celebrate, colors blended subtly, will reward long inspection. One of the twentieth century's greatest colorists, Pierre Bonnard, saw

Violets in the grays
Vermilion in the oranges
On a chilly day
With beautiful weather.

I happen to enjoy writing and entertaining in a room where my walnut desk, teak tables, and silver-chromed chairs with black leather seats stand against white walls hung with silver-framed, black-ink drawings and calligraphy; red Berber rugs accent the oak floor, and reddish orange draperies close the window wall. That palette responds happily both to shifting sunlight and to bright lamps, which create high or low pools of light.

Other, very different rooms have their own distinctive character: pale orange walls with white ceiling, accented by pink, green, and silver in cornice, wainscot, and frames. Blue, white, and gold is a sophisticated, cheerful triad for a summer house. Mulberry walls sharply delineated by white trim superbly display the crystal and silver on walnut sideboards and a highboy in a Newport house. In one Manhattan apartment, a blue-gray wall with white cornice and wainscot is the background for a reddish brown cherry chest holding a large glass bowl and pewter candlesticks, all beneath a silver-framed drawing. Elegant palettes can bring various shapes and scales together.

Palettes: colors in combination and in context. Strike major chords with primaries, minor chords with their complementaries. The harmonies, contrasts, and accents within a palette can be wonderful. One artist claims to have spent weeks studying a single brick. I could readily spend an hour enjoying one of the richest palettes nature offers: two eggplants —deep rich black, red, pink, lustrous, somber purples, with a few grace notes of green—marvelous subtle harmonies.

How arresting even an incidental bouquet can be! The dust jacket of one large book that lies flat on my coffee table brightens the room. It shows a detail of a John Singer Sargent portrait of an English lady. In eight or nine deft strokes, Sargent made a peony blossom: lavenders, blues, and whites. We marvel at it.

Even Kelly green and royal blue with psydelic pink can be a great palette, provided you are setting a summertime theme on a garden terrace! If you intend to cause headaches, invite eight women in their Lily Pulitzer dresses to luncheon in a room decorated with brilliant floral patterns in rugs, sofas, armchairs, napkins, and curtains. Ever since Mario Buatta chintzed America, decorators have given hotel and hospital rooms the English country look. With so much pattern and too much color, the rooms are busy. "That dress," one mother warned, "is wearing you." When the multicolored, heavily patterned room becomes the topic of conversation, a display of its own, the room will never become what it should be, a foil for people.

Even the liveliest palettes will not paint out mistakes in spatial design or unwanted structural intrusions. Color can, however, direct the eye toward desired vistas; it can clarify steps, columns, and other structural hazards; and it can camouflage an unwanted door, offensive pilaster, or ugly grate. Palettes of hue and value can clarify separations or blend and unite disparate elements. They will provide chords and discords where you want them.

Composing good palettes should be the objective, though taste may be uninhibited but not outlandish.

Side by side with that caution, accept some seasoned advice: Record the palette and its chemical genesis. It will not survive wear and cleaning, and is difficult to match, repair, or replace. Left to the paint shop and maintenance crew, it will become darker and cruder. However carefully integrated into the palette, a wooden, chromed, or plastic strip that protects the corner against wheelchairs' errant damage, eventually, in the absence of recorded specifications, will become an eyesore. The subtler the palette, the greater the need for documentation.

For a fine palette in context is sensitive. Developing and maintaining it requires restraint, even subtlety and sophistication. Mies van der Rohe is remembered for his pure elegant architecture and for two quotations: "God lives in the details" and "Less is more." I prefer his advice above the taste of a museum curator who exults over a Victorian riot of color, pattern, and form: "A little bit too much," he said, "is just about right for me." But then, his hospital room doesn't have to be mine. ∎

67 / Acoustics: Say It Again?

Lewis S. Goodfriend

Sound strongly influences the quality of everyone's life. For the elderly, sound and noise, which is unwanted sound, can play an even stronger role.

People have strong emotional responses to sound. Music has been shown to influence emotional state, and the environment for music is almost as important as the score itself. When noise interferes with hearing music, understanding speech, or immersion in creative activities, people can become irritable and, sometimes, disoriented.

There are some basic guidelines for the acoustical design of presentation spaces, listening rooms, classrooms, living rooms, and sleeping rooms. Desirable sound distribution and acceptable noise level can yield a more comfortable environment.

First, room reverberation times should meet the widely published criteria found in every architectural acoustics text. The background noise levels should meet the familiar criteria set forth in the *ASHRAE Handbook*, published by the American Society of Heating, Refrigerating and Air Conditioning Engineers. These levels cannot always be reached, but they serve as reasonable guidelines. When levels are above the recommended criteria, speech communication and comfort become degraded during long-term exposure.

Beyond those physical attributes of space, acoustical comfort also includes freedom from distracting, intrusive noises, which make concentrating on reading difficult for anyone, and especially difficult for the elderly. Sounds from mechanical equipment and plumbing disturb occupants, especially in sleeping spaces.

Intrusive noise can also diminish the recreational value of reading rooms, libraries, music rooms, and audiovisual areas. In areas used for creative activity, especially writing and musical composition, activity noise and routine operations, such as elevator doors and delivery carts, can seriously interfere with occupants' use and enjoyment of these spaces.

CONTROL OF NOISE

Some critical decisions control the practical lower limit of interior noise levels:

- Siting with respect to exterior noise sources such as highways, railroads, and flight patterns.
- Selection of buildings' shell materials.
- Selection and location of heating, ventilating, and air-conditioning systems (HVAC).
- Separation of operational facilities from sleeping and recreational facilities.

Adjacent spaces can be isolated from each other by appropriate partitions and, where required, carefully selected connecting doors. Noise from elevator doors within a recreation room cannot be corrected.

To minimize noise intrusions and interference with hearing:

- Select a site with minimal exterior noise problems. A site adjacent to the mainline railroad track or near a metropolitan airport will never be free of intrusions.
- Make a noise survey; then select the combination of building materials, especially windows and exterior doors, that will provide the required sound isolation.
- Lay out the interior spaces with the same consideration as in any quality residence. Separate noise functions by introducing better spaces. A foyer with book or magazine racks can shield an active corridor or elevator lobby from the reading room, even without doors.

- Impact-resistant, acoustically absorbing, cloth-wrapped glass fiber wall panels, along with an acoustical ceiling, can improve the effectiveness of such foyers.
- In multistory structures, select the floor–ceiling design not only for the appropriate fire rating but also for its high-impact insulation-class rating. Otherwise, even the slightest activity on the floor above will resound through the room below.
- In audiovisual recreation areas, provide seating with the appropriate audio equipment. Chairs can be equipped with jacks for listening devices for both normal and hearing-impaired persons. Do not use loudspeakers, whether large or small.

Review the fundamental design decisions that will control the background noise in all spaces. Among those are the choice between having central heating, ventilating, and air-conditioning or through-the-wall individual room units.

There are good operational and economic reasons for using through-the-wall heat pumps and air-conditioning units. In hotel rooms occupied only for a few days, they may be satisfactory, but long-term comfort may not be attainable with the typical through-the-wall units. They make the sleeping spaces and living rooms noisier than long-term residents may find acceptable. Tests performed on such units show them to be unacceptable for condominium and apartment use; this clearly makes them unsuitable for facilities for the elderly.

- Provide more acoustical absorption than for conventional sleeping and living spaces. The elderly, even those with modest hearing impairment, are often more sensitive to noise, and noise makes understanding speech more difficult than for those not so handicapped.
- Carpet in corridors, even thin carpet, will reduce footfall noise inside rooms facing the corridors. In multistory facilities, carpet will reduce the impact noise heard on the floor below.
- In kitchen and serving areas, use plastic-wrapped acoustical materials behind wash-able, perforated, acoustical pans and panels.
- Dining rooms, which are often used for other purposes, should be treated as the group meeting spaces discussed earlier.
- In the specification for the HVAC equipment, including the duct system and terminal devices, the noise criteria should be defined.
- All the usual cautions in selecting and erecting partitions between rooms in offices and hotels should be followed in all spaces, especially bedrooms. Having a telephone ringing in one room, but heard in the adjacent room, is unnecessary in the 1990s. Leaks must be controlled by the liberal use of non-hardening acoustical caulking materials, and care in positioning electrical outlets in adjacent spaces. Particular care is necessary at partitions that meet mullions and at convectors that pass through partitions.

ROOM ACOUSTICS

Rooms for group activities, including dining rooms, where speech communication is important, should have "good acoustics." This means that the reverberation time should be within limits, and there must be no echo or flutter echo. Where group listening will occur in meeting rooms and small auditoriums, optimum reverberation times are wanted. Long reverberation masks speech and confuses listeners.

Acoustical wall panels at the sides and rear of the space, along with an acoustical ceiling, will provide adequate control. A small speech-reinforcement system, also equipped with jacks at each seat, should provide adequate speech reinforcement.

Private rooms also need acoustical control. An acoustical ceiling will generally provide adequate absorption, in conjunction with other furnishings.

The optimum conditions can seldom be achieved, but with care in planning and thoroughness in detailing, the desired acoustical environment can be provided in living facilities for the elderly. ■

68/Graphic Design: Sign and Symbol

Malcolm Grear

Developing a strong visual identity is a major concern for most aspiring healthcare organizations. Before distinctive imagery can be designed, the organization must establish clear, specific, and unique goals. Sign and symbol must sing a message.

A unified, consistent communications program, from stationery to environmental graphics, will help identify the healthcare facility as an organization with a special purpose. The function of messages may be relatively simple, but signs must have distinctive visual identity, and they must be organized in an aesthetic, memorable, efficient, and economical way. Showing visual elements at random and in cacophonous discourse makes them compete. A unified system starting with a symbol and/or logotype and an identifying color palette pro-

vides a clear, forceful, and unmistakably individual statement.

A cohesive graphic communication system should also respond to the day-to-day, at times minute-to-minute, functions of the healthcare facility. Purely pragmatic concerns, such as directions, are not the only messages. Human and highly emotional issues must be met. As people and faces change, as spaces serve multiple functions, the graphic elements must allow flexible application.

At best, a symbol is a very important signature, announcing an organization's visual identity. It links publications, advertisements, and building signage. Widely exposed, a symbol increases its forcefulness.

To design a symbol is one of the most challenging jobs a serious designer can undertake.

Dana Farber Cancer Institute, Boston, Massachusetts. (Designer: Malcolm Grear Associates)

A symbol should convey an idea. If it is merely pictorial, the symbol may soon be obsolete, and it will have little flexibility. While unique, memorable, and timeless, outlasting any vogue, a good symbol will be strong, whether large or small, in two dimensions or three. An idea that is well-conveyed does not exhaust its meaning quickly. A good symbol is profound and timeless.

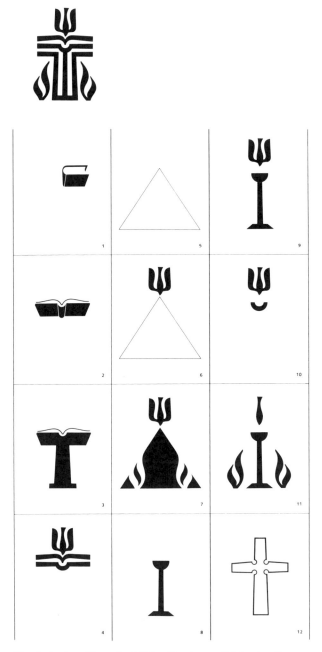

Presbyterian Church, USA. (Designer: Malcolm Grear Associates)

One of the major vehicles of communication is signage. Before imagery, the real problem is information. Information and signage require a communications expert, someone who is involved with communications on many levels: intellectual, ethnic, social, and economic. The message must be right. That is the province of the graphic designer and experts in semiotics, who should be members of the design team in the earliest stages of planning a new building. They can contribute greatly in planning spaces, including intensive care units and clinics.

Any graphic system is only as strong as the means for maintaining it. A graphic standards manual should introduce and define the system and guide its proper implementation. Custodial staffs in their paint shops can ruin the best graphic system. A computer program can define the proper sign for a certain situation, but also can identify all the signs that are affected when space usage changes.

Even though the idea of electronic signs, such as holography, seems exciting, I believe that such information systems at this time are impractical and inhumane. Most reception areas are well-enough designed, furnished, and maintained, but often a feeling of desolation and impersonal monumentality makes these areas look more like uninhabited showrooms than the warm reception areas they should be. Making such areas more inviting is a goal, and electronic signage will not help.

People visiting healthcare facilities commonly experience stress. Part of that stress is not directly related to ailments, but has to do with the social and moral consequences of needing treatment. A kind personal word, a vase of fresh-cut flowers, a video set with some chosen light programming, would help in relieving the patients' tensions and in breaking through the introverted loneliness waiting rooms now inspire.

The most unreceptive public spaces are usually the connecting circuits. Not only is orientation extremely difficult, but walking or being rolled through a labyrinth of steam pipes and soiled linen hardly inspires peace of mind or faith in antiseptics. To improve the social quality of these untidy but vital arteries, a merely functional signage system will not suffice. A

ElectroScan

ElectroScan, Willmington, Massachusetts. (Designer: Malcolm Grear Associates)

system that is both informative and decorative can, however, distract attention from vastness (pipes, air ducts, wiring, air conditioners, and fixtures), and a system would also guide the occasional visitor through the labyrinth.

Messages and graphic elements should be simple and direct. The clarity of the message is primary; the supporting material should be kept neutral. There is also a need for a positive approach in the messages the signs deliver. The stern, reprimanding tone on instructions and regulations could, in many cases, be presented in a more sensitive manner.

GRAPHIC IDENTIFIERS AND STATIONERY SYSTEM

A goal of a healthcare facility is to broaden the perception of its personality through visual identity and communications. Varied audiences must know what the organization is and what it stands for. To this end, the healthcare facility must be organized *visually*. The development of a unified communication program, from logotype and stationery to environmental graphics, will help identify the healthcare facility as an organization unique to its purpose.

No single solution or set of solutions will assure that all people will be able to read a sign, especially in a healthcare facility. Viewers differ greatly in their ability to see, and medication can alter these differences even further. There are also wide variations in an individual's reading capacities. Factors such as education, intelligence, and dyslexia are all factors to consider.

Under normal daylight conditions, a person standing still with 20/20 vision can read a one-inch-high letter on a small eye chart 50 feet distant. That distance can be increased or decreased by changing type style, color, letter spacing, line spacing, and character, such as having all capitals, all lowercase, or a mixture of capitals and lowercase. The elderly require larger letter heights.

A well-designed type style should be chosen in terms of how the letters work together and not as single letters. A single letter is a unit within a twenty-six-part system. Letters unite to form words, which are part of another system; words, in turn, form statements or sentences. If letters are too close together or too far apart, word recognition can be destroyed.

Color and contrast are, of course, very important. As an example, a bronze three-dimensional letter that is placed on a white wall could

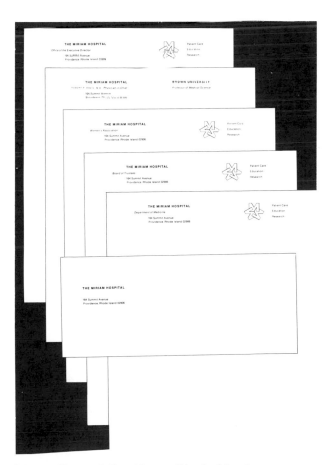

Miriam Hospital, Providence, Rhode Island.

produce shadows that may generate the same color as the letter, thereby making it difficult to read.

When color is used as part of an identification system, I do not believe that more than five colors, excluding black and white, can be remembered. And, obviously, these colors must be easily distinguishable from one another, such as red, yellow, blue, green, and brown.

Communication involves more than colors, numbers, and letters in an alphabet. Some messages are best conveyed by graphic images.

Our signs could say "Cardiology." Or they could draw upon the vast heritage of imagery that conveys the word "heart." "Pulmonary" summons all the images of balloons, winds, bellows, kites, and sails that man has invented. Those universal images can be humorous, delightful, and humane; they can also transcend linguistic and cultural barriers.

Ideas are the origin of good graphic design; they are its purpose. Symbols and signs should present more than information—they should enhance the environment. ■

69/Personality of the Chair

Edith L. Claman

We enter a room and immediately feel welcome when there is warmth, graciousness, charm, and hospitality. Thus it is with a chair! A proper chair welcomes us with its profile, scale, and shape; its quality and design; its character and function; its encompassing power to engulf us and make us feel at home.

What makes a chair (or any seating piece) hospitable for senior citizens? First, it must be constructed so that one can get into it and, especially, out of it easily and with dignity. We refer again to profile, scale, and shape. Even though we must distinguish between dining/game chairs, lounge chairs, and wingback chairs, in all cases the chief features are the pitch of the chair, the height of the chair seat (18½–20 inches), the height of the arms (25–26 inches), and the interior depth of the seat (18–20½ inches).

Chairs must have arms strong enough to support the weight of a rising person, great stability so as not to tip, lumbar support to reduce fatigue, smooth edges, rounded corners, and a generosity of feeling. The body must be "cradled" to limit stress and produce an aura of warmth. This is accomplished when the chair is so constructed that the thighs, buttocks, and

Stackable armchair with foam-filled back and seat. Priority Seating, Inc. (Designer: Edith Claman/Photo: Chuck Adams Photography Studio)

Wingback armchair on casters. Priority Seating, Inc. (Designer: Edith Claman/Photo: Chuck Adams Photography Studio)

torso are aligned through proper interior depth and pitch, with the seat and back angle formed to protect the pelvic area, knees, and thighs.

Seats must be firm but comfortable, with a heavy density foam of 3½–5 inches thickness, so that the chair doesn't "bottom out." The seat padding should be extended with no sharp edges, to avoid discomfort to the thighs and underleg areas. Backs should have 3–3½ inches of foam or padding where applicable. Arms are also more comfortable when padded.

Chairs must be easily movable. A diner must be able to move back and forth with ease; chairs must be moved for cleaning. Proper glides are an asset, but casters on heavy chairs are only advisable on carpeted floors, never on hard floors. A handle built in as part of the top-back design, or a wood ledge in back of a chair, helps in moving furniture. Here again, proper construction, use of strong but not overly heavy materials, and good pitch are all assets to mobility.

A crumb space built around the inside, back, and arms (if upholstered) is essential for easy cleaning.

New catalyst lacquer topcoats and specially treated fabrics afford extra protection and durability without sacrificing beauty, quality, and choice of design.

Love seats or settees are for sharing, a social plus; sofas are large and often uninviting. No one wants to sit in the middle, and it's difficult to hold a conversation from one end to the other. Although neither the love seat nor the sofa is merely a "stretched-out" chair and must be built with its own rules as to profile, shape, size, and pitch, the love seat often has much more of the personality of the chair and makes an excellent companion to it.

People come in all shapes and sizes. Some sit passively and others more actively, shifting and moving about. We must aim to build the chair that supports the body under all conditions and allows the sitter to find comfort. We all spend a great deal of time sitting in chairs. Seniors' chairs must outperform all others in comfort and quality.

The chair that has personality to speak out to us and say, "Sit in me first," is the user-friendly chair offering comfort, hospitality, and warmth. This ideal chair can be built. It is the chair with personality, the chair for all ages.

RATTAN AND WICKER SEATING

Whereas warmth, comfort, and hospitality are key attributes of upholstered and wood-trimmed chairs, rattan seating offers lightness, airiness, and flexibility with comfort. Durable beyond belief, furniture built of reeds and vines has been produced for many hundreds of years. The oldest existing bamboo factory has been manufacturing in Yi Yang, China, since the 1600s.

Rattan is a thorny, climbing tropical vine belonging to the palm family, found in the tropical rain forests of Southeast Asia. Its woody, pliable stalks do not grow vertically but follow a wavy course. As rattan grows, the weight of its fronds bends the stems toward the ground; the growth then continues vinelike along the ground until reaching a bush or tree when the rattan climbs upward, clinging to the tree with its thorny projections. Lacking support in the treetops, rattan bends to the earth and the pro-

Rattan armchair. Priority Seating, Inc. (Designer: Edith Claman/Photo: Chuck Adams Photography Studio)

cess begins again until the vine has grown to some 40 to 65 feet. Harvesting begins 6 to 15 years from the start of a new growth. The resilient vines are cut into 18–20 foot lengths, the stems stripped, then washed and sun-dried before being taken to the factories where they are processed, fumigated, cured, sorted, and graded. The tough outer skin is removed and used for bindings and to make cane mesh; the inner core is used to build furniture frames.

This climbing tropical vine from Southeast Asia is much stronger than bamboo. Solid and bendable, rattan is ideal for furniture. Rattan can be bent and, when woven, it makes the finest wicker furniture.

Rattan wicker is by its nature a flexible product and thus, some flex will be felt when pushing against the back or arms. This adds to the life of the product and also enhances comfort. Correctly made rattan furniture has corner struts, screws and/or steel pinnings, and stretchers for strength, durability, and beauty. Leather bindings are preferable to peel binds. Triple-leg construction adds strength and a better design.

Because rattan is hand-steamed and bent, its wonderful patterns and designs are great in greenhouses and sun porches. It also can be designed elegantly for more formal purposes, such as dining rooms, lounges, and living areas. No matter what the pattern, the wicker should be tightly woven. Size, proportion, and pitch must never be sacrificed. Wicker chairs are comfortable and sturdy a well as nostalgic.

We recommend rattan wicker furniture for senior living and healthcare facilities because it is lightweight, and thus easily movable; durable; resilient; and lightscale, correctly proportioned to the older physique. Rattan and wicker afford a warm ambiance, an uncluttered atmosphere, pleasurable surroundings, and a wealth of design opportunities. They remind us of our youth, recalling thoughts and memories of seaside houses and comfortable porches. ∎

70/Gaining Residential Scale

Barbara J. Watt

The lobby is generally the first impression a visitor has of the community, and a welcoming, homelike setting is vital. In The Fairfax, Fort Belvoir, Virginia, a printed nylon carpet is glued directly to the sealed concrete floor, permitting ease of movement for those with mobility limitations. Specific areas are defined by borders and insets. While the lobby does not take the abuse of a hotel lobby, the contract-grade seating has a decided residential appearance. Firm seats, along with a shallow depth, permit ease in rising. The variety of fabrics provides tactile and visual stimulation and contributes to the residential ambiance. In this area, the concierge desk provides the residents with many hotel-like services.

The main dining area seats 260 people in a continuous room with a combination of chair

The Fairfax, Fort Belvoir, Virginia. Lobby. (Designer: The Marriott Corporation/Photo: David Doyle)

and banquette seating. Large spaces are subdivided by half-walls with planters and etched glass panels, while lighting combines fluorescent fixtures in coffers, incandescent downlights, and chandeliers, with shades to reduce glare. The dining chair was designed to Marriott specifications to be ergonomically correct and for ease of maintenance. The printed nylon carpet continues the color palette established in the lobby, and extensive interior landscape and elegant window treatments contribute to a luxurious atmosphere. ∎

71/Physiology and Adaptive Hardware

George Baker III

Aging is not a disease to be cured, but rather a biological process to be understood and accommodated through adaptation and intervention. There are really no scientifically valid interventions. However, adaptive environmental options can improve physiological functional capacity. Perhaps the best known are reading glasses, prescribed for presyobis, or nearsightedness. Other adaptations to improve vision at older ages are: reduce glare—in the office, in the market/store, in the home, and on the road; accommodative size, spacing, and contrast in signs and labels; and appropriate color schemes. Many accommodations would not only improve the physiological and psychological capabilities of older individuals but enhance their safety, productivity, and quality of life.

Look around your built environment! Think of all the things you have trouble using, seeing, hearing, turning, opening, closing, lifting, wearing, riding in. For the most part, furniture is furniture as it has always been! Fixtures are fixed! Think of round smooth doorknobs when half of all individuals over 65 (12 percent of our population) have an arthritic condition. Many experience difficulty with that knob and other knobs and dials on electronic gear. Most accidents among older individuals occur in bathrooms. No wonder! Most bathrooms are ill-designed. Walk-in bathtubs and showers are infrequently installed in homes, even those newly constructed. Who said a toilet or sink must be so high or low? There is really no reason why a toilet should not move up or down. Technology exists to make it work!

Most things could be better throughout the entire built environment. For example, all of us have adjusted a thermostat, but not until

Honeywell Electronics & Controls. Thermostat with visual and audible aids. (Photo: Courtesy of Honeywell, Inc.)

SwimEx Hydrotherapy Pool. (Photo: Courtesy of SwimEx Systems, Inc.)

we have found it and struggled to read its temperature setting. Failures in design get entrenched into building standards. Many alarm systems are set at sound frequencies many older individuals cannot detect, no matter how loud the sound. Who said a stair has to be a stair like all other stairs? Building codes specify only minimums. Why do we have jar lids that challenge even Hercules? Do we even need jars, with all the alternatives available?

I do not approach adaptation or accommodation of the built environment specifically with the elderly in mind. I would encourage designers to meet the human factor criteria for a 40-year-old person and not a 20-year-old, as we do today. Reexamine most so-called "standards"; our society will not be any younger. Redesign would have widespread impact on the day-to-day functional capabilities of many more of our mature citizens, and more than likely enhance productivity and safety for younger individuals as well.

Do you struggle to open the jellies and peanuts served on airplanes? Orange juice and milk cartons? Pill containers that, ironically, only children can open?

As long as the built environment remains a *barrier* and American business and industry have not responded to the demographic changes in our society, the quality of life at older ages will be diminished. ∎

Adjustable Fixture Co. Nightingale® Brass 'n Color lamp. Special features: Two-way base paddle switch, night light located in the middle of the back of the lamp, with plug-in receptacle below. (Photo: Courtesy of Adjustable Fixture Co.)

Part **VIII**

Nurturing the Caring Environment

While hospitable design provides a *physical* health-care environment for privacies and memberships, the *social* dimensions depend upon morale and service. How can staff members develop hospitable attitudes, be responsive, even inventive, and offer congenial services?

72/The Trustees' and Administrators' Role

Donald L. Moon

The successful continuing care retirement community (CCRC) contains an intricate juxtaposition of motivating elements that are represented in its various levels of governance. Generally, all CCRCs have one major motivation: the *social and healthcare needs* of the elderly. But those needs may be defined in *economic terms* (e.g., to serve middle-income elderly), or they may be expressed in *medical/social* terms (e.g., to provide medical services primarily to those who are considered "frail"), or defined in terms of *constituency* (e.g., to provide services to retired ministers and missionaries).

The governance chosen by the CCRC is motivated also by a desire to *provide a sense of security, community, and independence* among its residents. Security depends on the community's success in providing both *financial and healthcare* assurances. Residents expect financial stability that will ensure coverage of future liabilities for healthcare.

How a CCRC provides its guarantees for residents' future care may vary, but should include the comfort that, no matter what an individual's future financial condition might be, the cost for long-term healthcare will be contained within defined and manageable parameters. Outside the CCRC, such costs can be catastrophic and devastating. The residents of the CCRC expect that future healthcare needs will be met at manageable cost in a familiar setting among fellow residents who are both friendly and supportive.

A third motivating factor affects a CCRC's pattern of governance: the quality of healthcare the organization wishes to provide. Today's market offers many options. To compete successfully, a CCRC's healthcare must be technically proficient and compassionately caring for all its residents in both the short and long term.

Finally, the CCRC's governance must be motivated by sound business practices. Its managers must be financially astute.

UNIQUE GOVERNANCE ISSUES

While issues of governance face all service institutions, the CCRC presents some unusual demands. First, unlike other businesses, the CCRC has a contractual agreement to care for residents for life. Thus, the CCRC must ensure its future and the implications of lifecare contracts. Its governance should not allow any group advocating short-term or immediate initiatives to dominate.

Having placed their trust in the CCRC for care throughout their lives, residents expect a role in decisions. To give them a role, maintain their independence, and sustain their self-esteem, while still guiding a reasonably congregate life within the community, governance must give residents both individual and communal self-determination.

Successful models assign each group within a CCRC some authority and responsibility for specific functions. Each group's purview and authority should be clear. Identifying responsibilities and developing the discipline each group needs to respect others' rights, is key to success. Obviously, a board of directors, charged with forming overall policy, should not enter everyday management matters; nor should administrators change policies or usurp the fiduciary responsibilities of the board of directors.

THE GOVERNANCE TRIAD

The effective governance system within a CCRC will have three distinct, overlapping governing bodies: the corporate board of directors, the administration, and the residents.

My experience with that governance triad in the CCRC, Foulkeways at Gwynedd, Pennsylvania, has been in a not-for-profit corporation with approximately 362 residents. Established by the Gwynedd Monthly Meeting of Friends (Quakers), the community has a twenty-member board of directors, which includes at least 75 percent Quakers. Operating since 1967, Foulkeways represents one of the earliest modern CCRCs in the United States, and as its Chief Executive Officer since 1977, I offer suggestions that flow from circumstances at Foulkeways.

The Board of Directors

As the *primary policy-making body*, the corporate board of directors is charged to act with due diligence to fulfill its fiduciary obligation: to ensure a financially sound community, operated in an efficient and effective manner to fulfill its corporate mission and future obligations.

In not-for-profit circles, much debate arises over a board's ideal size and composition. CCRC boards have anywhere from *ten to twenty-five members*. Having fewer than ten makes it difficult to obtain broad experience. More than twenty-five makes the board unwieldy. A large board can, of course, delegate authority to its Executive Committee. Board members should be chosen for ability, willingness to spend time, and to represent a *wide variety of expertise*, including finance, law, medicine, construction, and business.

Having residents as members of a board is often debated. Foulkeways at Gwynedd has traditionally had two resident members and has never regretted their presence. Resident board members, however, are informed that they are not "representatives" of the community or any constituency. Rather, regardless of the issue, all board members are charged with caring for the total well-being of the community.

Concern for the total life and mission of the community leads to the board's systematic preparation and review of *a long-range plan for the corporation*, which the Foulkeways board and staff revise every five years.

The board's Finance Committee monitors both operating and capital budgets and reviews monthly balance sheets, revenue and expense reports, and cash-flow statements. The board approves investment policies, reviews the quality of services and approves the appointment of senior personnel. Only the corporate board may appoint the Chief Executive Officer (CEO), Chief Operating Officer, and Medical Director. Those three critical officers inform the directors about the community, and the CEO attends board meetings as an officer of the corporation.

The board delegates much work to standing committees. We operate with five: the Finance Committee, the Health Center Committee, the Property Committee, the Personnel/Pension Committee, and the Admissions Committee, which has responsibility for admitting all residents.

Foulkeways at Gwynedd has several ways to inform its various constituencies, especially residents. All residents meet together at least once each year. An additional meeting may be called to announce a change in fees or policy, a major renovation, or an expansion. The Chairman of the Board and Chief Executive Officer then explain any actions proposed and invite questions. An annual financial report is distributed to residents. Many states now require such full disclosures. A Joint Advisory Committee, composed of three residents and three administrators, with a single board member serving as the chairman, meets regularly. Given only advisory power, the Joint Advisory Committee sends recommendations to the appropriate group for implementation.

The Administration

Throughout its twenty-two years, Foulkeways at Gwynedd has developed an effective administrative structure. Organized on a departmental model, various department heads report to the Administrator, who is Chief Operating Officer. The one exception is the Controller, who reports directly to the Executive Director (Chief Executive Officer).

There simply is no substitute for active personal involvement. Knowing each resident and having a friendly rapport will head off a variety of difficulties. At Foulkeways, residents and senior administrators meet monthly to discuss any questions about the community except those dealing with individual employees or individual residents. Similar meetings with employees enhance morale and interpret various policies and actions.

The Residents

In an earlier chapter, I discussed the residents' role in governance and described the Residents' Association. Foulkeways regularly gains advice, better communications, and much voluntary service through the leaders of its association. Keeping everyone informed and involved at an appropriate level is easier where the triadic governance model operates. ■

73/Medical Center's President's View

Robert J. Shakno

As chief executive officers of healthcare institutions, we are responsible for providing the highest quality medical care and services, but we also must do so in a pleasant environment that fosters wellness and good health. Our institutions serve the acutely ill, those who require episodic ambulatory hospital services, visitors who include a patient's family and friends, and other professionals. Their experience of our institution must be positive.

Most important, we need to create a hospitable environment and atmosphere for employees and our best advocates, our physicians.

Central among the critical departments are those traditionally known as "back of the house." They include housekeeping, dietary, transportation, security, engineering and grounds maintenance, telephone, and communications. Far from being background or negligible, when given attention and encouraged to have pride in their service, those departments change the environment dramatically. Those back-of-the-house departments constitute our "hotel services." Organized and motivated to give high-quality service, they see themselves as equal partners intent on hospitable medical service. Organizationally, the administrative leaders of service departments should see themselves as conducting a hotel within a hospital organization. Their training of employees should encourage team work that assures a positive environment. Therefore, those department heads need standards and training programs that will inspire a high performance level. Then, even employees in the blue-collar groups will find their sights raised and attitudes changed. They will be goodwill ambassadors for the medical center in all contacts with our patients, doctors, and visitors.

Housekeepers, dietitians, and TV installers have frequent contacts with patients and physicians. Yet, this "weakest link" in the chain of services is often neglected. Remember how a bellhop in a hotel greets you at the registration desk and escorts you as he takes your bags to your room? If he cheerfully makes you aware of fine services, then you have a good feeling about the hotel. The same is true for a hospital. Whether transporters, staff at the information desk and gift shop, the housekeepers, the dietary aide, the telephone operator, and the groundskeeper, each employee can help to set the hospital's image. How a telephone is answered decides the caller's opinion of the institution!

Patients and their families can more easily evaluate the performance of service individuals than they can judge the medical care they receive. The impression of service received is often the opinion the patient transmits. If enthusiastic about the nursing staff, food, cleanliness, and helpfulness, the patient becomes an advocate.

An important influence on hospitality is the Patient Representative Department. Observing the quality of patient services and testing

The Mt. Sinai Medical Center, Cleveland, Ohio.
(Photo: Media Services Department)

The Mt. Sinai Medical Center, Cleveland, Ohio.
(Photo: Media Services Department)

patients' satisfaction through interviews and questionnaires, the patient representative responds to specific requests and visits selected patients each day. A salaried professional representative can lead well-trained volunteers; the volunteers become goodwill ambassadors.

Lobbies and other public areas can influence the public's perception of the hospital. A well-designed, inviting lobby encourages confidence and hospitable response: concierge desk, information and reception area, a gift shop, a restaurant, and other retail services including specialty shops related to medical care services.

When making public spaces attractive, do not forget parking and security. Whether on grade or in a structure, the parking areas are often the first impression. Safety, good illumination, clear signs, landscaping, and well-trained attendants are welcome.

Every large, urban hospital should have valet parking. We have found the public grateful and willing to pay for the convenience. Driving to the valet station at the entrance door to discharge a patient or visitor eases arrival. Similarly, before leaving the patient's room, the visitor can call for the car and have it waiting at the front door. Valet parking also improves safety and efficient use of parking facilities.

One of the most successful ventures I have undertaken has been to create a fine public restaurant in our hospital lobby in the Mt. Sinai Medical Center, Cleveland, Ohio. Designed to be a first-class setting for dining, the Lobby Cafe offers table service and a gourmet menu. On some days, the chef sets up a carving stand for roast beef, tenderloin, ham, turkey, and other entrees. The Lobby Cafe is popular with the public, but many employees also welcome it; a special area is reserved for physicians. The Lobby Cafe's popularity further advances the hospital's reputation.

For the employees' cafeteria, the selection of food, its preparation, and its presentation should reflect employees' preferences; dining areas should be inviting and cheerful.

There are gift shops, and there are gift shops! Our experience demonstrates that they should be managed by a professional manager and stocked with items that are appropriate for employees and physicians, as well as for patients. Far too many gift shops are managed by volunteers who fail to present appropriate merchandise. Even when aimed only at patients and visitors, the gift shop can offer gift wrappings, catalogue shopping, and deliveries. The gift shop can increase a hospital's revenue, but it also should make friends and convey the hospitable atmosphere one wishes to create.

The total hospitality approach to healthcare management, I believe, is financially sound. I much prefer to invest in hospitable staff and services than to spend the same dollars on advertising. Just as patients and visitors measure the quality of food, cleanliness, and the friendliness of employees, the medical staff does so as well. A medical staff that is proud of its hospital's hospitality will be more likely to recommend that institution over one where the entire attention is focused on clinical/medical services. Similarly, a hospitable institution will attract community members to serve as board members and volunteers, and fund-raising will

be helped. Finally, and perhaps most important, employees perform better and their rate of turnover drops while their productivity increases. That is an important dividend when nurses and therapists can work where they choose.

Hospitable service gives an institution opportunities to be creative, to experiment, and to increase its revenues. Market share increases because the community "grapevine" broadcasts that this hospital is a well-managed, caring place. ■

74/Hospitality Management

Stevan D. Porter

Designed, constructed, and opened, a beautiful space alone does not assure excellent service. As physical spaces are opened, operational procedures must be redesigned to meet the expectations of an increasingly more

sophisticated public. Healthcare hospitality invites us to focus on design, customer needs, consumer experience, and service management.

At Healthcare International, a healthcare

Healthcare Medical Center of Tustin, Tustin, California. (Photo: Courtesy of Healthcare International, Austin, Texas)

provider based in Austin, Texas, we have adopted and integrated hotel services to improve the guest/patient experience.

Research shows that consumers give high marks only where their expectations are exceeded. A May 1985 *Hospital* article identifies the top patient satisfiers/dissatisfiers: nursing care, visitor treatment, diet and meals, care and treatment, room and housekeeping.

NURSING/NURSING CARE

Nursing care is generally perceived to be a combination of clinical confidence, responsiveness, and courtesy. It is difficult for a patient to know whether a catheter or IV has been inserted properly or whether a clinical procedure has been completed accurately, but staff courtesy is recognizable and remembered, and the confidence exhibited by employees has great bearing on the satisfaction level. Attractive rooms encourage pride and courtesy.

VISITOR/FAMILY TREATMENT

How comfortable and accessible is the facility? Are restrictions necessary? Is information easily accessible? Do staff follow up on requests and assurances? Is signage readable, legible, contemporary, and interesting? Do the spaces lend themselves to relaxation and comfort during a tense situation? Hospital lobbies should be as comfortable and elegant as midscale hotel lobbies. Exterior spaces should capture the same excitement as do the grounds around major commercial industrial projects, with attention paid to landscape and maintenance.

DIET AND MEALS

There is universal enthusiasm for good food, yet a general abhorrence of hospital meals. Training and staffing can deliver an effective blend of the best in dietary and culinary skills. Top chefs can be as imaginative in a hospital kitchen as they are in a hotel or restaurant kitchen, and should be recruited and employed.

Healthcare Medical Center of Tustin, Tustin, California. (Photo: Courtesy of Healthcare International, Austin, Texas)

Healthcare Medical Center of Tustin, Tustin, California. (Photo: Courtesy of Healthcare International, Austin, Texas)

Nurturing the Caring Environment / **199**

CARE AND TREATMENT

Care and treatment involve a wide array of perceptions and activities. Again staff courtesy, facility accessibility, convenience, staff responsiveness, fluidity, and availability of information all play important roles.

ROOM AND HOUSEKEEPING

Satisfaction begins in the place where patients spend most time. Designing and furnishing spaces that are not traditional to the healthcare industry are critical. This includes the patient room, treatment areas for emergency patients, and waiting, preparation, and recovery areas for ambulatory or surgery patients.

Three of the five patient satisfiers/dissatisfiers relate to peripheral services and design elements, rather than to the traditional core services such as nursing and clinical services.

CONSUMER EXPERIENCE

Customer satisfaction surveys repeatedly emphasize staff courtesy. Irwin Press aptly states that staff courtesy results from many organizational and operational variables, including spaces and organization. According to Press (Summer 1988, *Patient Representation*), ". . . patient staff interaction issues are the items most highly correlated with overall patient satisfaction."

The patient consumer experience is about 85 percent directed to hostelry (registration process, phone interaction, room and building cleanliness, campus accessibility, signage, food quality, staff appearance, etc.), while only 15 percent is clinical. Recognizing variations across disease categories, the relationships still generally remain constant.

Regrettably, that point is neglected by many hospitals, which typically allocate resources and attention differently. Usually a hospital allocates about 10 percent of total support (financial, personnel) to hotel activities and closer to 90 percent to clinical elements. Those areas identified as contributing substantially to satisfaction rating have typically been accorded low operational priority.

An effective hotel services program can balance the hotel and clinical needs, enhance patient–staff interaction, and support customer

Healthcare Medical center of Tustin, Tustin, California. (Photo: Courtesy of Healthcare International, Austin, Texas)

satisfaction. The best hotel services program will combine both the physical and personal elements of customer service.

HOTEL SERVICES

The physical and personal service elements are developed in a program of features and benefits.

1. *Physical features:* Physical features provided through a hotel services program include: attractive front entrance; enhanced landscape; organized and well-signed parking; campuswide open accessibility; staff uniforms; name badges; interior decor; focal design elements to include oversized lobbies, atriums, and printed collateral/patient informational pieces; attractive tray and food service; terry and linen; and a dedicated services manager.
2. *Personal features:* Personal features include guest-relations training program, employee service-orientation reinforcement program, (hotel) service committee, frequent internal and external communications focused on service as a point of differentiation, and employee involvement in service planning.

Maintaining purpose and enthusiasm is essential. Physical and personal services should be coordinated and employees in a guest-relations training program must have regular follow-up instruction. An employee-recognition program is motivational *and* critical to success;

it should be more than the typical "employee of the month/employee of the year" award, and it should include the ability to receive feedback from employees, supervisors, physicians, and customers.

Motivation and reinforcement are key to enthusiasm's longevity. *Applause* is one of the most effective programs. Developed by Christine Peterson of Chicago, this customer-service/guest-relations training program applies directly to the hospital setting and lends itself to local facility customization.

OPERATIONAL STANDARDS

To develop service-related features tied directly to customer benefits, the manager must develop operational standards. Such standards should be developed for linens, amenities, tray service, guest robes, in-room registration, concierge service, and lobby coffee service.

The hospital should be especially alert to the patients' experience. This includes the point of entry, the registration process, being escorted, entering the guest room, the bed's comfort, the appearance of food trays and their delivery, convenient access to toilet facilities, grooming items, procedure scheduling, interaction between staff and patient, interaction between staff and family members, departure procedures, and satisfaction follow-up.

An effective integration of service and design elements has been achieved at Healthcare Medical Center of Tustin (Tustin, California): guest services/patient representative, generous private guest/patient rooms with fine service and dining. (Also created at Eastwood Medical Center in Memphis, Tennessee, Elmwood Medical Center in New Orleans, Louisiana, and Pali Momi Medical Center in Honolulu, Hawaii).

SERVICE MANAGEMENT

While environmental and service programs are important, effective day-to-day management is critical. Service systems must be managed. Integrating various services is fostered by service committees comprised of key department

Elmwood Medical Center, New Orleans, Louisiana. (Photo: Courtesy of Healthcare International, Austin, Texas)

managers, administrators, and line employees, who can assure uniform planning and participation at all levels of the organization.

SUMMARY

Jan Carlzen, President and CEO of Scandinavian Airlines, was the first to use the expression "a moment of truth" to mean that time when a customer faces an employee or organizational point of service. At that moment, the customer concludes that the encounter is positive or negative. If it is the only service encounter the customer has, nothing can alter that conclusion. In one moment, the organization's reputation rides at risk.

In a healthcare environment, consumers have a multitude of service encounters with scores of employees. The moments of truth are critically important. In Carlzen's words: "There are 50,000 moments of truth out there every day." Indeed, healthcare may have many more, which supports the need for an integrated and effective hospitality service management program. ■

75/Guest Services in Long-Term Care

Christian A. Mason

Effective guest relations begins with an enhanced service program that has at least ten ingredients.

Ingredient 1: A director of guest relations to oversee hospitality and staff development. The director should be well-versed in hospitality and have a profile similar to the population being served (i.e., native, and conversant with comparable social circles).

Ingredient 2: A well trained and service-oriented staff. From the nursing assistant to the administrator, every *employee* must be trained to identify customers' needs and to satisfy them. That is the essence of healthcare hospitality.

Ingredient 3: Employee recognition for positive performance. The successful recognition program at Berkshire Medical Center, called "Caught in the Act," rewards employees for positive behavior that extends beyond routine duties, for going the extra mile to satisfy customers. Employees are selected by the awareness team, a group of employees that anonymously selects award recipients.

Ingredient 4: Enhanced food service. Restaurant-style dining with table settings, mobile dessert carts, and a Sunday brunch is recommended. Other dietary enhancements might include a select menu, a cook-to-order program, and a visiting chef program.

Ingredient 5: Improved accommodations. Space is a primary concern. Permitting seniors to have their "home" decorated to their tastes personalizes their unit. Typical room enhancements include quilted comforters, designer chairs, armchairs, love seats, coffee tables, vanities, built-in desks, clock radios, wallpaper, overbed lamps, throw pillows, brass lamps, wall clocks, and designer mirrors. Each item adds to the personality of the unit.

Ingredient 6: Attractive noninstitutional furnishings and decor. One sure way to make your residents feel like guests is to install furnishings that, while *functional*, are patterned after furnishings found in their homes. Plastic-coated institutional furnishings have given way to many fabrics and textures.

Ingredient 7: Enhanced service through special programs. Providing additional services can increase the sense of hospitality: telephone service, cable TV, fresh flowers brought to the resident's unit, a personal parking space, daily newspaper, room service 7 A.M. to 7 P.M., special parties for families and friends, dry-cleaning services, personal laundry service, beauty shop services, trust accounting, remote-control television, VCRs with daily or weekly movie rentals, and magazine subscriptions.

Ingredient 8: Activities and socialization. An active social calendar contributes to hospitality. Programming specialists help residents maintain an active schedule. Lunch at the polo grounds may take only half a day; a major adventure is a trip to foreign lands (with private nurses in attendance).

Ingredient 9: Fitness Services. Often, residents refuse to accept the need for routine examinations. When such services are included in the fitness program, it becomes easier to conduct routine annual health examinations, physical therapy, and eye, ear, and dental examinations.

Ingredient 10: Ambiance: An environment that feels good. It smells good. It sounds good. Natural light abounds. The place seems active, and you can find your way.

In summary, service-oriented programming will meet the expanded demands of the senior market. A strong guest-relations program is also essential to success. ■

76 / Training in Today's Healthcare Environment

Rose Duran-Harvey

Hospitals are witnessing a drastic change in the type of patients they serve. Their patient population is being decreased by rising healthcare costs, reductions in government reimbursements, insurance companies' "caps" on benefit payments, and healthcare alternatives such as same-day surgery, walk-in clinics, and outpatient services. As a result, hospitals must operate in a more businesslike manner. Hospital personnel now work with fewer, but more acutely ill patients, and the public demands more quality service. Hospital administrators are finding that cost-containment measures, which include "downsizing" and reorganization, must be accompanied by staff training if the hospital is to survive the current climate in healthcare delivery.

The "Smile and Say Hello" training program of yesteryear is no longer enough. Good guest service behavior is the challenge today's institutions and their training departments must meet. ■

77 / Staff Awareness

David Demko

Once a healthcare facility is built, bricks and mortar cannot easily be rearranged to accommodate changes. Much like the thermostat that adjusts the temperature, however, staff can adjust the environment and minimize physical constraints. Getting staff members to realize the fullest potential in their daily dynamic relationships with residents requires training.

For Prosperity Oaks, a rental retirement

community housing over 200 seniors in a six-story complex located on twenty-seven wooded acres in South Florida, we conducted a training program to sensitize personnel to the special needs of older people and to promote resolution of environmental problems that could be eased by staff intervention.

THE TRAINING

I designed and conducted the training program, called SMART, an acronym for Senior Marketing and Retirement Training at the request of the Care Bridge Corporation, the management group for the retirement community. All staff members participated, including management, marketing, clerical, van drivers, receptionists, foodservice, housekeeping, building and grounds, and the health nurse.

Topically, the training included the psychosocial needs of older adults, age-related changes in their special senses (hearing, vision, taste, smell), and the art of helping. Experiential training included slides portraying elders' visual problems, and a hearing test demonstrating difficult situations. A theatrical experience, the "Feeble Follies," calls upon trainees to perform retirement community activities while sensory-impaired by goggles and earplugs; there are also special exercises in vision and hearing.

VISUAL CONCERNS AND SOLUTIONS

Visual problems require special attention. Decrease in the ability to see objects clearly requires special concern for print material, such as newsletters, posters, and menus. If these materials are difficult to read, the older adult may not understand what a poster is trying to communicate, order incorrectly from a menu, or get frustrated and give up reading altogether. Large print for brochures, newsletters, display ads, and posters will help. Don't forget business cards. If older patients can't read your phone number, they can't call. Allow adequate spacing between lines, stress important points, and minimize unnecessary information and graphics. Use color contrast to dramatize your message.

A second visual problem is a decrease in the ability to function in dramatic levels of light such as bright sunlight or dimly lit areas. Too much light, such as direct sunlight reflected from a shiny surface, causes squinting and tears, and may have hazardous results, such as a fall. Too little light as at twilight or in a low-lighted cocktail lounge, decreases the older adult's ability to drive or walk with confidence.

Since an 80-year-old needs three times more light to see as clearly as a young person, an intense reading lamp may be needed to flood a brochure or newsletter. Avoid the flare of print on glossy paper.

Helping older adults to function well in all levels of light should include: use of nongloss paper for printed menus, minimizing contrasts in light intensity, providing screen lighting in bright atrium areas, and using windows that cut down direct light. Courtesy vans and buses at night are helpful.

A third visual problem is depth perception, or the ability to judge distance or uneven surfaces. Painted lines can appear to be obstacles; steps that appear to blend make it difficult to see where one step ends and another begins; and uneven surfaces where carpet and tile meet provoke trips and falls. Help older adults walk with confidence. Stairways and entry areas should be well-lighted, as should public restrooms. Distinguish one floor surface from another, and mark steps and uneven surfaces by colors.

HEARING CONCERNS AND SOLUTIONS

The two common hearing problems of normal aging require staff training. The first problem, loss of sound volume, causes difficulties in hearing a human voice, doorbells and telephone, radio, and television; all need to be clearer and louder to be heard by the older ear.

The second problem is high-frequency loss. A female or a child's voice, a flute or piccolo, a voice over the telephone—all are hard to discern. Make eye contact before speaking so that the elder knows you are addressing him or her.

Move in close so that you can be heard. Face the person so that lipreading cues can be seen; slow your speech, keep pitch low, and speak clearly, without running words together. Rephrase your comments so those with high-frequency hearing problems have additional verbal cues to interpret your message. And avoid background noise such as piped-in radio music that competes with your conversation.

SUMMARY

Staff members can most significantly stimulate a positive living environment for the elderly because of their daily contact and dynamic relationships with residents. Knowing the impact of sensory loss and understanding how to minimize the problems created by those losses helps staff break age barriers. ■

78/Auditing Hospitality as an Incentive

Dianne Davis

No matter how proficient, attentive, or successful, healthcare managers, like other managers, need fresh insight from time to time. Even the best can become accustomed —nearly oblivious—to lapses and defects that clearly mar performance and irritate patients, residents, staff, and visitors. Managers do not regularly put themselves in the role of the people they serve. How telephones are answered, what information is given, persistent deferrals of appointments, delayed responses, and long lines and extensive periods of waiting without reliable information or diversion affect patients and their attitudes. But managers do not often subject themselves to those conditions. Few telephone anonymously into their own institutions just to find out whether calls are answered with reasonable speed, whether being put on hold is interminable, whether operators readily reach extensions numbers, and, most crucial, whether operators return to take a message when an extension does not pick up.

A fresh appraisal helps, as shown by a few examples. As consultant to an ambulatory surgical center, an exemplary "high-tech" and "high-touch" design, I noticed a small but important flaw. Within a reception area, I heard an intermittent, irritating noise, and discovered it was caused by chromed steel hangers squeaking when they were moved on their chromed steel rod. Unfortunately, patients in recovery, on the other side of the coat rack wall, were disturbed each time the hangers moved. The center's director admitted that she was unaware of the noise and disturbance. Little things make a difference and can mar an otherwise perfect experience.

Managers and their staffs know the routes to their facilities; first-time visitors need signs. At one hospital, I discovered that getting lost was easy for, from midtown or the airport, there were no signs except for one small blue Hospital sign with arrows pointing in two different directions! The sign marking the emergency entrance had become obscured by trees, and a fund-raising billboard was placed right in front of the smaller sign that bears the hospital's name. Inside the hospital's dining area, where hard surfaces created high noise levels, signs at food stations were hard to read. Elevators lacked floor registries. Had the manager merely visited a department store, he might have seen many ways to signify services and guide customers.

To discover a fault, discern its cause, and suggest ways to correct it is the function of fresh professional appraisal. Disarray and cluttered tables in a lounge or reception area may be cleared by providing magazine racks and coat pegs. The design, size, number, and location of trash cans can help people be kempt or slovenly. To add light, shelf, and paper to a public telephone location, where a sign politely asks users to limit calls, can help every-

The Hebrew Home for the Aged at Riverdale,
Riverdale, New York. (Photo: Courtesy of Joseph Breed)

one. People can be led to neatness and civility. A patient's room that lacks provisions for storing personal items, conveniences, such as electric outlets for razors or hairdriers, or reading lamps controlled by local switches can cause annoyance and diminish a patient's natural orderliness.

In one hospital I analyzed, lobbies were scattered with dying plants, debris in their pots, frayed and soiled furniture, and ugly signs. Grimy entrance door kickplates, mold growth in tile floor's grouting, a poor selection of fare in vending machines in the Emergency area, and corridors crowded by beds and other hospital furniture sent a message: Who cares? When those blemishes were pointed out to senior managers, they immediately recognized the need for improvement.

The healthcare institutions that will be successful while meeting the needs of the healthcare and senior community markets will integrate hospitality attitudes and services within their medical settings. Now growing about 9 percent a year, the healthcare industry is responding to two strong influences: the need for a coordinated hierarchy of healthcare services in a variety of settings and the patient's desire for a caring experience in those settings.

How well an institution conveys its intent to offer "total hospitality" is not easy to evaluate. Unfortunately, administrators are sometimes blinded by familiarity and cannot see the forest for the trees. Years ago, a hotel executive

might be asked to "mystery shop" a healthcare institution and make recommendations. Today, far more effective evaluation (and motivation) can be derived from a well-organized hospitality audit suited to the unique criteria of healthcare and senior communities.

Currently, there are valuable checklists for designs, such as Cannon's 50 points illustrated in Part V of this book. Other lists attempt to standardize interior finishes and furnishings; still others evaluate guest relations. Still others audit restaurants and hotels. There are also regulatory standards and the Joint Commission on Accreditation of Hospitals publishes Long Term Care Standards Manuals. There is continuing care retirement community accreditation; AARP offers a handbook. These standards and manuals address healthcare policies and procedures, but offer few detailed examinations related to hospitality-oriented design and services.

The difference between a technical design audit and one directed at healthcare hospitality can be illustrated by a single incident. Within a Manhattan ambulatory, surgical center, a dignified elderly woman, emerging from a dressing cubicle, barely covered by her "Johnnie," said to a man, emerging next door, in his "Johnnie," "Oh dear, next, I suppose, we'll meet at a dinner party!" Dignity, comfort, privacy, propriety—a hospitality audit seeks these social and emotional needs, a technical audit does not.

Such an analysis of hospitable environment is the focus of a quick, inexpensive evaluation, called the *Hospitality Quotient*, developed by Hospitality Healthcare Designs. Designed to produce an instant "Polaroid" picture of a facility's hospitality as *seen through the consumer's eyes*, it pinpoints factors that influence consumer satisfaction, perception of care, market practices, and profitability.

That hospitality/healthcare audit accomplishes three things: a greater awareness of consumer perceptions, an understanding of the "total hospitality" approach to healthcare, and a systematic directory for helping to raise a facility's "hospitality pulse." The first step, however, is to develop awareness of the existing situation. Frequently, that is difficult. A manager's first response to an audit is apt to be, "Don't waste time telling us the obvious. Just tell us what's wrong." My reply: "We don't know what's obvious to you. We will report what we find and what is missing."

A comprehensive hospitality/healthcare audit covers over ten essential areas, each with numerous detailed questions. A list of chief headings will suggest the breadth of the *Hospitality Quotient* process:

Main entrance or lobby
Hospitality information
Reception/checkout
Greetings
Telephone
Signage/directional and information
Calendars
Corridors/elevators and traffic circulation
Lighting
Hardware/appointments/equipment
Special places and designated spaces
Landscaping
Outdoor space
Treatment and dressing rooms
Foodservice
Patient's mood

Most audits are technical, like the "Fifty Points" Cannon cites here in Chapter 48, and those are vitally important. But a hospitality audit includes those technical points and, further, asks for success in social, emotional, and intellectual directions. It also provides insight and useful information for improvements and incentives. The Parkview Episcopal Medical Center in Pueblo, Colorado, reports that its quality training programs improved morale, lowered staff turnover, and decreased the percentage of late-starting surgeries from 48 to 8 percent. At other institutions, preregistration has hastened admissions. Transportation worries are relieved by limousine service or valet parking. Guest lodges, concierge services, restaurant-style menus, and "business from your bedside" have become popular amenities at hospitals. Express checkout with credit card charges greatly speed departures. Faced with a windowless waiting room, the Miami Heart Institute asked an artist to paint a trompe l'oeil mural, to everyone's enjoyment. Our research demonstrates that when consumers have a choice, they select facilities that provide *service*, *comfort*, and *convenience*.

The Miami Heart Institute, Miami Beach, Florida. Mural in the radiology waiting area. (Artist: Oriente Davila/Photo: Dianne Davis)

Each of us involved in senior living/healthcare today must recognize that only responsive organizations will prosper. Over all, a hospitality audit addresses one question: How flexibly responsive are your services in meeting unscheduled requests and needs? To serve today's demanding, sophisticated consumer, healthcare must offer many hospitality elements that increase satisfaction. As one colleague said, "People just don't stop their lives when they come. Whether it's a computer terminal or fax machine, secretarial services or telephones, communications must respond to patients' needs even in acute-care areas. Our job is to provide a welcoming, caring environment. Remember, we're in the business to sell beds just as hotels need to sell rooms!"

First impressions can make a difference in how a facility is perceived. What is seen, heard, and felt strongly influences selection of and contentment in hospitals, nursing homes, and senior communities. Hospitable design and services could have prevented the comment: "This place feels like a jail," an elderly visitor said to her children. "I'd rather die than go there." ∎

Part IX

Windows to the Future

Admittedly a series of vignettes, this concluding section first discusses three obstacles to gaining successful healthcare and senior communities. Following those essays about codes, regulations and finances, a major essay about the future CCRC's introduces some pioneering designs, including urban, multigenerational, mixed use projects. An essay about choosing designers concludes the book.

79 / Impact of Codes and Regulations

Martin H. Cohen

As diverse as it is, no other segment of our society is as dependent as the elderly are upon the built environment. Yet, environmental insults and barriers constantly impinge on each individual's independence. The physical and psychological needs of senior residents are not being met by existing codes and standards. Rather, those codes and standards frustrate innovative efforts to prolong and improve the quality of independent living, impede the provision of quality care, delay construction of needed facilities, and increase both their initial capital and long-term operating costs.

Horror stories abound in housing, senior living communities, long-term care facilities for assisted living, personal-care, and nursing homes: of badly needed replacement projects delayed eight to ten years by draconian regulations and bureaucratic approval processes, while costs mount and three or four generations of hapless residents remain trapped in outmoded facilities with recognized deficiencies, until power struggles and personality conflicts are resolved; of redundant and overlapping federal, state, regional, and local environmental standards, which force architects and engineers to assemble working design codes based upon the most stringent, costly, and sometimes irreconcilable requirements; of conflicting interpretations by code administrators, often between representatives of competing agencies, but even between officials of the same agency (e.g., central office plan reviewers and regional field inspectors), frequently resulting in costly delays and construction changes to obtain certification.

Originally, environmental zoning and design codes were established for the purpose of assuring the public that:

- ambitious (and sometimes careless or unscrupulous) developers would preserve such cherished amenities as light, air, and open space, while excluding inappropriate uses from residential neighborhoods or communities (consider the zoning regulations developed by municipalities such as New York in the 1920s);

- expenditures of federal, state, and private dollars for development and/or operation would meet certain minimum standards of construction, safety, sanitation, and function (consider the Title One urban renewal regulations of the late 1940s and early 1950s, or the Hill-Burton requirements of 1954).

Following the advent of the Medicare and Medicaid programs in the 1960s and the frustrating rise in healthcare costs that ensued, these codes and their descendants have been increasingly misused as instruments of cost containment. Difficulties in improving quality and controlling major but elusive long-term costs of operation (such as inadequate access, unnecessary care, excessive utilization, lengths of stay, medical fees, labor, maintenance, and repair costs) have led to excessive concentration on simplistic control of finite but relatively minor initial capital costs such as construction and equipment. Thus, codes and standards written to prescribe barely adequate minimums now are enforced as rigorous maximums, to be exceeded only by the unreimbursed expenditures of sponsors, charities, and philanthropists. Meanwhile, inefficient and obsolete physical plants become more costly to operate and replace, even as they become ever more inappropriate, as technologies and modes of use change. Even brand-new facilities are constrained by obsolete space and layout standards, based upon outmoded concepts of staffing, technology, safety, function, and amenities.

A substantial body of knowledge about environmental design for aging exists, research is in progress, and design-for-aging books are published by the American Association of Homes for the Aging (AAHA), the American Health Care Association (AHCA), and the American Institute of Architects (AIA), which has an up-to-date design for aging database on-line in the AIA library. National and regional conferences on long-term care increasingly incorporate symposiums or workshops on environmental design; and evidence of developing sensitivity and expertise among sponsors, developers, architects, and designers is very exciting. But, few existing codes and standards defining residential and/or healthcare environments are based on research. The allowable square footage or cost of a facility, or its layout, construction materials, furnishings, equipment, and systems (e.g. technologies for monitoring and communications), do not reflect research into the needs of older people or the efficient use of long-term-care staff resources. Indeed, most regulations are derived empirically, by averaging existing (i.e., obsolete) facility dimensions or by modifying hospital standards, without consideration of how satisfactory such might be for senior living and/or long-term care.

Encouraged by enlightened providers, published paradigms, and dedicated donors, innovative professionals are trying to create environments for aging that support and delight their residents, while enhancing their lifestyles and reducing functional costs. They recognize that the principal venues for long-term care will, first and foremost, be residences; that they must be enjoyable to live in; and, if they are to enhance the quality of elderly living, they must not over time become barriers to independent living. This simple set of goals, however, seems to have escaped many regulatory, funding, and reimbursement agencies, whose obsolete regulations and "bottom-line" mentalities still condemn too many future residents to impoverished standards of comfort and amenity.

For example, the average person entering a nursing home today is an 83- to 86-year-old woman, who will spend the rest of her life (perhaps 3 to 5 years) living in one room. In that room, she will seek to preserve her identity, dignity, and privacy, surrounded by the few remaining mementos of her life, including her clothes, some photographs and letters, maybe some souvenirs or treasured curios, and perhaps a favorite chair or dresser. Should she really have to share that room with someone else? Must she really accept an inboard bed,

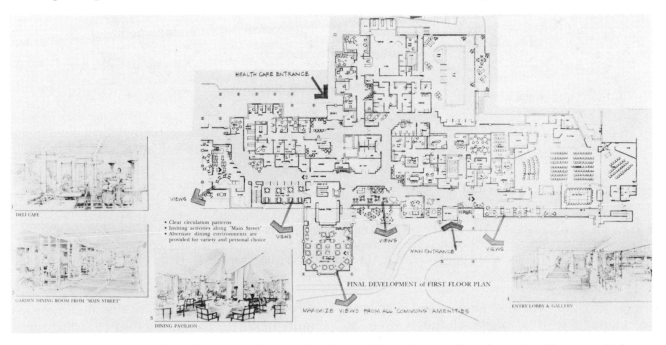

Orchard Cove Continuing Care Retirement Community, Canton, Massachusetts. First-floor plan. (Sponsors: Hebrew Rehabilitation Center for Aged, Roslindale, MA, and Terence G. Lewis, Sr., Senior Vice President, New Ventures/ Architect: Huygens DiMella Shaffer and Associates, Inc., in association with Korsunsky Krank Erickson and Associates Architects, Inc./Consultants: Martin H. Cohen, FAIA, Armonk, NY, and Lorraine G. Hiatt, PhD., Innovage, NY.)

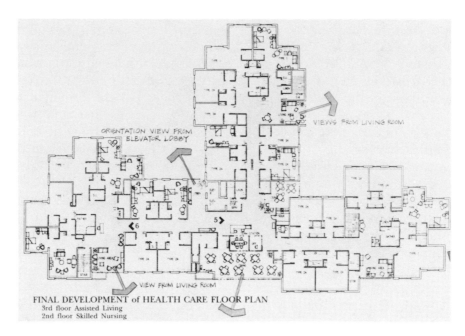

FINAL DEVELOPMENT of HEALTH CARE FLOOR PLAN
3rd floor Assisted Living
2nd floor Skilled Nursing

Orchard Cove Continuing Care Retirement Community, Canton, Massachusetts. (Sponsors: Hebrew Rehabilitation Center for Aged, Roslindale, MA, and Terence G. Lewis, Sr., Senior Vice President, New Ventures/Architect: Huygens DiMella Shaffer and Associates, Inc., in association with Korsunsky Krank Erickson and Associates Architects, Inc./Consultants: Martin H. Cohen, FAIA, Armonk, NY, and Lorraine G. Hiatt, PhD., Innovage, NY.)

Orchard Cove Continuing Care Retirement Community, Canton, Massachusetts. (Sponsors: Hebrew Rehabilitation Center for Aged, Roslindale, MA, and Terence G. Lewis, Sr., Senior Vice President, New Ventures/Architect: Huygens DiMella Shaffer and Associates, Inc., in association with Korsunsky Krank Erickson and Associates Architects, Inc./Consultants: Martin H. Cohen, FAIA, Armonk, NY, and Lorraine G. Hiatt, PhD., Innovage, NY.)

away from the window? How is she supposed to manage with a single clothes closet 20 inches deep and 22 inches wide? How are her physical and psychological needs (and those of her family visitors) to be met in 100 square feet (or less in an older, unrenovated facility) in a 4-bed room? Yet, those are the minimum requirements for patient rooms in a skilled-nursing facility in the current *Guidelines for Construction and Equipment of Hospital and Medical Facilities*, which is used by most states to certify compliance with Medicare and

Medicaid standards. Those requirements certainly are *minimum*, and perhaps might even be understood as essential minimums in an era of stubborn, uncontrolled, and inflationary healthcare costs. But how can we justify enforcing such requirements as *maximums*? By what set of warped values should we punish providers who choose to exceed such standards—refuse to reimburse any costs that exceed "caps" based upon such "minimums," even when the rationales for such departures include more functional space criteria and layouts, resulting in more cost-effective staffing?

When states relax or abandon certificate-of-need (CON) regulations, many people mistakenly assume more rational, market-based standards will take their place. Instead, penny-wise and pound-foolish attitudes often persist in states' rate-setting commissions and/or reimbursement agencies, in bond underwriting or insurance agencies, and among mortgage lenders. Thus, even though only four to six states may still suffer from draconian CON regulations, there still is a widespread need to improve the design of senior living environments and an urgent requirement to establish a national climate for excellence.

Together, providers, developers, architects, and residents must convince governmental review agencies, rate-setting commissions, insurance payors, mortgage lenders, and bond underwriters to adopt more realistic guidelines, similar to those that developers of successful market-rate residences employ to attract investors and residents. If they don't, the residential and healthcare facilities they build will still cost more than the public thinks they should, will continue to become obsolete before their time, and ultimately may be rejected in favor of any better alternative that becomes available in the future. Given such real threats to a facility's potential marketability and long-term viability, it should be clear that quality environmental design for aging is at least as important to the sponsors, operators, regulators, and underwriters of a facility as it may be to the residents and their families. ■

80/Surviving the Approvals Process

William Glass

Gaining approval to develop a site for senior housing can be fraught with risk. Such sites are often marginal "left-over" properties, or the undesirable parcel of a planned unit development (PUD). Most zoning codes do not recognize some healthcare categories, such as the continuing care retirement community. While he or she may presume that special uses are permitted, the developer facing zoning review still must prove that the proposed senior facility will not adversely impact its neighborhood. The possibility of clustered or high-rise buildings and concern about traffic, sirens, and ambulances excite opposition. An ill-conceived plan or a failure in public education can leave the best-intentioned project stillborn on the drawing board.

Seldom does a zoning ordinance offer a classification that adequately describes or allows the desired seniors' project. Often, the zoning compliance becomes politicized. Owners of adjacent property can become surprisingly irrational at the thought of "old" people becoming neighbors. Apprehensions develop into visions of illness, ambulance sirens, and death: The NIMBY Syndrome, "Not In My Backyard." NIMBY groups can thwart development, and the costs in time and effort to combat them can be expensive.

Perceptions created during the zoning approval process can benefit or stain public reception. If the initial efforts are tainted, can a facility ever generate a positive market image? If early occupancy is financially critical, can momentum be regained subsequent to a public confrontation?

Urban prototype for Marriott Life Care/Style B. (Architect: The Martin Organization/Photo: Courtesy of the Marriott Corporation)

Anticipation of potential opposition is essential. It requires our understanding the local planning/zoning environment, including understanding zoning psychology. Maintain the position of a "reasonable person." "Walk a mile in the other person's shoes" before responding or taking a firm position. Anticipate, evaluate, and act on predictable questions before they become issues. Many citizens do not recognize the differences and benefits between seniors' housing and conventional housing. Be ready for questions and be viewed as flexible. In discussions with neighbors and public officials, do not overstate; exhibit sincerity and patience. Strive not to lecture; *beseech their understanding.* As a rule, never embarrass public officials; help them look effective. Invite ideas. Communicate benefits and positive images such as community, compatibility, quality, lifestyle, and neighborhood. Even the most avid opponents relax when offered the possibility that a facility may serve their neighbors, their parents, or eventually themselves.

Prior to selecting a site or seeking approval, preliminary intelligence and research are necessary to assess risk. Before expending devel-

opment funds, know the local municipal and neighborhood environment well. Investigate the history of similar projects in the area. Was any precedent set on prior submittals, whether approved or denied? Research the existing zoning ordinance to determine all possible tactical directions before setting a course with no recourse! What is your site's history? What is the sequence of public hearings? What are the individual agendas or "hot buttons" of board members? Who are the local power brokers? Which individuals or constituencies could speak positively for your project? Common interests among diverse players can construct collective interest and action. Gauging the level, intensity, and direction of potential opposition can eventually save time and dollars.

Creating the site approval team is key. Who should be perceived to lead the effort? The developer, zoning attorney, architect, or landscape architect are all candidates, depending on the specific project. Create a written plan to communicate anticipated parameters to all players. Elicit feedback from various disciplines. Support the design disciplines by allocating enough money to fund a model and renderings; most citizens have difficulty visualizing without drawings or models. Plan a critical path over time. Continuously update your assumptions with outcomes as they materialize: modify your plan and anticipate and diffuse problems before they occur.

Prior to application, schedule initial community contacts to discern support and to measure the intensity of opposition. Meet local community groups, owners of adjacent property, and other interested parties on an open basis. Listen to the message they send by their questions and concerns. Communicate to gain support. Where real or perceived apprehensions are left to the imagination, rational concern turns emotional. Once reason turns to emotion the probability of a lengthy campaign increases. When a project is ready, time becomes the developer's nemesis. Involve concerned citizens in an advisory capacity; advertise, plan tours of similar facilities, offer

presentations, and organize informal coffee hours. You seek their help in building a project you believe is beneficial. The more time and care spent on the municipal and community relations effort, the smoother and more rational the approvals process will be.

No matter how well-prepared, inevitably the time comes to negotiate final issues. How flexible is the business plan? You may find that some beneficial modifications come through participation: alliances with local suppliers, affiliations with a group medical practice, or contracts with a local industry or church. But where demands damage a business plan, compromise must be carefully considered, because once it is offered, it is usually gone. Consider long and hard before mentioning any legal action; threats can easily backfire. Hostility is easy to generate. What your senior living project needs is enthusiastic friends. ■

---

81 / The Continuing Care Retirement Community on a College Campus

Albert Bush-Brown

Like so many alliances that seem natural and inevitable, the combination of a senior community or a continuing care retirement community (CCRC) with a school, college, or university has yet to be realized as an integrated operation resident on campus.

Mention such an alliance to the elderly Dartmouth alumni who book the Hanover Inn to capacity, and their faces light up. Mention it to the retired businessmen, "rusty nails," they call themselves, who meet at the Piping Rock Club, in Locust Valley, New York, to hear a speaker after lunch, and they ask when such a CCRC might be built. Ask the adults and their teachers in the Hutton House lecture program at Long Island University's C. W. Post College in Brookville, New York, and they will tell you that a CCRC on a college campus is a great idea. The Elder Hostel pro-

gram is popular, as are Alumni Colleges and their airline and cruise ship educational tours to the ancient Aegean and Far East.

Why influential alumni have not marshalled their enthusiasm to get a CCRC built on a campus is not clear. There are, however, some hopeful premonitions at Ames, Iowa, and, as we write, Oberlin, Ohio. Soon, we can expect the elderly to override current prejudices against clustered housing or amend the restrictive zoning that denies building permits for healthcare communities and certificates of need to skilled-nursing centers. For it makes no sense to force older residents to leave their half-century-old affiliations to enter distant nursing homes away from sons and daughters and all the friends and services they knew. If they must move, for those with tight bonds to a Berkeley or Yale or Princeton, why should

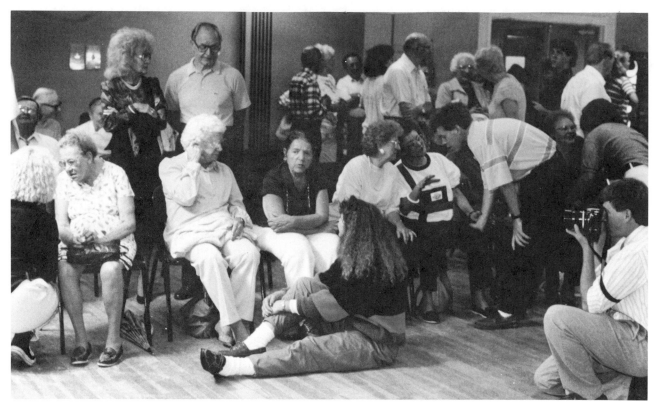

"Up with People." (Photo: Tadder/Baltimore)

they not return to a community that is part of their college heritage? Even at 80, the great Spanish art scholar, Chandler Post, believed that to be more than a fifteen minute walk from Harvard's Widener Library would be fatal.

Today, there are several adjacencies. Babson College in Wellesley has leased land to North Hill CCRC. Near Haverford College, the Quadrangle's well-stocked library testifies to the residents' professorial origins and interests. Beaumont, near Bryn Mawr College, attracts alumni. Adjacent to the George School, Penn's Woods has sometimes supplied teachers and enjoyed the school's programs, and a college near Foulkeways has been a source of waitresses and choral and dramatic groups. Iowa State University at Ames has a university-affiliated retirement community, Green Hills, and in Exeter, New Hampshire, Engelbrecht & Griffin have designed a CCRC for retired faculty members and alumni.

An integrated affiliation could benefit both the CCRC and college. "It seems like a natural marriage of interests," David Clark of Oberlin College has said about Oberlin's planned CCRC. We want ". . . to keep some of our great minds . . . and alumni . . . who want to spend their retirement years in this kind of intellectually enriched environment, rather than basking in the sun."

Day-care centers are needed at colleges and universities for employees' children; a successful center exists within Medford Leas. Many colleges need specialists teaching on a part-time basis; librarians, museum guards, and custodians of music rooms are wanted. The CCRC, in turn, needs the college student to guide or to read to the sight-impaired husband, to give his wife time to pursue her own interests, and to introduce some college activities the student is enthusiastic about. The college libraries' tapes and films could be a resource, and the theater, concerts, and public lectures offered on many college campuses could greatly increase the CCRC's satisfactions.

Enrollment in college courses is a formal arrangement that may not be popular, but many colleges during the 1970s developed special offerings that drew adults. Most attractive and rewarding to professors and adults alike are Alumni College and Weekend College—short courses on themes chosen by adults.

A university or boarding school alliance with a CCRC could address the need for trained administrators in lifecare institutions. A university's hospital could develop specialists in geriatric care.

Vacant land on many state-owned university campuses that have smaller enrollments than planned might be leased by not-for-profit CCRCs, which could use state bond provisions to build communities that are integrated into the educational programs. Many dividends will flow from such integration.

Since college means "freedom" for some undergraduates, some students may resent the presence of an elderly population, but a CCRC on campus may result in tangible benefits and also some intangible ones we need, especially a society where youth and the aged have concern for each other. ■

82/Financing the Hospitable Healthcare Community

James E. Eden

The concept of retirement communities in the United States dates back to the early 1900s. Churches and fraternal organizations recognized an obligation to care for older members of society and established homes for the aged. Often, these were converted houses, and provided a bedroom, meals, and limited services. In time, nursing services were added, marking the start of the continuum-of-care concept. These facilities were most commonly financed by "asset turnover"; in return, the entrant received a promise of care for life.

Growth was slow. During the first half of this century, life expectancy was low, and older citizens were not numerous. Family units remained geographically close, and elders could be cared for at home. By midcentury, the number of elderly increased. Greater mobility dispersed the family unit. Medical science reduced the childhood diseases that had caused early death, and antibiotics, nutrition, and physical exercise lengthened life expectancy.

Eleemosynary sponsors began to build institutional buildings to care for the elderly. Meanwhile, the wealth of older citizens was rising, and the "asset turnover" concept gave way to the lifecare concept. Instead of turning over all assets, the entering resident paid a fixed-sum endowment fee in return for a promise of care for life. Social Security payments and pensions made it practical to charge a monthly maintenance fee as well. This led to an expansion of services. In the 1960s, the creation of Medicaid and Medicare benefits enabled lifecare institutions to provide substantial nursing capacity.

During the 1970s and 1980s, the population born after World War One expanded the percentage of elderly. The "graying of America" has become publicly recognized. Medical care and research are directed at the diseases that attack the middle-aged, with consequent rising longevity, and the elderly male, as well as female, can expect longer life. The population explosion of the elderly has profound consequences on national and corporate policy, and its financial implications will be felt well into the next century.

Early, developers recognized these changes and retirement community construction grew rapidly in the last two decades. As new conventional apartment and condominium construction tapered off, reflecting overbuilding in urban areas, developers with capital looked for new investments. Lifecare projects could be financed by fees, land being held for apartment uses could be profitably developed, and the growing number of senior citizens offer a perceived market.

That retirement community construction

has been a developer-driven business has many implications. For example, developers have seldom been developer–operators, even though this industry is operations-intensive and healthcare delivery requires management. The developer's focus has been short term. High, initial developer fees damaged projects. Poor site location and faulty predictions of markets hurt other projects. Where building designs were operationally inefficient and had little marketing appeal, projects failed. Most important, few developers had the benefit of consumer research indicating what prospective residents might or might not find appealing, and virtually no project reflected advice from the gerontological community.

Both proprietary and not-for-profit developers have shown a willingness to enter expensive financing arrangements, whose costs burden operations. Except for upper-income communities, those costs for money borrowed for construction retarded the expansion of services and programs. Sometimes, lifecare endowment fees were drawn down to supplement operating revenues, thereby depleting any reserves intended to pay off debt principal and future healthcare obligations. Sometimes a "backwards proforma" was concocted to justify charging monthly fees to cover amortization of high front-end costs. Such costs contributed to slower than anticipated project fill rates and led to some spectacular failures.

Capital formation has yet to occur consistently in an organized way. Aware of difficulties and failures, lenders and investors lack underwriting experience and are wary of the unpredictable costs promised by future healthcare commitments to residents. Occupancy rates are difficult to predict and have generally been slower than feasibility studies and proformas indicate. Lack of reliable consumer research has not helped to allay investors' concerns.

Still, many projects are successful, and recent years have brought some industry consolidation. Viable trade associations, such as the National Association of Senior Living Industries in Annapolis, Maryland, advocate better practices. Large, well-funded corporations, such as Beverly Enterprises, Hyatt Corporation, Manor Care, Inc., and Marriott Corpo-

ration have entered retirement community construction and operation, bringing capital and credibility. They often offer a rental-only payment plan, with small or no up-front fees, and commercially available long-term-care insurance is becoming a reality. On the federal and state levels, there is encouraging discussion of catastrophic health insurance and housing-related reimbursement programs.

The hospitality-related corporations entering the healthcare business are experiencing some notable success. Both Hyatt and Marriott have conducted substantial consumer research, and their experience in marketing is effective. Setting high standards for excellent service, they are gaining product acceptance and faster fill rates. With new and better services, good locations, more advice from the gerontological community, and sensitive marketing, the industry seems better poised. Strong developer/operators have taken hold. Proactive wellness intervention programs and increased investment in aging research, consumer research, and professional marketing bode well for the future.

Successes will lead to further evolution. Case management for private, paying, well elderly, increased home care services, and wellness programs will be among the array of senior services added to retirement communities. Success will lead to capital formation, and then smaller developers will be able to reenter the market for the newly accepted models. Certainly the new projects will attract the elderly to hospitable, residential designs with an emphasis on living as independently as possible. They will be operationally more efficient, but with increased marketing appeal. Most important, in keeping with the spirit of the Older American's Act of 1985, they will be affordable.

New program development is essential. Today's array of amenities represents a basic offering in the form of meals, housekeeping, laundry, transportation, social activities, and security. Few operators have any real knowledge of what programs and activities might extend independent living or make a higher level of care seem more residential and independent. Advance in this area will require public/private partnerships between the operators and the gerontological academic centers, as well as continued funding for aging research.

Meanwhile, major obstacles impede development. For example, adequate sites will be difficult to find in the deepest markets. Zoning approvals are difficult to obtain in many communities. Certificates of need for all the healthcare components are difficult to come by. Many of these barriers are inadvertent because community leaders do not understand the product. Their labor-intensive requirement is a serious problem as the supply of labor shrinks in many of the best locations.

All these matters will require broad cooperation and possibly government incentives. Given the equity many elderly have in their houses, combined with pensions, savings, and Social Security, it seems reasonable to try to modify current tax laws to relieve the elderly from those capital gains and income taxes that prevent their converting equity into lifecare. Just as the energy crisis provoked a national policy, there is urgent need for a cohesive and comprehensive policy on aging. Such a policy, the subject of the third White House Conference on Aging, will greatly affect our industry's future.

The business of providing housing and related services to the growing population of elderly in this country represents not only a business opportunity, but a cultural one. The American heritage holds our elderly in esteem, and as their numbers increase, developers, governments, academic centers, and business leaders should conspire to supply them with environments and services in a profitable and socially desirable manner. ■

---

83 / Design Opportunities

Wayne Ruga

To create a total living environment for mature adults, it is not enough to rely on the traditional list of activities. We should address eight "opportunity elements," each of which can be shaped to reflect local tradition, culture, and values.

The first opportunity element is *socialization*, a healthy, outward expression of one's individuality. Caretel® provides a symbolic front porch at the entrance to each resident's unit. The porch is a transitional zone between the public street and the private room, enabling residents to see what is going on in the street and to be seen by passersby. Socialization is also advanced by landmarks. "Meet me at the fountain" encourages movement, activity, encounters, engagements, and expectations. A wellness center also contributes to socialization; residents meet at a pool, spa, massage area, sauna, steam room, library, workout room, or game room; classrooms, examination and treatment rooms, training areas, and a sports lawn are further points of meeting, as are internal and external gardens.

The second opportunity element promotes *personal growth and development*. One setting is a media resource center that includes a library with books, audiovisual material, periodicals, artwork, and a reading room. There might also be a teaching–training area, a demonstration area, and tutorial rooms. A network could extend beyond the center to enable access from home or patients' rooms to media resources. Now that more care is given within the elder's own homes, access to remote media resources could play a vital role

The third opportunity for enhancing life satisfactions is to *provide transportation* that eases barriers to mobility. The entire system must be improved, including parking convenience and security, public conveyance, traffic segregation, convenient access to pickup and drop-off points, appropriate weather shelters, and clear internal circulation. Access is key. All architec-

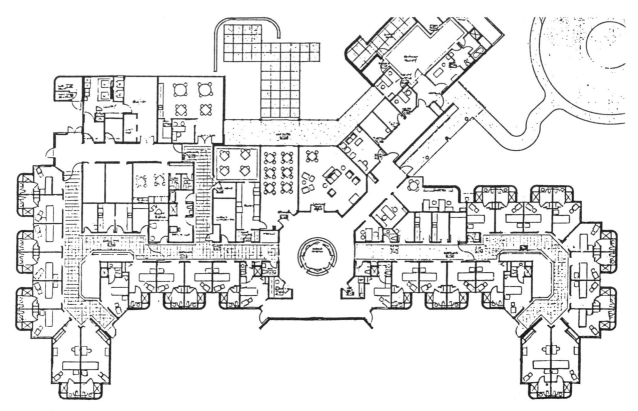

Harbour's Edge Life Care Community, Delray Beach, Florida. Skilled-Nursing Center. (Architect: Shepherd Legan Aldrian/Plan courtesy of Lifecare Services)

tural barriers should be eliminated.

The fourth opportunity is *entertainment and cultural activities*. The relevant environments are spaces for drama, concerts, and motion picture film. Participation will increase if workshops and studios are provided.

Work is the fifth element. Attainment of age sixty-five does not require stopping work. In fact, new careers frequently open. New business opportunities, volunteer programs, and professional support services all enhance life satisfaction. A business center with meeting rooms and office space will help start new enterprises. A reference shelf, secretarial support, word processors, and fax should be available. A branch bank, investment counseling, and, if possible, a post office are also useful. Crafts need other work spaces, and there should be places for writing.

The sixth opportunity element is *communication*. Information is transmitted through interactive electronic media, telephones, intercoms, pagers, and emergency call systems. Devices that encourage communication can be located throughout the circulation system,

at landmarks, plazas, scenic overlooks, widened intersections, and appropriately designed lobbies.

The seventh element is *healthful rest*, which will benefit from adequate acoustical insulation, siting to gain privacy, and freedom from intrusive cameras, emergency call alarms, and intercoms. Individual thermal and ventilation controls contribute to healthful rest.

The eighth way to enhance life satisfaction is *personal expression*. Rooms and apartments should allow residents to express their lifestyles. Their choice of furniture, art, color, lighting, and foliage—all important decisions —reflects individuality. Their freedom to shop, choose clothes, and enter a restaurant or theater affects their self-image. Food and dining areas, restaurants, and food markets are important settings for personal choice and expression.

When environmental planning and design achieve more than mere functional and aesthetic results, when, instead, they enhance life experience, there will be new caring, curing, and satisfying places. ■

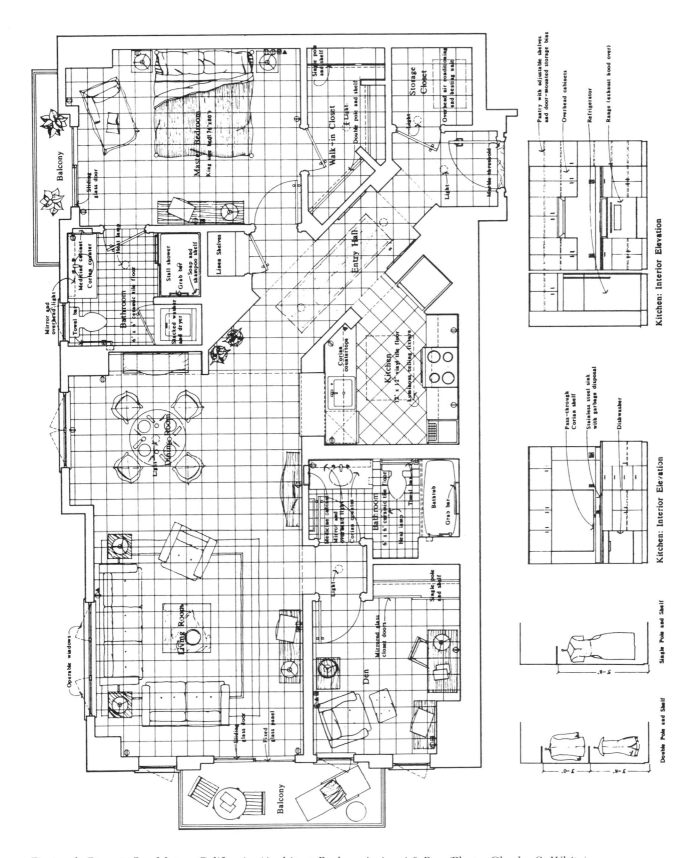

Peninsula Regent, San Mateo, California. (Architect: Backen, Arrigoni & Ross/Photo: Charles S. White)

84/The Continuing Care Retirement Community: Past, Present, Future

Martin Trueblood

What is the status of the continuing care retirement community (CCRC) industry after twenty-five years' development? Approximately 600 CCRCs are in operation today, with many more in development. No longer an innovation, the CCRC has evolved to reflect the life experience and expectations of residents. The following are my observations about the changes that have accrued over the past twenty-five years and my predictions of changes in the future.

UNIT DESIGN

The primary changes in living unit design are larger units and full kitchens instead of kitchenettes. Full kitchens are partly a response to the higher cost of small nonstandard kitchen fixtures in contrast to the more competitive cost of standard units. Increased apartment sizes respond to demand and the realization that enlargement costs run about a third the cost of average initial space.

UNIT MIX

Where, twenty years ago, the two- or three-bedroom unit was infrequent, a significant preference for such units reflects the dramatic increase in couples electing to move to a CCRC, the longer life expectancy for men, and their much greater acceptance of the idea of CCRC residency. Earlier election by couples has also contributed to the increase. Some new CCRCs offer two or more bedrooms in over sixty of the independent units.

ELIMINATION OF STUDIO

Early CCRCs offered studios, which appealed to single persons (widowed or never married). Today, fewer elderly persons are satisfied with studio units, which has resulted in older com-

Broadmead, Baltimore, Maryland. Apartment of Mrs. Alexander S. Cochran. (Architect: Cochran, Stephenson & Donkervoet, Inc./Photo: Albert Bush-Brown)

munities having empty studio units and waiting lists for larger units. Many older CCRCs now combine two adjacent units into one larger unit. Given full kitchens, construction costs for small one-bedroom units are not significantly greater than those for a large studio.

AMENITIES

Certain amenities have become passé, while new ones are now desired. Where a shuffle-

Broadmead, Baltimore, Maryland. (Architect: Cochran, Stephenson & Donkervoet, Inc./Photo: Albert Bush-Brown)

board court was standard and sufficient, swimming pools, once rarities, are now almost a necessity. Other new features include a computer room, a fax machine, a bank, a residents' association office, and exercise facilities.

MEAL ARRANGEMENTS

Dining in CCRCs has changed significantly. Today new communities provide menus with a choice of several entrees, a one-meal plan, open seating, and a coffee shop; most recently, main dining rooms are being divided into two or more sections with different themes.

ENTRANCE FEE

Twenty-five years ago the most common entrance fee arrangement provided for no refund on death and no refund on voluntary withdrawal after fifty months. Today, most plans provide for a refund on death, and many offer a choice of plans. While this increases the entrance fee, the availability of a refund plan has broadened the market.

STATE LAWS REGULATING CONTINUING CARE RETIREMENT COMMUNITIES AND ACCREDITATION

Twenty-five years ago there were no state laws regulating the CCRC. Today many states have such laws, and each year more states are writing regulations. There is also a movement toward professional review and accreditation.

RESIDENTS' ASSOCIATIONS

Residents have become more and more active through their associations, and today have a strong voice in management decisions. Much debate surrounds residents' role on a board, particularly regarding confidentiality and the right to vote on matters concerning staff members and other residents. The value of active resident activities committees, however, is well recognized.

GROWTH OF CONTINUING CARE RETIREMENT COMMUNITIES IN THE FUTURE

By the year 2000, I predict there will be 1000 CCRCs in the United States, and by 2020 there will be 2000. This is not a wild guess. The Philadelphia area is a good example. There are approximately 40 CCRCs for the area's 5,000,000 population: one CCRC per 125,000 people or eight per million. At that ratio, the entire United States population of 250,000,000 would have 2000 CCRCs right now. Even in Philadelphia, the demand for CCRCs is far from met. The CCRCs' residents are predominantly white Anglo-Saxon Protestants. Many others in the Philadelphia area will eventually elect to enter a CCRC for their later years. Fifty years from now there could be 5000 CCRCs in the United States.

BROADENING THE ECONOMIC RANGE OF CONTINUING CARE RETIREMENT COMMUNITIES

Until now, most sponsoring groups have been more successful establishing upscale projects, while acceptance of more affordable CCRCs has been disappointing. More recently, the more affordable projects appear to work best in markets where they compete with upscale projects. They become more acceptable once the idea of living in a CCRC has become established and visible.

CONTINUING EDUCATION

Tomorrow's residents will have lived with continuing education throughout their careers. They will want extensive continuing education programs. College courses in history, philoso-

Model for BDHS/WMLC, Springfield, Massachusetts. (Architect: Sherertz, Franklin, Crawford & Shaffner)

phy, mathematics, astronomy, and art will be the norm. I think that keeping up with current affairs, and stretching and exercising the mind will be important parts of any wellness concept.

CULTURE

Ideally, a CCRC should be located near cultural resources. Residents may not take advantage of all the things available, but they think they will. There should be a museum, an orchestra, and other cultural resources, including sporting events, within a reasonable distance of the CCRC.

HEALTH EDUCATION

Part of the continuing education program should be the availability of health education resources. Residents of the future will be vitally interested in health programs.

EXERCISE

Tomorrow's residents will be from the aerobic age. Some new CCRCs have provided spas and equipment. That hasn't worked as well as expected and isn't always good for people of advanced age, but exercise is. An exercise program using exercise mats, with a leader, and set to music, is fun and will be standard in the future. Exercise programs in pools will be popular, and each community should have a walking trail, either outdoors or inside.

NUTRITION

What older persons should eat to maintain good health has not been certain. Still, nutrition is a major factor in health maintenance. Future residents will demand not only nutrition education programs but also a role in menu planning.

RECREATION

Future residents will be involved in the recreational program, its operation, and its planning. (Essay 20, by Donald Moon, describes residents' committees and activities. Essay 21 emphasizes the role of residents in creative arts.)

ORGANIZATIONAL STRUCTURE

In the future, there will be both not-for-profit and for-profit CCRCs, and since my company primarily manages not-for-profit facilities, I clearly prefer the not-for-profit structure. While there are a few fine for-profit companies in the field, and there will be more, I predict that the industry will remain mostly not-for-profit in the foreseeable future. Most existing CCRCs are self-managed, but I see a strong trend toward not-for-profit boards hiring professional management firms. One of the reasons for this is that the lenders are insisting on it. Lenders are simply saying they won't lend money without a professional management contract.

COMPOSITION OF CORPORATE BOARDS

I predict that future boards will generally be larger. The day of the small board is probably over, and future boards, of approximately 20 people, will consist of equal numbers of men and women.

RESIDENT PARTICIPATION ON BOARDS

There will be resident participation on corporate boards. The question will be what form this participation takes. Boards without resident input should consider ways to encourage resident participation without causing severe problems. Residents on a board tend to think short term, and a board must think long term. Usually, board members serve independently, without representing a constituency. Any resident serving on a board cannot avoid representing the residents. This creates divergent responsibility and can impede decision making. My preference is to have one or two residents, appointed by the residents' association, attend all board meetings, and take part in discussions. Under this system, residents can have a strong voice and can report back to the residents' association without being placed in the position of voting on price increases, executive salaries, and major use of funds. This system also makes it legal to deny confidential information on other residents to the representatives of the residents' association.

THE RESIDENTS OF THE FUTURE

I predict that entering residents will be a good deal older. In 1960, the average entry age was around seventy-four. At that time, sponsors hoped for younger residents and were disappointed when few under seventy chose the CCRC arrangement. Now, twenty years later, the typical entry age is seventy-eight. What does that imply? I coined a phrase many years ago. People move to a CCRC at "the age of apprehension," and I believe that is still true. People don't move to a CCRC until they awake at 3:00 A.M. and ask themselves how they are going to cope if they become frail or if they lose their mental abilities. Since it is generally agreed that the health of older persons is improving, it follows that "the age of apprehension" will rise from the current age of seventy-eight. In the future there may be a time when the average age of admission is over eighty. Since there is little evidence of significant life extension after age eighty, there could possibly be a time when the average life expectancy on admission could decrease.

THE RESIDENTIAL UNIT

Today's significant trend toward larger units should continue. Future residents will come from large homes with large rooms. The small, 600-square-foot units won't sell. Older facilities with smaller units will need to serve a different economic level, or modify their small units. The mix of unit sizes will probably include very few, if any, studio units, and a high percentage will offer more than one bedroom. Many new communities already include some three-bedroom units.

CHANGES TO THE INPATIENT CARE UNIT

The future CCRC will move away from the medical model for nursing care. Currently, we are locked into the federal standards of Medicare. We are told how far from a nursing station the furthest room must be. Technology long ago supplanted such standards and their rationale. Future design will have small, private rooms, standard doors, a more homelike appearance, and totally different nurses' sta-

tions. The current nurses' station is an anachronism in the electronic age. A receptionist is needed, but the nurses could perform paperwork in a totally different way. I'm convinced that the nurses' station interferes with the nurses' work. Perhaps an electronic dispenser for medication for each patient is possible— some way to assure compliance, but without using the nurses' time.

HOME HEALTHCARE

It has been popular in recent years to support home healthcare as a viable solution to the problem of caring for the elderly and as a satisfactory alternative to personal care or nursing home care. While there is a great need for short-term home healthcare for a person living alone, and for some degree of long-term home healthcare for one or two persons living together, it is not a viable solution for a longer period of time. For a person living alone, home healthcare can result in total isolation from society and, for couples, it doesn't work when one member is totally impaired for a long time. In the future CCRC, there should be an extensive program of home-delivered health services. This would not be twenty-four-hour bed care or companion service, but rather an economical system of delivered services aimed at extending independence and at reducing the utilization of personal-care and nursing services.

PERSONAL-CARE UNITS

In the future, the personal-care units will be significantly different. Some communities have called these units "assisted residential" which, by its name, implies a standard apartment setting with assistance. Personal-care rooms in the past have been just that, too often semiprivate, and with a shared toilet and no bath. Not surprisingly, residents in nice apartments refuse to move to personal care, even though there are sound reasons for extra care.

I would like to see personal-care apartments have removable kitchenettes and include one-bedroom, and possibly, a few two-bedroom units.

STAFFING CONSIDERATIONS

We must learn to use labor better. Our communities are labor-intensive, and we're running out of labor. In the future, we will have to be imaginative and provide services with fewer people. I think the practice of weekly housecleaning will end. Most residents can maintain their units with only minor assistance. Providing a washer/dryer in every unit not only meets the expectations of the future resident, but perhaps more importantly, reduces total staffing needs.

MIXED USE SITES

To date most CCRCs have been built on single-use sites. This has had the effect of separating residents from society, which has inherent pluses and minuses. I predict that there will be more CCRCs built on mixed-use sites, particularly in smaller towns. The use of the dining room as a public restaurant is just one constructive idea, showing what is possible on a mixed-use site. Shopping malls, college and school campuses, and office complexes offer some future siting opportunities.

FINANCIAL MODELS

I expect that the future will bring greater variation in financial models offered in new CCRCs. The desire for ownership is very strong among older people, and while there has been a grudging acceptance of nonrefundable entrance fees, it now is clear that new structures must be offered. I still believe that the fifty-month declining-balance entrance fee plan is best for most people, but I recognize the attractiveness of the refundable plan, even with the resultant higher fees. Future plans should offer an option of either the refundable or the nonrefundable plan.

In addition to refundable entry fee plans, there will be a growth of plans involving actual ownership by the resident. Some condominium and cooperative plans are now in place and more are planned.

OUTPATIENT CARE

Most CCRCs have made extensive use of a "clinic" or "outpatient department" to reduce nursing care and to provide on-site access to physicians. I predict that this type of program will become even more important and will expand into the total wellness concept, including nutrition, exercise, and mental stimulation.

COGNITIVE IMPAIRMENT

The optimistic predictions of improved health at advanced age do not take into account the growing evidence that very little available to us today reduces cognitive impairment after age eighty. As new CCRCs draw on older and older populations, chronic cognitive impairment may become the greatest challenge to CCRC management. New designs and communications systems can help mildly cognitively impaired persons cope with their environment and needs, but much more will be needed to be done to deal with this problem.

In conclusion I believe that the future of the CCRC is strong, but that improvements and changes will be needed not only for new communities but also for existing ones. ∎

85/Freestanding Assisted-Living Facilities

Arvid Elness

Designed by Arvid Elness Architects, Inc., Elder Homestead in Minnetonka, Minnesota, and Rosewood Estate in Roseville, Minnesota, are nonlicensed freestanding assisted-living facilities functioning as an alternative to a nursing home. What makes these facilities unique is not only their noninstitutional, homelike character but a perfected operational system that delivers the needed care to the resident at a lower cost. There is also evidence of residents' increased social well-being, which has been attributed to the architectural environment and an emphasis on independence and self-help.

ARCHITECTURAL

Elder Homestead was designed in 1984 in conjunction with the Altcare Corporation, a partnership of General Mills and the Wilder

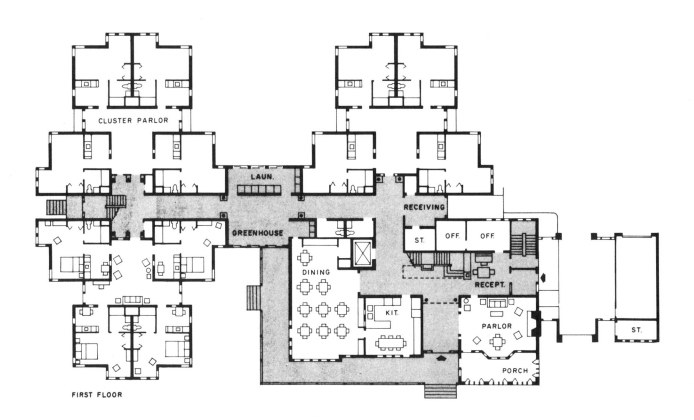

Elder Homestead, Minnetonka, Minnesota. Plan of first floor. (Architect: Arvid Elness Architects, Inc./Photo: Franz Hall)

Foundation. The first of its type in Minnesota, the 28-unit facility became operational in 1986 and remains full today. The design attempted to dissolve the edges between the public or common areas of the building and the private or individual aspects of living in the facility. This feature was achieved with the introduction *of a cluster parlor concept*, which permitted four individual efficiency apartments to be assembled around a common parlor. This concept was recognized by the code officials as a single unit where four unrelated individuals can live as a family. In this situation, permission was given to open windows and doors to the four private apartments. It also reduced the number of units in the building by a factor of 4, which altered other planning issues as well. Beyond this feature, the common areas are residential and typical for a charming house, of the type most residents have known all their lives.

Rosewood Estate, which was also designed by Elness in conjunction with SWB Management, opened in 1989. The project achieved a similar objective, but here an expanded corridor of lounges was used rather than parlors.

Elder Homestead, Minnetonka, Minnesota. (Architect: Arvid Elness Architects, Inc./Photo: Franz Hall)

Elder Homestead, Minnetonka, Minnesota. (Architect: Arvid Elness Architects, Inc./Photo: Franz Hall)

This feature allowed the resident to socialize outside his or her unit in a public street serving the common areas and dining rooms in the main house.

Another significant factor of difference is that each building of this type costs less to construct than facilities that are licensed in the state of Minnesota. The facility is essentially an apartment building that can be constructed of wood and generally produced for up to $12.00/square foot less than a comparable "I" classification required for a licensed facility. This savings translates to reduced cost of development, which can then be passed on to the resident as a saving in rent on his or her total monthly cost.

OPERATIONAL

Again, experience has shown that the care provider must be distinctly separated from the real estate developer. This was achieved by contracting a licensed home healthcare provider to assume all responsibility for medical care of the residents on a individual contract basis. At Rosewood, the home healthcare provider actually rented space in the facility to better serve its residents. The residents, however, are not restricted to use this particular provider. Charges to the resident are divided between rent for housing and care provided by the home healthcare agency.

Certain resident services, of a nonmedical nature, are provided by the management company or landlord. At Rosewood Estate it was reported that 80 percent of the residents actually came from a nursing home. Both facilities are currently full and operating effectively today. In the case of Rosewood, all sixty-nine units were occupied within a year of its opening. ■

86/Designing a Room as a Social Unit

Jean Marc Gauthier

Four principles guide us in designing architecture for old people.

Respect for the freedom of elderly people is a primary objective, and the desired consequence is a building's intimacy. This priority includes three qualifications: adaptable private environments, permanent space for personal belongings, and proximity and access to collective activities.

Giving flexibility to each resident's bed area permits privacy, but also encourages voluntary reshaping of the individual's relation to the community. Each arrangement becomes the choice of the individual to exhibit participation in the movement or animation that comes by. A delicate balance of respect results from the shared awareness that each resident voluntarily shapes his or her living environment as a language of participation. A completely adaptable environment, where the refuge of the bed

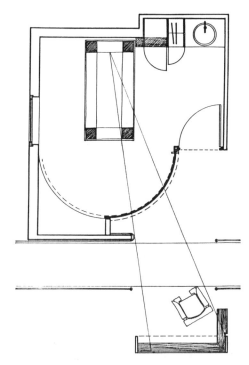

Round room. (Architect: Emmanuelle Colboc et Jean Marc Gauthier, Architects)

View from corridor. (Architect: Emmanuelle Colboc et Jean Marc Gauthier, Architects)

will change as the patient improves, reduces the trauma of discharge following illness.

It is our belief that permanent spaces for personal belongings will assist a stable representation and an organized image of each individual. By setting personal furniture and cherished objects in areas peripheral to the bed space, traditional spaces for socialization are reinforced, the individual is free to manage his or her relation to them, and the individual claims his or her existence within the community.

Of equal importance, the immediacy of intimacy is controlled through the alcove. By adapting the personal space of each bed area, the patient establishes visual or direct participation with the resident community. The alcove creates levels of intimacy while reducing the taxation of involvement in close proximities of community activities and animation.

Time spent in the bed area can be staged as a series of increasing reentry into collective activity of the facility and the reality of everyday life.

A second priority for the built environment of elderly people is to establish the right dialogue between the old person and the architectural elements that shape space. Architecture supports memory. Solitude invites reverie and recall of former reality. Spaces are sponges for intense contemplation. Architecture can stimulate memory by giving screens for contemplation that induce a rekindling of the past, or a revisitation of the memory. The intermezzo periods of communication with one's past are often intense, and for many patients, constitute the greater part of time lapses. Some textures and projections of light and shadow soothe the eye and mind of the elderly person, and extended contemplation can be endless.

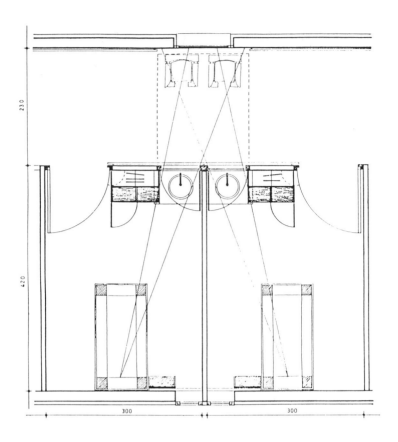

Rectangular room. (Architect: Emmanuelle Colboc et Jean Marc Gauthier, Architects)

To shift perceptual awareness from past to present and vice versa, we look to community activity and movement of people, contiguous to the memory screens, to sharpen perceptual awareness and gain better alertness.

A third priority is to use architecture to promote the shift from privacy to community-focused socialization. This is more important as stages of dependency advance. We want to ensure that the built space optimizes one's capacity for choices; within the theater of interactions, each individual holds a known place. It is our belief that a community organization will generate self-help and bonding among the residents and increase the feeling of security and belonging within the group. Therefore, we ensure that each community unit provides the functional components of life, so the elderly residents feel comfortable in the small-scale units. The variety of spatial organization between units, with loosely defined borders, spawns curiosity and promotes a desire to visit other units.

Fourth, we aim at spatial neutrality and flexibility in varying units. We try to contradict any attempt at segregation as related to the dependency of the residents. We expect the variations within each place to reveal the subtle and often quick variations of well-being and to further one's capacity to demonstrate moments of wellness in whatever motion that entails. We endorse the freedom to be social, antisocial, spontaneous, or conventional by giving freedoms unconditionally. Ideally, the built space will help to reveal inclinations and promote their expression.

Design should attempt to balance highly functional, adaptable spaces with familiar components of intimacy. We want to introduce traditional places of collective socialization, similar to the piazza of a village, contiguous to the bed areas.

Some major issues needing future development and understanding are the need for visiting, the rituals of food, expediting change, securing choice in socialization, and offering spontaneous experience of an informal garden. ■

87 / A Modular Approach to Senior Living Design

William Glass

Toward easing the steps now slowing the opening of new full-service senior facilities—typically, site adaptation, component relationships, zoning approval, and reliable cost projections—architects often advocate an assemblage or predesigned parts. Gaining a way to speed development is especially urgent for the Marriott Corporation, which has planned an aggressive building program at a time of expanding regulatory review. In July 1989, Marriott's Senior Living Division announced a budget of over $1 billion to construct 150 facilities over five years. How to reduce time, control cost, and achieve quality is the urgent question.

With the help of computer-aided design (CAD), we developed a "kit of parts." This kit is intended to ease the design portion of passage through the regulatory requirements for coordinated compliance: building, health, licensing, and zoning codes. Further, to gain maximal site utilization value, the kit is designed to facilitate rapid evaluation of alternate configurations, to achieve early consensus by all architectural and engineering disciplines, and to reduce the time required for design development and cost estimates. Where size, shape, or slope vary, the parts can be rearranged and connected in many configurations. For example, a change in site and, hence, the assemblage of parts, may require new mechanical and electric design documentation. Merely a recalculation of the size and connections within a predetermined routing pattern will be required prior to generating final documents.

Ideally, the kit of parts will give us a historical record of capital costs per unit and some valuable insights into maintenance and operation costs. The record should result in realistic competitive bids, and contractors and suppliers should be able to reduce costs. With CAD, zoning submittals can be generated in a matter of hours. ∎

Brighton Gardens by Marriott, Virginia Beach, Virginia. (Architect: Fusch-Serold & Partners, Inc. Photo: Courtesy of Marriott Corporation)

88/The Synergenial® Healthcare Community

Earl S. Swensson

More than any other factors, the size and well-being of our mature population promise to influence the character of 21st century society. Through sheer force of numbers, the population wave initiated after World War II and swelled by advances in the healthcare sciences will cascade over us during the next ten years, changing the way we live and think. For the architect, pressure to anticipate these changes is intensifying. The very nature of our profession is evolving beyond technical considerations of structure and art toward more universal concerns for social and individual wellness, in all senses of the term. Architecture has entered a new age—one my associates and I refer to as the Synergenial® Age—that will require adaptation of sophisticated technologies to daily life within a mature society. Through the integrating process of synergy, architects will have to coordinate complex issues of technology, engineering, design, aesthetics, and economy into genial environments that allow larger, older populations to remain independent, productive, and satisfied.

In 1990 more than 50,000 Americans were over 100 years old; those over 90 exceeded 1.3 million. In the next 10 years, those numbers will swell, indicating a need for architects to devise community plans that accommodate our maturing population. There are other considerations as well. Healthcare, for example, is evolving beyond the mere treatment of manifest crisis into a preventive discipline. Driven by technological change, education is becoming a continuing, lifelong pursuit. Shopping is serving as entertainment—a social interaction. Recreation is big business—diverse, individ-

ual, and an acknowledged component of a healthy lifestyle.

The combined effect of demographic change and public activities and appetites is to create a need for communities that incorporate comprehensive medical care, educational resources, regional shopping, recreational and fitness facilities, auxiliary services such as day care, car maintenance, restaurants, public service facilities and cultural and amusement areas; and the elderly and chronic, and coordinate them all as a single residential and service community. Independent automobile access will remain vital, but so will interconnected, covered walkways. In short, what the next ten years will make obvious is the need for Synergenial Suburban Villages such as the 220-acre prototype designed by Earl Swensson Associates as an integral part of a 650-acre planned neighborhood incorporating residential, commercial, office, and recreational facilities. By the year 2000, the Synergenial Suburban Village will represent a social and residential revolution in this country every bit as pervasive as the development of planned suburban communities in the early postwar period.

The 220-acre Synergenial Suburban Village attempts to redress two distinct biases that deflect both the American public and the American architect. First is the bias favoring segregation of the elderly from the rest of society; second is the tendency to design for a presumed ideal human prototype—the 30-year-old male, 5 foot 10 inches tall, and weighing 145 pounds. In the Synergenial Suburban Village, the continuing care retirement community (CCRC) is no longer isolated, but is integrated into the community. Its residents enjoy access to residential, employment, shopping, recreational, and medical facilities that, while tailored to mature needs, are also blended into the overall neighborhood. And, given the reality that the typical CCRC resident is not male or 30 years old, but female and 75, the Synergenial Suburban Village incorporates designs and technologies appropriate to "her"—down to the smallest detail.

As a planned community, the overall Synergenial Suburban Village represents a "critical mass" design. It incorporates two CCRC residential communities; 1.3 million square feet of office space; an 800-room hotel; a covered shopping galleria with parking; continuing education/conference facilities operated jointly by university and hotel interests; recreational, fitness, cultural and amusement facilities; and a medical center with 320 acute-care rooms, a medical office building, diagnostic center, and outpatient facilities.

Within the CCRC complexes, all design accommodates the physical, social, and emotional needs of residents, ranging in age from 75 to 110. The two CCRC structures are six stories tall, situated on ten landscaped acres, and offer 320 apartments to accommodate a population of approximately 800. Self-contained communities, with their own miniclimate, underground parking, a personal-care center, and chronic-care center, the CCRC's design evolves from total attention to detail in our Synergenial approach to meeting the special needs of mature residents.

Extensive natural lighting, for example, brings the outdoors indoors, reducing the dependence on artificial light sources and the glare and disorientation they produce. An entire minicommunity can exist under glass in a gardenlike atmosphere, with soothing but constant natural sounds to mitigate disorientation even further. There, individuals can gather or separate for their myriad pursuits. The CCRC plan includes a chapel, lap pool, activity center, carillon, small pond, and various services, such as a restaurant, pub, research library, reading library, computer center, and investment club. Barber and beauty shops, banking, and other services are also assembled within this environment in an admittedly hotel-like arrangement. Will residents make use of all these facilities and services? Of course they will

Opryland Hotel, Nashville, Tennessee. (Architect: Earl Swensson Associates, Inc./Photo: Timothy Hursley)

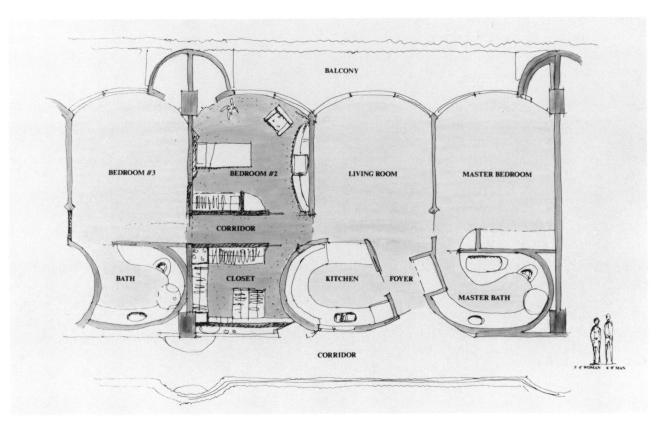

The Synergenial Healthcare Community, Prototype 3. Bedroom living unit. (Architect: Earl Swensson Associates, Inc.)

—just as their mature predecessors do today—but locations will no longer be scattered all over town.

Medical services will share the first floor, screened from the community spaces, but nonetheless open to gardenlike landscaping of their own. Strategically placed nursing stations will maximize care, and modular space planning will streamline storage of equipment and dispensation of medications. Throughout the CCRC, there will be no ups and downs except for elevator connections between floors—no stairs whatsoever, except for fire escapes. And elevators will be constructed of glass to further enhance the spatial orientation of the residents.

Perhaps the most striking departures from accepted architectural practice, however, will be the Synergenial residences in the CCRC. Here, more than any other place, it is mandatory to introduce the technologies that assist rather than restrict the mature resident. That means near-total elimination of hinges that

need bending, plugs that need pulling, switches that need twisting, and so on. The technology already exists to provide more convenient ways to accomplish such tasks as opening doors and windows, drawing drapes, and stacking pantry shelves. We aim at a minimum of exertion and discomfort. Even telecommunications can be accomplished by voice-actuation and facsimile transmission. The challenge represented by a Synergenial vision of the future is to incorporate these technologies as universally possible.

In the Synergenial personal residence for the older person, open corridors six feet wide will extend the effect of an outdoor environment even to one's personal space. Resting places midway along corridors and curved walls will enhance mobility, whether one walks or employs the motorized three-wheeled scooter that is destined to replace the wheelchair. No residence will be farther than four doorways away from elevator access to the community area and parking facilities below, and entry into each apartment will require only the touch of a security plate, with fingerprint recognition technology replacing the need for tumbler locks and keys.

Individual apartments will be spacious. No one likes to pare away a lifetime's accumulations. Accordingly, apartments will include storage spaces, and the resulting tidiness will enhance the already generous living space. These residences should cause the least amount of adjustment to lifestyle possible. Moreover, assisted-living quarters can be more spacious in their own right, with more and larger rooms, and kitchens and baths that don't require 100 percent assistance. The goal should be to protect the residents' fragile senses of independence—even if only in an intellectual and emotional sense.

Inside, all surfaces will be soft and glare-free, and the traditional hinged door—the source of more hazards and problems for the older person than any other household device—will be eliminated in favor of sliding doors and windows. Curved bay windows, without mullions, and a balcony—whose radiant overhead heating and wind screening will render it useful 365 days a year—will actually integrate the residence into a natural environment. Yet polarized glass will control the wax and wane of sunlight, and, where necessary, cove lighting in the nine-foot ceilings will integrate artificial lighting to the naturally lighted space.

How can all this be economically feasible by the turn of the century? The solution is modularity. Utilizing the "warehouse concept" of unitized construction, each individual residence in the CCRC, based on a two-bedroom master design that can be modulated into one- or three-bedroom designs, will be prefabricated and literally "rolled" into place. Utility and communications connections will be centralized at the rear of the unit, and the entire

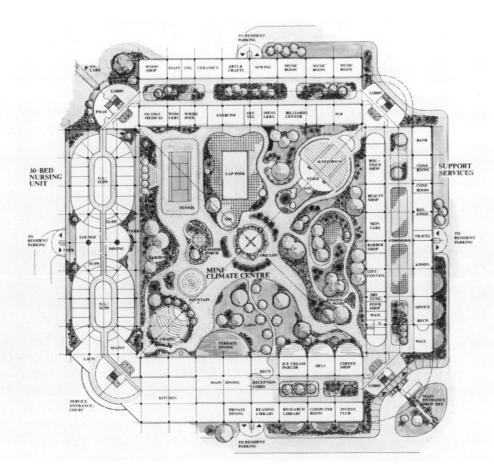

The Synergenial Healthcare Community, Prototype 3. Ground floor plan. (Architect: Earl Swensson Associates, Inc.)

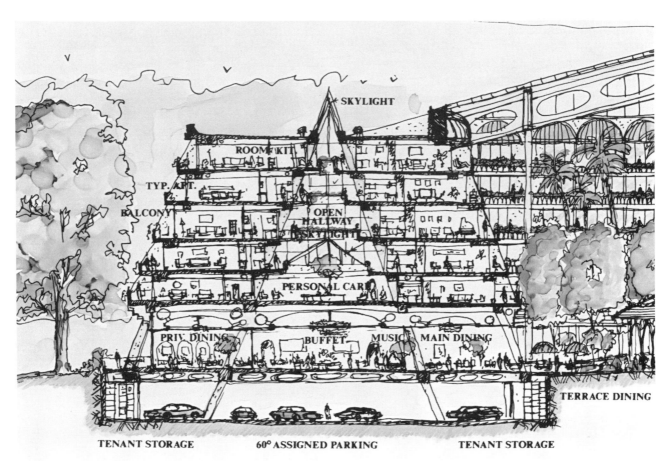

The Synergenial Healthcare Community, Prototype 3. Cross section. (Architect: Earl Swensson Associates, Inc.)

assembly of 320 such units in each CCRC structure will fit into an overarching skeletal span that is completely fireproof.

This unitized or modular strategy, which is already becoming the normal design for medical facilities, gives the architect outstanding opportunities for designing living spaces as a collection of molded, ergonomic task centers that include specially designed bathroom and kitchen facilities, living and dining room areas, communications and entertainment centers, and modular personal storage that maximizes efficient use of storage space. Best of all, modularity means that older technologies can literally be exchanged for newer ones simply by replacing the unitized module with an updated version whenever one is inclined to do so.

As congenial and self-contained as each level of CCRC design is intended to be—from the personal residence to the community structure to the entire Synergenial Suburban Village itself—the object is not to isolate mature residents from the larger neighborhood, but to integrate them to whatever extent they choose. Although the elderly's mental clarity and physical vigor depend upon stimulation, younger members of a community will not need to go out of their way to "absorb" or make room for their older neighbors. By opening CCRC amenities such as fitness facilities, restaurants, and amusements to outside memberships, integration can be assured. Moreover, in the future, the experience and training of our mature colleagues will be as essential to our businesses and national economy as they already are to our family lives and cultural experiences.

Designing communities like the Synergenial Suburban Village will force architects to address real challenges that go far beyond issues of structure and form. At stake are the health and well-being of our society. How, for example, will we invest finite resources in housing, medical, employment, and recreational requirements of our maturing population? How will we, at the same time, incorporate modern technologies *and* remain flexible enough to make room for newer ones as they appear? How will we minimize the costs—financial, physical, and intellectual—of living longer, healthier lives? Synergenially—in other words, by the application of an interdisciplinary design philosophy that incorporates science and art, efficiency and convenience, engineering and psychology—is an answer.

Designing Synergenial communities and structures is not a process that awaits technology. It is a process we can—and should—begin today. ■

89/Chagny: Multipurpose Senior Urban District

Jean Marc Gauthier

For an existing hospital at Chagny, in the French Saone et Loire region, the architect Jean Marc Gautier has designed three additions that integrate existing medical facilities with housing for disoriented elderly people and also for young couples. Private gardens, shops, and offices are connected by ramps and raised walkways. Although architecturally complex, the hospital at Chagny is a successful urban integration of young and old, new and renewed, and commercial with healthcare. ■

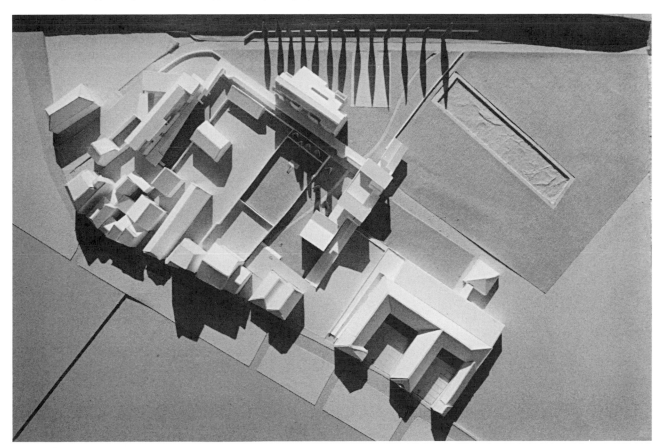

Multi-use Senior Urban District, Chagny, France. (Architect: Jean Marc Gauthier)

90/Mixed-Use Urban Development

Wilt Berger

Few municipalities or communities yet recognize the social and financial advantages of well-designed mixed-use commercial developments that include residential units for seniors. Miller Hanson Westerbeck Bell (MHWB) Architects has designed several projects where the needs of a municipality are coordinated with provisions for residences and social agencies, such as day care and a YMCA. A need to increase downtown parking and gain a larger customer base for a commercial core can be accommodated within a high-rise retail development that includes residential facilities and a parking structure.

By financing foundations, parking, and utilities with public financial instruments, and uti-lizing land depreciations, tax increments, and air rights transfer, the planners of multiuse projects can subsidize the costs of senior housing and attendant healthcare facilities. The combination of parking spaces for residents and the public also provides flexibility as the residents' and public use expands.

There are also social advantages. The senior resident, in particular, desires proximity to shopping and necessary services. At Riverplace and Galtier Plaza, MHWB designed large spaces for healthcare facilities and retail stores. The retail operations give the elderly resident necessary services inside the complex. The retail core or common area also serves as a social gathering spot and an activity area for the ten-

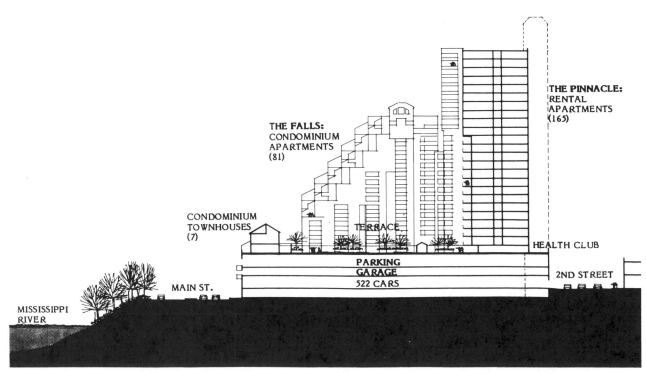

The Falls/The Pinnacle/Eastbridge, Riverplace, Minneapolis, Minnesota. Cross section. (Architect: Miller Hanson Westerbeck Bell Architects, Inc.)

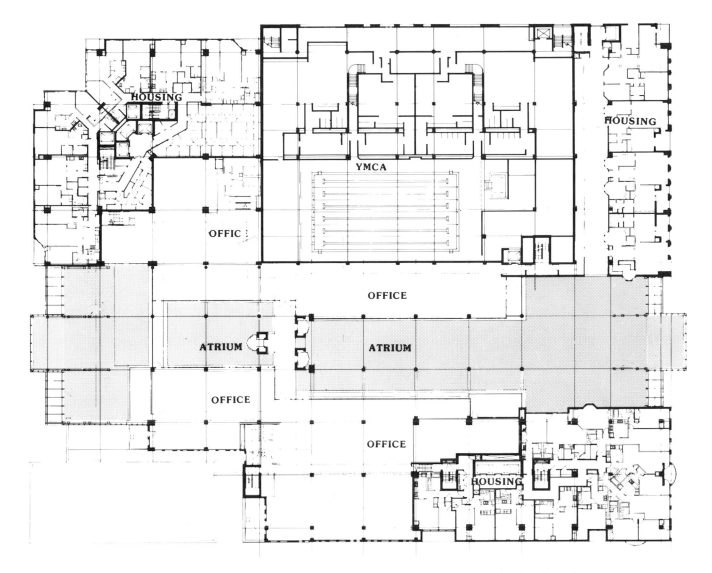

Galtier Plaza, Saint Paul, Minnesota. Fifth-level plan. (Architect: Miller Hanson Westerbeck Bell Architects, Inc.)

ants. The Galtier Plaza project also incorporates a multiscreen theater and several night clubs.

A well-designed mixed-use complex can provide almost all the social needs the elderly tenant demands while also enabling the sponsoring municipality to accomplish its urban-planning goals of increasing density, downtown parking, and possibly the expansion of existing commercial and office space. ∎

91 / Elderly Housing as Part of Mixed-Use Projects

Martin S. Valins

Senior housing is an age-based form of housing. Whether segregation by age actually supports a better lifestyle (or merely reinforces society's view that elders are best put out to graze) is debatable.

Because of the size and scale of many larger retirement communities, they have often been located in suburban and even rural locations. Their communal facilities also tend to reinforce their self-containment, setting them apart from the local community. In recent years both social and economic factors suggest that retirement housing be integrated in mixed-use projects.

INTEGRATION OF SENIOR LIVING PROJECTS CAN TAKE A VARIETY OF FORMS

Mixed-Use Housing

Largely as a result of government funding and zoning codes, countries such as Sweden and Denmark have long integrated housing and care facilities for older people within mixed-use housing projects. Communal facilities are separate where appropriate, but integrated where possible to create spontaneous interaction. Catering to all age groups makes the scheme a community resource. Supporters of integration argue that this overcomes the problems of creating age-segregated ghettos and creates a more holistic approach to housing solutions.

One example is a senior housing project in Lund, Sweden, known as Alderdomshem Papegojelyckan ("Home for the Aged in Papegojelyckan"). Designed by the architect Sten Samuelson, it represents a typical scheme of 70 residential apartments within a two-story three-wing development which has been located adjacent to a newly developed multifam-

ily housing area. The apartments and communal facilities provide programs equivalent to the American personal care or assisted-living projects. The average age of residents is 85 plus; the site at Lund combines multifamily housing and elderly housing. It is a residential setting in a multifamily neighborhood—that is, while the actual units are segregated, the overall site provides an unobtrusive and almost natural link with the multifamily housing via a community park, landscaping, and parking areas.

Mixed-Use/Multifunction

At Coventry in England a continuing care retirement community (CCRC) is currently being planned to include commercial office and retail space. The office space will generate income for the operator and therefore enable service charges (in part) to be subsidized. The rental spaces in the CCRC will include branch banks, food stores, and a beauty parlor. Such facilities will be available both to residents of the CCRC and to those who use the office space. Because the office staff will be a continuous group, i.e., not total strangers, security will not be a problem and opportunities for social interaction will occur. It is also anticipated that residents in CCRCs will come to work in the offices, perhaps on a part-time basis. This will enable commercial users to tap the often underutilized expertise of retired managers in industry. This example therefore illustrates a totally compatible but controlled and secure integrated mixed-use project. (Source: "Brief for New Continuing Care Community at Whitley Hospital Site Coventry," August 1988, Martin Valins & Associates.)

A further example of a mixed-use multifunction retirement facility is currently being

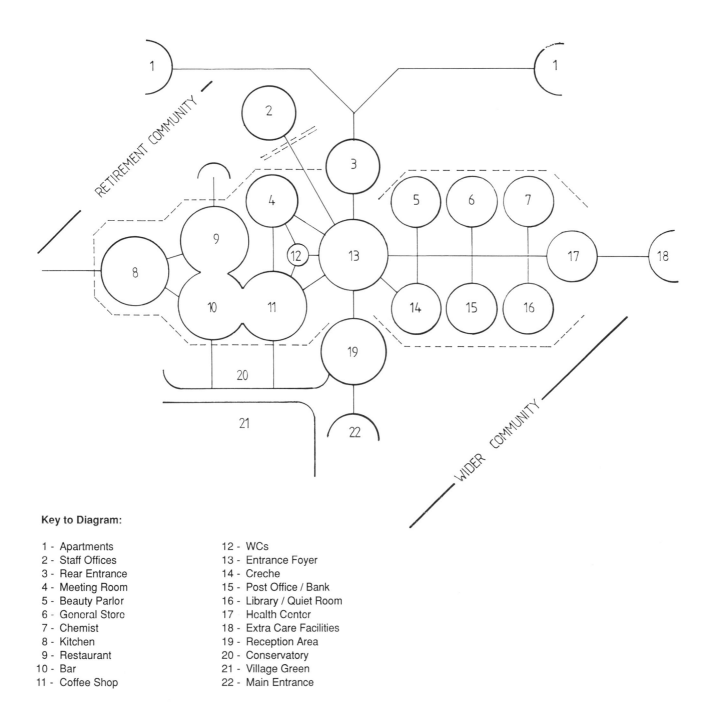

Key to Diagram:

1 - Apartments
2 - Staff Offices
3 - Rear Entrance
4 - Meeting Room
5 - Beauty Parlor
6 - General Store
7 - Chemist
8 - Kitchen
9 - Restaurant
10 - Bar
11 - Coffee Shop

12 - WCs
13 - Entrance Foyer
14 - Creche
15 - Post Office / Bank
16 - Library / Quiet Room
17 - Health Center
18 - Extra Care Facilities
19 - Reception Area
20 - Conservatory
21 - Village Green
22 - Main Entrance

Concept for village center within a multi-use retirement community, Coventry, England. (Architect: Martin Valins + Associates)

planned in London. Here a Swedish-based lifecare operator invited the architects Salmon Speed/MV + A to develop a program to include senior housing, commercial office space, and an education center. The aims and inspiration for the development shift housing for elderly people into a far more sophisticated package of accommodation with associated communal care, commercial activities, and cultural services.

The concept involves the integration within one site of the following:

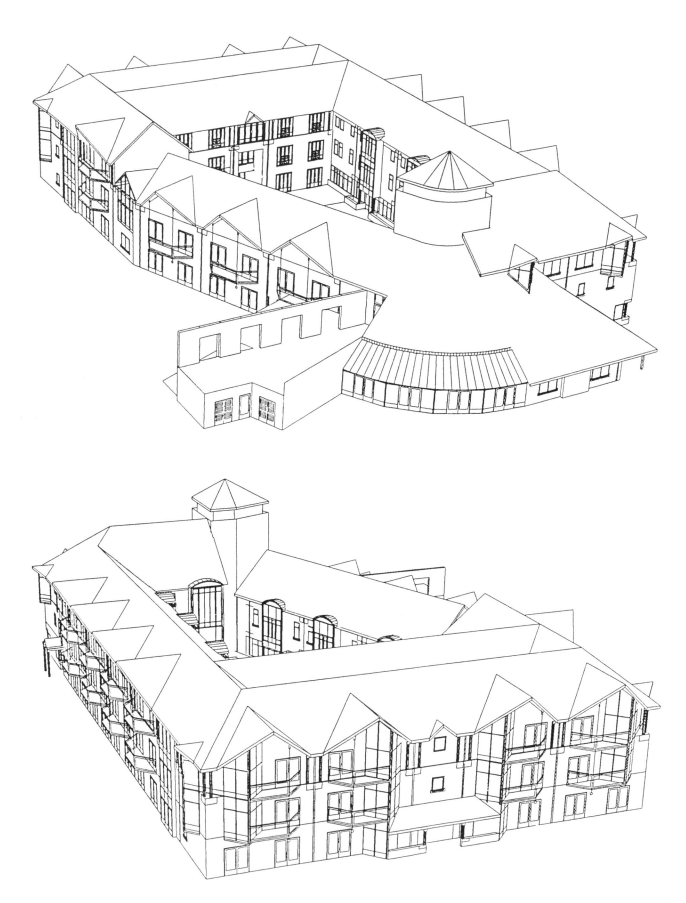

A Multi-use senior housing concept. (Architect: Salmon Speed/MV + A, U.K.)

1. Self-contained residential living units aimed primarily at the 65 plus market.
2. Activity center: This in many ways will represent the spirit of the concept. Residents will continue to lead active lives and be able to recreate the social fabric that may have been lost to them as they grew older and more isolated in their previous communities. Forming the hub of the activity center will be a lounge/lobby and dining room which will bring residents together for daily meals and social gatherings. The activity center will also include meeting and seminar rooms, which will also be a part of the education center.
3. Education center: It is envisaged that this will provide programs for learning not only for residents but also for senior students from both within the United Kingdom and elsewhere. The center therefore will share certain facilities with the activity center and will have a conference facility and classrooms. The education center will also offer outreach learning programs in other senior living facilities.
4. Commercial office space: Anticipating a significant number of residents who may wish to maintain their occupation and rent offices, the plan provides office space for them and for outside users, who can also use the conference room and classrooms.
5. The care center: This will essentially be a treatment and nursecare base from which health services will be delivered both to residents and to the wider community.

Mixed-Use Care Support Services

In the United Kingdom, recent government legislation has provided further encouragement for a service-based care support system for elderly people who wish to remain in their own homes. However, such services require a base from which to operate. This provides opportunities for retirement communities to offer their support and care services to a wider range of users. As the concept of the CCRC begins to gain ground in Europe, planners urge integration with the local community; potential exists for carrying the higher service costs through shared use of facilities, by offering membership in the CCRC village center

on a "country club" or community center basis. This arrangement brings both economic and social benefits.

Even in the most attractive retirement communities, the quality of life will depend upon enabling residents to be part of the wider community, both on an emotional and a physical level. In particular, if the communal facilities can also be enjoyed by those retirees who may not live within the facility, these can bring added richness to the quality of life within the community. Luncheon clubs, coffee mornings, and support groups are able to create such opportunities for social integration. Communal facilities within a CCRC can therefore double-function as a retirement community center. Such integration also allows excellent promotional opportunities for local retirees to learn about CCRCs so that moving to one becomes less of an upheaval.

FACTORS WEIGHING AGAINST MIXED-USE

Zoning Restrictions

Mixed-use housing has been a predominantly public-sector domain. However, in the private sector zoning restrictions have shaped the trend to age-segregation and continue to do so.

Security

From various research studies of user groups, age-segregated projects seem to be more satisfactory from a security standpoint than age-integrated ones. In age-segregated communities—ones which are insulated from younger persons—difficulties with youths were among the least frequent complaints, whereas in projects that contained elderly housing amongst a series of family buildings, particularly in poor neighborhoods, elderly residents were afraid to venture forth into other portions of the site. By being aware of the potential problems, however, architects should be able to design against this criticism of age-integrated facilities.

CONCLUSION

Age-integrated housing has not been carefully scrutinized with regard to the issues of intergenerational exchange. More careful study of successful age-integrated projects is needed to understand how mechanisms that bring together younger and older people can develop. Understanding the spaces and activities of successfully mixed generations will allow us to develop and encourage settings where this type of interaction can take place.

In our effort to better understand age-segre-gated housing we, as an industry, have all but abandoned the issue of stimulating intergenerational exchange through innovative age-integrated housing. More careful research is needed to understand how the goal of age-integration can be met through the development of new housing prototypes to create new social and financial models of mixed-use projects for the 1990s and beyond. ∎

92 / The Presbyterian Hospital/Columbia-Presbyterian Medical Center

David Ginsberg

The design objectives set for the modernization and reconstruction of the Presbyterian Hospital/Columbia-Presbyterian Medical Center reflect a continued commit-ment to the program started by James Gamble Rogers in his architecture for the 1930 Medical Center campus. The current architects, Skidmore Owings & Merrill, took on this task in

Columbia-Presbyterian Medical Center, Milstein Hospital Building, New York, New York. Rooms overlook the Hudson River and the George Washington Bridge. (Architect: Skidmore Owings & Merrill/New York/Photo: Robert Miller)

partnership with the hospital's project team. The basic approach was to temper the often "hard" institutional or clinical environment with a more "soft" facility statement.

The massing and location of the new one-million-square-foot Milstein Hospital Building makes it the principal component of the Medical Center campus, which formerly was dominated by the original, twenty-two-floor-high Presbyterian Hospital. Milstein's central cylindrical core connects a series of highly articulated components, with each of ten floors providing over 80,000 gross square feet, within walls that provide much windowed space.

Unlike its predecessor, the Milstein Hospital Building is located on the palisade along the Hudson River. Its views are oriented toward the water and the George Washington Bridge to the north and toward Manhattan's skyline to the south. Window stools are low, at eighteen inches above the floor; windows are large and ceilings are high to add to the feeling of openness; the top floor has a glass-roofed atrium, and exterior spaces are used by staff as well as by patients.

At the ground plane, a combination of multilevel spaces and open landscaped areas establishes openness from the beginning. Natural wood, brick, warm colors, and soft furniture reinforce the environmental statement.

Throughout the new Milstein Hospital Building, space has been developed for people: lounges, waiting rooms, a restaurant, coffee shop, and other "soft" space for staff, students, patients, and visitors. The connecting glazed bridges and the new Medical Center Concourse provide all-weather linkages to the over five million square feet of existing and new buildings. As many as 25,000 people a day can now move above ground and indoors among the many buildings of the Columbia-Presbyterian Medical Center for the first time. Overall, the hospital responds to the human spirit and environmental needs of the patients, as well as to compassionate care and curing of their physical illness. ■

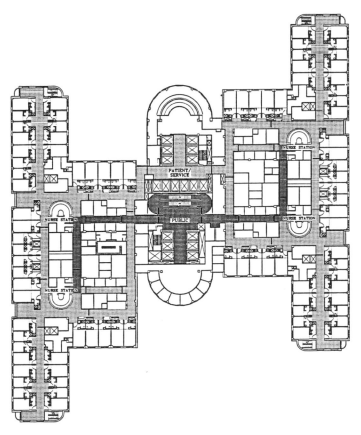

Columbia-Presbyterian Medical Center, Milstein Hospital Building, New York, New York. Rooms overlook the Hudson River and the George Washington Bridge. (Architect: Skidmore Owings & Merrill/New York/Photo: Robert Miller)

93 / Selecting a Designer

Albert Bush-Brown

One of the most momentous decisions in the life of any institution is choice of architects and designers. That choice leads to bricks and mortar, steel and glass, and other immovable, inflexible arrangements, such as entrances and parking and kitchen locations, which may soon be regretted, particularly if expansions or conversions were not anticipated. Who is chosen as designer for your healthcare or senior community will set the style and spirit of your institution for decades to come.

There are many measures of a designer's performance. There are superficial ones like a bias for historic style, or a high regard for utility and economy. The measure architects themselves apply is more reliable: What is the total impact of the design? Did the architect satisfy the client's essential needs in a remarkable way? Did the designer create sequences of attractive spaces in corridors, dining areas, patients' rooms, and gathering spaces, so that the spirit of place gives a sense of membership, belonging, ease, and comfort?

You can obtain a reliable healthcare building or senior living community from many architects and interior designers today. Elevators, air conditioners, and telephones will work. Patients, senior members, and staff, however, deserve and should expect more.

Architecture, it has been said, is the visible expression of intellectual decisions. It is based on good research and sound planning. Yet architecture, it has been said further, is the magnificent play of light and shade over geometric forms and spaces that are beautifully shaped and arranged for the people who live and work among them. Such a performance requires an uncommon, passionate designer. The best architects and designers are captured by the thrill of an idea: a way to ennoble and dignify the life and work of those who will occupy their spaces.

Thus, to provide superior architectural services demands more than the sculptural virtuosity of a talented designer, more than the precise computations of an engineer, more even than the efficiencies, economies, and care of a resourceful builder or fabricator. Surely, it requires each of those, but it also requires proven, mature coordination among them, everyone who is needed to bring steel, glass and bricks, typewriters, telephones, and medical instruments together, secure them in assigned places, and fit them precisely, ready to perform their roles in the occupied building.

There is no substitute for a firsthand encounter with a designer's work. Interviews with architects, interior designers, and graphic designers may help to identify whose work should be seen, but you must visit, enter, see, and question.

Be wary about the questions you ask. Some of our prejudices for "Georgian" or "Colonial" style or for Cape Cod, Williamsburg, or Bay Area "character" may mislead. A prejudice against modern architecture is silly, for quality in design is quite independent of style. Just because a building is Gothic or Georgian or Modern in its massing and stylistic details says nothing about its fitness to give good service or its aesthetic worth.

Those judgments about quality are deeper than style. They refer to circulation and sequences of space, harmonies of proportion, the important matter of scale, the delicate matter of balances, which can be asymmetric and eccentric, and other matters of rhythms and accents that grace fine shelter. To choose an architect because of stylistic prejudice is an error.

What then are the measures to be applied as you visit buildings to select architects and designers?

One: responsive interpretation. Does the designer listen intelligently, discern the client's essential needs, and interpret them faithfully?

Two: technical experience. Does the designer command advanced technological potential and assure reliable technical operations? Is technology's setting humane and not intrusive?

Three: research and analysis. Do the designer's clients testify to skills in functional analysis, research, persistence in seeking physical, financial, and regulatory fact, including zoning and environmental issues, and ability to submit alternate schemes for evaluation?

Four: visual imagination. Is there evidence of that rare and cherished ability to imagine beautiful space and form, convey proposed imagery convincingly (even to potential donors and investors), and sustain its quality in construction, so that buildings and interiors are inspired, vibrant, and distinguished?

Five: durability. Have buildings aged well, survived occupancy and change, and weathered use, abuse, and storms?

Six: adaptability and flexibility. Have changes in use been easily accomplished? Are buildings and site easily adapted to renovation or expansion?

Seven: documentation and supervision. Does the designer produce those graphic, verbal, and statistical documents that will elicit reliable construction bids and, under supervision, faithful interpretation in construction, with few "change orders" and "cost overruns"?

Eight: economics. What is the record in adhering to capital budgets and, equally important, in achieving economical operating performance?

Nine: character. Has the designer, specifically the architect, succeeded in siting buildings so that entrances, streets, gardens, and terraces convey a sense of vital place with order, purpose, and beauty, and is that quality carried through in lighting and furnishings?

Ten: accessibility. Is the designer serious about his or her client, patient in the long hours of analyzing alternatives, making choices, and available to lead the client through the many negotiations and compromises that normally occur in a major building project?

Those ten measures of designers' service are profound and cannot be taken except by visiting a designer's completed work and interviewing owners and occupants, including staff and customers.

One more warning is needed against superficial measures, namely the quest for specialists. The mere fact that a great designer has never designed a healthcare facility or a senior living community is no mark against retaining that designer. If the firm's work measures up and you have experienced consultants, then be assured that the best talents will be applied and the result may be brilliant. The specialist with a long list of medical clients and hospitals may not meet more than a few of the ten serious measures. You do not need a repeat of a specialist designer's tired files.

To gain fine buildings requires more than the talents of designers who meet the ten measures. It also requires good clients. Good clients demand our ten measures of performance, but good clients themselves must also meet tough measures. The most important is that they insist on professional attention to the physical, social, emotional, and aesthetic needs of staff, patients, and other members of their proposed healthcare facility. A good client remains steadfast in that insistence. ∎

Glossary *

Adult day health care For those who do not require 24-hour care, but are not capable of full-time independent living.

Adult day programs Provides a social environment for frail elderly persons enabling them to remain in independent living environments.

Senior living industry Term covering whole living environment of the elderly.

Unbundled Services A la carte, fee-for-service foodservice, housekeeping, and linen service in a senior living community.

TYPES OF SENIOR LIVING FACILITIES

Adult foster care Unrelated adults allow elderly persons to stay with them. Room and board, and sometimes personal care, are rendered, usually for a fee.

Ambulatory care facility A freestanding or hospital-based facility providing preventive diagnosis, emergency therapeutic services, surgery, or other treatment not requiring overnight confinement.

Assisted-living facility Residence for independent seniors, with 24-hour supervision.

Congregate apartment hotel As with a residential hotel, the apartments are private, with the possibility of social dining and sitting room areas when desired by residents.

Congregate community Congregate communities include a mix of housing types, including attached houses, congregate houses, and a congregate apartment hotel. Residents choose the type of living arrangement they want, and all have equal access to the social and service arrangement they want, and all have equal

access to the social and service facilities and support staff of the community. These facilities always include a restaurant and linen service, and sometimes include some linkage to a healthcare facility like a nursing home and hospital.

Continuing care retirement communities (CCRC) These range from a single high-rise development to a large villagelike campus of many different housing types. Admission is usually limited to seniors in good mental and physical health and of sound financial status. At a minimum, CCRCs have independent living units and access to healthcare facilities. Full-service, modified, and fee-for-service are three types of CCRCs.

Adult congregate living facility (ACLF) Homelike housing, meals, personal care services; either rental, condominium, cooperative, or endowment fee communities.

Domiciliary care home (personal care, residential care) Supervised group living arrangements. License and minimum staff required.

Extended care Facility (ECF) Healthcare facility offering skilled-nursing care, rehabilitation, and convalescent services.

Independent living (lowest intensity of healthcare) Similar to an apartment, but with emergency alert system, handrails in the shower/bath, and lighting and accessories that complements the needs of the elderly. Residents should be allowed to use their own furnishings.

Intermediate-care facility (ICF) Those not fully capable of independent living are provided with 24-hour supervision by registered nurses in a licensed nursing facility.

Lifecare facility A continuing care retirement community for seniors for which there is a "lifetime contract" for living accommodations and varying intensities of healthcare from independent-living units through skilled-nursing care for the duration of the resident's life. This contract, if properly worded, may entitle the resident to a homestead exemption if it is determined that the resident has been granted equity in the property. Financial arrangements usually include a substantial entrance fee plus monthly charges.

Residential care facility Full-service, unlicensed facility much like a boarding house.

Retirement village Villages from 1000 to 5000 people with emergency medical services only.

Skilled-nursing facility (SNF) Licensed freestanding facility or part of a CCRC or institution providing long-term inpatient care for chronic disease or convalescence. State approval and a Certificate of Need (number of beds) required.

Surgicenters Freestanding or hospital-based intermediate surgical care for procedures too complex for the physician's office, but does not require inpatient hospitalization.

AT HOME SERVICES

Home-delivered meals ("Meals on Wheels") Authorized under the Older Americans Act and implemented through federal and state status. These meals are provided to the convalescent elderly or handicapped person on a daily or less frequent basis.

Hospice care Care that addresses the physical, spiritual, emotional, psychological, social, financial, and legal needs of dying patients and their families, that is provided by an interdisciplinary team of professionals and volunteers in a variety of settings, both inpatient and at home, and that includes bereavement care for the families.

Respite services Temporary residence (more than 24 hours) for elderly people who need care for a short time.

AT HOME INDEPENDENT LIVING

Echo Housing (Elder Cottage Housing) **or "Granny Flats"** Echo units are small, freestanding, temporary housing located in the backyard of the family's prime residence.

---

* For further reference: the *Dictionary of Terms for Senior Citizens and the Industries that Serve Them*, Association for Senior Living Industries, published by the National Association of Senior Living Communities.

Selected Readings

Anderson, J.V. "Think Service," *New Jersey Health Care*, January/February 1988.

Backus, H. *Designing Restaurant Interiors: A Guide for Food Service Operators*. New York: Lebhar-Friedman Books, 1977.

Baraban, R. S. and J. F. Durocher. *Successful: Restaurant Design*. New York: Van Nostrand Reinhold Company, 1989.

Berg, B. "A Touch Of Home in Hospital Care," *The New York Times Magazine*. November 27, 1983.

Bernstein, C. "Editor's Corner: Opportunity Market: Retirement Health Care," *Nation's Restaurant News*, August 3, 1987.

Blakeslee, S. "Recovery 'Hotel': It's Not the Ritz, but It's Restful, *New York Times HEALTH*, January 24, 1991.

Brooks, H. D. and C. J. Oppenheim. "Horticulture as a Therapeutic Aid," Rehabilitation Monograph 49. Institute of Rehabilitation Medicine. New York University Medical Center, 1973.

Bush-Brown, A. "An Urban Alternative," in *Connections*. Albany: SUNY Press, 1990.

Calkins, M. P. *Design for Dementia: Planning Environments for the Elderly and the Confused*. Owing Mills, MD: National Health Publishing, 1988.

Cappo, J. *Future Scope: Success Strategies for the 1990s & Beyond*, Longman Financial Services Publishing, 1990.

Carey, J. and S. Katz, "Four-star Recovery Suites," *Newsweek*, February 11, 1985.

Carpman, J. R. "Providing 'Life's Satisfactions' Is Everyone's Business," Hospitality in Healthcare and Senior Market Seminar presentation for Carpman Grant Associates, International Hotel/Motel & Restaurant Show, New York, November 11, 1989.

Carpman, J. and M. Grant. "Lost in Space," *Industries Design*, January/February, 1989.

Carstens, D. Y. *Site Planning and Design for the Elderly: Issues, Guidelines and Alternatives*. New York: Van Nostrand Reinhold Company, 1985.

Chellis, R. D. and P. J. Grayson. *Life Care: A Long-Term Solution?* Lexington, MA: Lexington Books, 1990.

Chrest, A. P., M. S. Smith, and S. Bhuyan. *Parking Structures: Planning, Design, Construction, Maintenance, and Repair*. New York: Van Nostrand Reinhold Company, 1989.

D'Angelo, H. "Windows of Opportunity in an Aging America", Hospitality in Healthcare and Senior Market Seminar presentation for Arbor Corporation, International Hotel/Motel & Restaurant Show, New York, November 12, 1989.

Davis, D. "Hospitality Pulse: The Human Touch," *ASID Report*, American Society of Interior Designers, February 1988.

de Courcyhinds, M. "The Voice of Age Finds a New Audience," *New York Times*, June 18, 1988.

Dunkelman, D. "The Maturing Guests: What Do They Want?" seminar presentation for Rosa Coplan Jewish Home & Infirmary, International Hotel/Motel & Restaurant Show, New York, November 12, 1990.

Dychtwald, K., M. Zitter, and J. Levinson. *Implementing Eldercare Services, Strategies that Work*, McGraw-Hill Information Services Company, 1989.

Eison, I. I. *Strategic Marketing in Food Service*. New York: Lebhar-Friedman Books, Chain Store Publishing Corp., 1980.

Flanagan, B. "A Suburban Mall Is Now 'Downtown'," *The New York Times*, March 14, 1991.

Franck, K. A. and S. Ahrentzen, Eds. *New Households New Housing*. New York: Van Nostrand Reinhold Company, 1989.

Franks, J., "Rocky Mountain High," *Restaurant/Hotel Design International*, June 1989.

Friedman, E. "A New Twist in Hospitals' Hotel Services, *Hospitals*, June 16, 1984.

Gerber, J., J. Wolff, W. Klores, and G. Brown. *Lifetrends: The Future of the Baby Boomers and Other Aging Americans.* New York: MacMillan, 1989.

Giese, J., "A Communal Type of Life, and Dinner's for Everyone," New York Times, September 27, 1990.

Gilbert, E. *Tabletop: The Right Way.* Charlevoix, MI: Jetiquette, 1976. (Library of Congress Catalog no. 80-81206. Training Guide Written for Syracuse China Corporation.)

Gindin, R., and M. Schechter. "Foodservice Inn Style," *Food Management*, August 1988.

Ginsberg, D. L. "New Opportunities Through the Blending of Healthcare and Hospitality," seminar presentation for Columbia-Presbyterian Medical Center, International Hotel/Motel & Restaurant Show, New York, November 11, 1990.

Gollub, J. O., *et al. Lifestyles and Values of Older Adults A Study of Older Adults and Their Preferences for Living Arrangements*, Final Report, National Association for Senior Living Industries, 1988.

Gottlieb, L. *Foodservice/Hospitality Advertising and Promotion.* Indianapolis, IN: Bobbs-Merrill Educational Publishing, 1982.

Health Care Advisory Board. *Service Quality at U.S. Hospitals: 24 Tactics for Improving Hospital Service. Quality of Care, Vol. I.* Washington, DC: The Advisory Board Company, 1988.

Huebner, P. O. *Gourmet Table Service: A Professional Guide.* Indianapolis, IN: Howard W. Sams, Hayden Books, 1968.

Killeen, W. "Halycon Place: A Refuge For Families Who Wait," *Boston Globe*, October 26, 1990.

Koenig, R. "When Hotels Replace Hospitals, What a Lift," *The Wall Street Journal*, April 5, 1990.

Kollar, R. "The Maturing Guests: What Do They Want?" seminar presentation for Classic Residence by Hyatt, International Hotel/Motel & Restaurant Show, New York, November 12, 1990.

Lee, M. H. M. *Rehabilitation, Music and Human Well-Being.* Saint Louis, MO: MMB Music, Inc., 1989.

Lewis, T. "Hospitals Pitch Harder for Patients," *New York Times*, Business Section, May 10, 1987.

Lewis, T. G. "90 Inspirational Ideas for Succeeding in the Senior Market", Hospitality in Healthcare and Senior Market Seminar presentation for the Hebrew Rehabilitation Center for Aged, International Hotel/Motel & Restaurant Show, New York, November 14, 1989.

Lund, L. Ed. *Journal of Health Care Interior Design. Proceedings from the Annual National Symposium on Health Care Interior Design*, Martinez, California, Vols. I, II, III, Davis Press, 1989–1990.

Lux, T., "The Maturing Consumer: Marketing Strategies that Work," Hospitality in Healthcare and Senior Market Seminar presentation for International Hotel/Motel & Restaurant Show, New York, November 13, 1989.

Madden, R. L., "For Hospitals, New Ventures and New Profits," *New York Times*, January 25, 1987.

Martin, D. "When Paralysis Is No Match for P-o-e-t-r-y," *The New York Times*, March 16, 1991.

Mills, I. J. *Tabletop Presentations: A Guide for the Foodservice Professional.* New York: Van Nostrand Reinhold Company, 1990.

Passini, R. *Wayfinding in Architecture.* New York: Van Nostrand Reinhold Company, 1984.

Pesman, S. "Medical Inns Keep Patients, Profits Near," *Modern Healthcare*, November 17, 1989.

Porter, S. D. "Healthcare/Senior Living Strategic Planning: Fusing a Total Hospitality Approach," seminar presentation for Hotel/Retail Services, Healthcare International, International Hotel/Motel & Restaurant Show, New York, November 15, 1988.

Radulski, J. "Design for Aging Database Grows." *Restaurant/Hotel Design International*, May 1990.

Rajecki, R., "Retirement Housing: Small Town America Gets a Facelift," *Contemporary Long-Term Care*, October 1989.

Raschko, B. B. *Housing Interiors for the Disabled & Elderly*. New York: Van Nostrand Reinhold Company, 1982.

Rees, R. A., "Providing 'Life's Satisfactions' Is Everyone's Business," Hospitality in Healthcare and Senior Market Seminar presentation for International Hotel/Motel & Restaurant Show, New York, November 11, 1989.

Remnet, V. L. *Understanding Older Adults: An Experimental Approach to Learning*. Lexington, MA: Lexington Books, 1989.

Risk, T. J. "New Opportunities Through the Cleveland Clinic Foundation, Blending of Healthcare and Hospitality," seminar presentation, for International Hotel/Motel & Restaurant Show, New York, November 11, 1990.

Romeo, P. R., "Detroit Hospital Home to Unique Caesars Unit," *Nation's Restaurant News*, September 5, 1988.

Salfinao, C. S. "Softening the Blow," *Architectural Lighting*, June 1990.

Shannon, L. R. "Footprints in the Sands of Time," *The New York Times*, SCIENCE *section*, March 20, 1990.

The American Institute of Architects. *Design for Aging: An Architect's Guide*. Washington, DC: The AIA Press, 1985.

Valins, *Housing for Elderly People: A Guide for Architects and Clients*. Stoneham, MA: Butterworth Architecture, 1988.

Walker, T. D. *Designs for Parks and Recreation Spaces*. Mesa, AZ:PDA Publishers, 1987.

Walkup, C. "Dynamic Fare Flavors Retirement Centers," *Nation's Restaurant News*, November 28, 1988.

Webb, L. C. *Planning and Managing Adult Day Care-Pathways to Success*. Owing Mills, Md: National Health Publishing, 1989.

Weisman, G. D., "Wayfinding and Architectural Legibility: Design Considerations in Housing Environments for the Elderly," in *Housing for the Elderly: Satisfaction and Preferences*, V. Regnier and J. Pynoos, Eds. New York: Garland Publishing, Inc. 1982.

Westin, R. J. "New Opportunities Through the Blending of Healthcare and Hospitality," seminar presentation for Westin Financial Group, International Hotel/Motel & Restaurant Show, New York, November 11, 1990.

Wiss, C. R. "Meals, Memories and Menoirs: A Culinary Odyssey," *Therapeutic Recreation Journal*, Fourth Quarter, 1990.

Wolfe, D. B. *Serving the Ageless Market: Strategies for Selling to the Fifty-Plus Market*, New York: McGraw-Hill Book company, 1989.

——"Arbor Corporation's New Caretel Concept," *Provider*, February 1988.

Wolfman, P. and C. Gold. *The Perfect Setting*. New York: Harry N. Abrams, 1985.

Van Den Haag, E. "How to Make Hospitals Hospitable: One Way would be to create a New Kind of 'Medical Hotel'," *Fortune*, May 17, 1982.

Zemke, R. "Healthcare Rediscovers Patients, The Marketing Emphasis of Hospital and Medical Center Management," *Training*, April 1987.

Zimring, C. M. "The Built Environment as a Source of Psychological Stress: Impacts of Building and Cities on Satisfaction and Behavior," in *Environmental Stress*, G. W. Evans, Ed. New York: Cambridge University Press, 1982.

——. "A Five-Star Look, Pali Momi Medical Center, Aiea, III," *Designer Specifier*, November 1990.

——. "Affordable Housing: The Years Ahead," A Program Paper of the Ford Foundation, New York. 1989.

——. "A Sickroom With A View," Technology. *Newsweek*. March 26, 1990.

——. "Providing Accessibility and Usability for Physically Handicapped People" (American National Standard for Buildings and Facilities). New York: American National Standards Institute, Inc. (ANSI A117.1-1986).

——. *Dictionary of Terms for Senior Citizens and the Industries that Serve Them*, National Association for Senior Living Industries, 1989.

——. "Environments that Support Healing," CONTRACT, a Gralla Publication, February 1989.

——. *Gift and Stationary Business Magazine*, A Gralla Publication, August 1990.

——, " 'Guest Relations' Brings a New Look to Hospitals," *New York Times*, April 23, 1987.

————. "Housing Needs of the Rural Elderly and the Handicapped," A report based on research conducted by the Office of Policy Development and Research, U.S. Department of Housing and Urban Development.

————. "Hospital Guest Houses Cut Costs," *Hospital Patient Relations Report*, Business Publishers, Inc., Silver Spring, Maryland, Vol. 5, No. 3, March 1990.

————. "Hospitals' Traditions Cross Lines of Culture," *Miami Herald*, Living Today, June 2, 1988.

————. "Hospital Hotels," *Food Management*, June 1987.

————. *Restaurant and Hotel Design International, Special Healthcare/Senior Living Issue*, August 1987 and monthly section.

————. "Senior Day-Care Plan Tested," *Frontline, Holiday Inn*, June 1989.

————, "Serving Senior Hotel-Style," *Food Management*, August 1989.

Index

Albert Bush-Brown

Albert Bush-Brown (MFA, Ph.D, Hon. AIA) is President of AB-BA, consultants in organizing, designing and financing educational, healthcare and cultural communities. Past director and chairman of Barclays Bank of New York, he currently chairs the Bank's Regional Advisory Boards.

Former Chancellor, Long Island University, Vice President, SUNY/Buffalo, and President, Rhode Island School of Design, Professor Bush-Brown started his career as an architectural and urban historian and critic, teaching at Harvard and MIT.

While President of RISD, he founded the Research and Design Institute, was a member of the Providence City Plan Commission, and was Presidential inaugural appointee to the National Council on the arts, Washington (1965). He has been Special Advisor to the Secretary, HUD (Washington), a Managing Director of the Metropolitan Opera (NY), and has conducted architectural seminars and consultancies in Turkey, Saudia Arabia, Mexico, England, Canada and the United States. His books and essays advocating the social and cultural benefits of good design have been translated into five languages.

He lectures extensively here and abroad. Recent presentations include: "Facilities for Aging: Agenda for Action in the 1990's" Round Table, sponsored by AIA Task Force on Aging, Barclays Bank Conference on health and life care, The First Annual National Symposium for Healthcare Interior Design, and the American College of Healthcare Administrators. He has been a consultant in planning more than one billion dollars of new buildings.

He received his degrees from Princeton University, is a member of the Society of Fellows, Harvard University, has been Bemis Visiting Professor at MIT, Fellow at Harvard University's J. F. Kennedy Institute of Politics, and Ford Foundation Fellow at Harvard's Center for Urban and Regional Studies. He has published 8 books and over 60 essays.

Essayist, watercolorist, cabinetmaker, and avid gardener, Dr. Bush-Brown lives in midtown Manhattan—the inspiration for his poems on the theme, "Walking to Work on Third."

Dianne Davis

Dianne Davis (M.A., P.D.) founded Hospitality Healthcare Designs, a marketing and environmental consulting firm. Professor Davis has been a leader in creating and integrating products and services for the hospitality, healthcare and education industries. Currently, her work focuses on the mature: marketing strategies, development of products and services, specialized training, adult day care, hotel conversions and adaptable hospitality concepts.

Known as an industry catalyst, change agent and futurist, her goal is to develop "crossover" ventures and stimulate traditional "sleeping" organizations or programs to move into the forefront of performance and impact. Professor Davis has stimulated major changes in industry and university curricula. Her innovative consulting experiences include the first medical professional center in St. Croix, midwifery center in Trinidad, hotels with intergenerational components, and advancing hospitable design in healthcare and senior facilities.

As an educator and industry liaison she developed New York University's Center for the Study of Foodservice Management, and created the NYU/Small Business Administration Regional Woman of the Year Awards. As founding president of the Roundtable for Women in Foodservice she created the prestigious Pacesetter Awards. She has also developed special programs for mature marketing and guest training.

Professor Davis has lectured and conducted innovative seminars for numerous national and international organizations which include the American College of Healthcare Administrators, The First Annual National Symposium for Healthcare Interior Design, Caribbean Hotel Association, National Restaurant Association, President Reagan's Initiative National Conferences for Women's Business Ownership, and the World Health Organization. She has also traveled the world as a 1988 Philip A. Connelly Awards' evaluator for the Department of the Army.

She received her degrees from New York University and Columbia University.

263